BIBLICAL HEALING
HEBREW AND CHRISTIAN ROOTS

FRANK C. DARLING

Published by

VISTA PUBLICATIONS
P.O. BOX 302 • BOULDER, COLORADO • 80306

Printed in the United States of America

Library of Congress Catalog Card Number: 89 - 50568

ISBN: 0-9622504-0-6

This volume is dedicated

to the memory of my mother

NORA P. DARLING

who introduced me to the

challenge, power, and comfort

of Biblical healing

TABLE OF CONTENTS

PREFACE

The title of this book *Biblical Healing* is not used in the titles of many other studies dealing with healing based on the teachings of the Bible. Much more common are titles using the words "Spiritual Healing," "Divine Healing," or the single word "Healing." The titles of the large number of books about healing based on the New Testament often contain the words "Christian Healing."

According to Webster's dictionary, the word "Biblical" means "of, relating to, derived from, or in accord with the Bible." This book adheres closely to this definition. It focuses primarily on the healing words and works of major figures in the Bible and the healing mission among their followers for slightly more than two centuries after the apostolic era. The sub-title "Hebrew and Christian Roots" refers to the early healing message emerging from both the Old and New Testaments.

At first sight the Bible as a whole appears to say relatively little about healing. The thirty-nine books of the Old Testament and the twenty-seven books of the New Testament printed in double column on more than one thousand pages include history, allegories, poetry, law, parables, genealogy, and religious and moral teachings. Except for the four Gospels and the book of Acts, only a small amount of this extensive literature contains specific references to healing.

Yet in its broadest sense the dominant theme of the Bible is the timeless topic of health and healing. From the accounts depicting the creation of man in Genesis to the apocalyptic visions of a new heaven and a new earth in Revelation, the Scriptures explain spiritual and moral values capable of producing harmony and wholeness among mankind. These values have been related and interpreted by numerous religious thinkers since the times of the Old and New Testaments. They are also relevant as a means of destroying disease and restoring health in the world today.

The basic purpose of this book is to present a survey of the written and spoken word on Biblical healing from the time of its origin around 1300 B.C. to the Council of Nicea in 325 A.D. The survey is non-denominational in scope and content, and it contains readings from both primary and secondary sources produced by a variety of religious and historical writers. Some of these works originally written in Greek and Latin have only recently been translated into the English language.

A second purpose of this collection of written selections and commentary is to remind ourselves of the time-honored practice of Biblical healing vis-a-vis the extensive influence acquired by the medical profession during the past one hundred years. Modern medicine has contributed much to the health and well-being of mankind, and it has reduced the suffering caused by many diseases. Yet modern medicine is continually confronted by perplexing problems and limitations. Some diseases of ancient times still afflict innocent victims and continue to be labeled as "incurable." New advances in medical skills are counterbalanced by the outbreak of new diseases such as AIDS and Alzheimer's disease.

Many modern illnesses are caused by mental and emotional disturbances induced by the intense pace of contemporary industrial societies, and a permanent cure for these maladies tends to elude the reach of drugs and surgery. Expenditures for medical services by the United States national government increased from $40 billion in 1965 to approximately $410 billion in 1985. Yet many people are unable to pay the rising costs of medical treatment, and health care programs are often inadequate and poorly planned.

Not until 1989 did the U.S. Department of Health and Human Services establish a centralized nationwide data system to collect and disseminate information on professionally unqualified physicians. The number of hospitals is declining in many areas, and fewer young people are pursuing medical careers. In spite of a gradual reduction in the size of the medical profession, one report states that by the year 2000 the United States will have 145,000 more doctors than it needs. Other conflicting trends continue to hamper the progress of modern medicine.

In this changing and challenging situation more people are seeking a broader vision of health and healing. Some physicians are increasingly aware of the potential influence of religion in alleviating sickness and disease. Some have urged their patients to pray for recovery from their illnesses. One of the most ironic developments in the recent revival of spiritual healing is that a growing number of doctors seem more willing to use prayer than are many members of the clergy.

Some public leaders are also aware of the healing power of the teachings of the Bible. The Thanksgiving Proclamation of a recent President of the United States mentioned that "the blessings that are ours must be understood as the gift of a loving God Whose greatest gift is healing."

The literature on Biblical healing is vast and diverse, and only selections of major writings can be included in a survey covering such a long historical period. The reader is invited to use the written sources included in this book as a guide to further independent thought and study. The appendices at the end include a list of all the healings cited in the Old and New Testaments. They also include an annotated bibliography of books on Biblical healing which can be helpful in pursuing a more in-depth understanding of this expanding field.

The study of Biblical healing usually involves a broad concept of man's wholeness and well-being, and it often entails a discussion of regeneration over sin. At times, the literature on Biblical healing also includes accounts of God's protection and deliverance from a variety of pending human calamities in what are often referred to as "supernatural miracles." Many books dealing with this aspect of the Bible and subsequent religious writings combine healing with vivid accounts of man's dominion over his physical environment and the counteracting of many natural laws.

The concept of healing used in this book on religious and historical writings is focused essentially on the physical and mental healing of people. The power which caused these human-oriented "signs" and "wonders" is the same power which caused the impressive displays of God's dominance over the material forces of the physical universe. Both kinds of miracles are recorded in the Bible. Yet this much broader topic is not the major subject matter of this chronological survey. The chief focus presented here is the written and spoken record of mankind's quest for health and wholeness.

My own commentary throughout this work is kept at a minimum. Except for the epilogue, it consists of introductory information about each historical period and the record of healing-oriented writings by each religious thinker. The major coverage is devoted to the words of the persons who shaped the healing mission of the Judeo-Christian heritage in its early stages. What I have labeled "Historical Commentary on Primitive Christianity" comprises relevant supplementary information and insights on Christian healing by professional historians.

I am grateful to Jennifer St. John for designing the cover of this book and for her assistance in handling many technical details in preparing this study for publication.

I deeply appreciate the assistance of my wife, Ann, who devoted many hours as a grammarian and proofreader in the final publication of this book.

FRANK C. DARLING

Boulder, Colorado
June 1989

Acknowledgements

Appreciation for permission to reprint copyrighted material is made to the following: Dorset Press, for the use of relevant passages comprising about five pages from *The History of the Church from Christ to Constantine*, by Eusebius, translated by G.A. Williamson, 1965; Prentice-Hall, Inc., for the use of a selected passage from *Understanding the Old Testament*, 1975, by Bernhard W. Anderson; Yale University Press, for the use of selected excerpts comprising approximately nine pages in Chapters III and IV from *Christianizing The Roman Empire: A.D. 100 - 400*, 1984, by Ramsay MacMullen; Dover Publications, Inc., for the use of three engravings by Gustave Doré from *The Doré Bible Illustrations*, 1974.

PART ONE

THE OLD TESTAMENT

The Old Testament does not purport to be simply a book of secular history or culture. It is sacred history, to both Jews and Christians, because in these historical experiences, as interpreted by faith, the ultimate meaning of human life is disclosed. From Israel's standpoint, this history is not just the ordinary story of wars, population movement, and cultural advance or decline. Rather, the unique dimension of these historical experiences is the disclosure of God's activity in events, the working out of his purpose in the career of Israel. It is this faith that transfigures Israel's history and gives to the Bible its peculiar claim to be sacred scripture. . . .[T]he Old Testament is Israel's witness to its encounter with God. For this reason, we cannot begin to understand the Old Testament so long as we regard it as merely great literature, interesting history, or the development of lofty ideas. The Old Testament is the narration of God's action: what he has done, is doing, and will do.

Bernhard W. Anderson
Understanding the
Old Testament

PART ONE

THE OLD TESTAMENT

The first roots of Biblical healing began to spread into the consciousness of Western civilization with the Hebrew concept of monotheism. In marked contrast to the pantheons of many gods among the pagan cultures surrounding the people of Israel, the early Hebrew patriarchs upheld one God who is the Creator of man and the universe and the Source of all life. Health was understood to be the natural result of living in accordance with the law of God; disease was considered to be punishment inflicted by God for disobedience to His spiritual and moral commandments. The ancient Hebrew people also believed that disease was often brought by demons acting on their own initiative or sent by God or sorcerers.

Health was conceived as something much more than physical comfort and pleasure. Instead, health had a much broader significance and meaning. Hebrew thought envisioned man's entire being more in terms of spiritual progress and moral rectitude than of physiological structure or bodily functions. The Hebrew word for this concept was *shalom.* It consisted basically of a sense of wholeness achieved by living in a correct spiritual relationship with God. In his book *Health and Medicine in the Jewish Tradition,* Professor David M. Feldman states: "Certainly this is a fundamental teaching, that physical well-being comes from -- or comes back again from -- subjecting one's heart to God and following the precepts of right living or righteous living." (p. 30) This idea of health was reinforced by numerous dietary and sanitary standards that were also considered as part of God's law. Well-being was demonstrated by a life of strength, soundness, peace, and longevity.

Physical healing of individual men and women by spiritual means did not become a significant element of Hebrew theology. The dominant thought of the Old Testament was concerned with the people of Israel as a "chosen race" receiving either collective victory or collective punishment depending on their adherence to God's commandments. The concept of man was founded primarily on the Adam allegory as related in the second and subsequent chapters of Genesis. Man was conceived largely as a mixture of good and evil; he had a choice to do good and be blessed or to do evil and be punished. The doctrine that sickness is punishment for departing from God's statutes came largely from the book of Deuteronomy. In much of the Old Testament, this teaching tended to be explicit and intense.

Yet a second element or strand of Old Testament theology more favorable to the evolution of spiritual healing was based on the vision of creation described in the first chapter of Genesis. In this account, God's creation comes forth in an orderly and ever-increasing volume of light. Man is made in the image and likeness of God. Everything in this creation is "very good." It contains no "talking serpent" or evil voice to deceive man or disrupt the harmonious relationship with his Maker.

This concept of man was confined to relatively few spokesmen in the Old Testament. The message is much more implicit and subtle than the punitive element in early Hebrew law, and at times it seems almost lost during the many trials and struggles of the people of Israel. Yet it grows in stature and begins to extend beyond a single nation or people into a universal covenant embracing individual freedom and well-being under a spiritual law of life and love. God is increasingly envisioned as a protector and comforter available to all mankind. Disease is seen in some degree as caused by the human mind rather than the chastening of a stern and punishing God. This changing sense of God, man, and healing emerged in the life and words of Moses, Elijah, and Elisha, and in the epic of Job. The promise of healing to new generations is voiced largely in the book of Psalms and by some of the prophets. This future sense of hope prepares the way for the healing words and works in the New Testament.

CHAPTER 1

MOSES

(CIRCA 1300 - 1200 B.C.)

Moses is widely recognized as one of the greatest religious leaders in human history. He was the emancipator who led the people of Israel from bondage in Egypt to the promised land. He was the lawgiver who received the Ten Commandments from God. He elevated the concept of monotheism first voiced by Abraham to a firm and permanent place in Hebrew theology. Moses was also the maker of the Hebrew nation.

A lesser known contribution of Moses to world thought was his role as the first thinker in the Bible to discover and perform spiritual healing. At Mount Horeb (Sinai) he witnessed the first recorded healing at the time he listened to God instructing him to deliver the children of Israel from oppression in Egypt. This healing was his own immediate recovery from leprosy. It was preceded by several important steps.

Moses' thought was made receptive to a better understanding of God and His ever-present power by a willingness to "turn aside" and ponder the unusual sight of a burning bush that "was not consumed." This spiritual curiosity gave him a stronger realization of the existence of a non-material universe created by God which is unseen by human eyes. In a book titled *Heritage - Civilization and the Jews*, Abba Eban has described Moses' experience on Mount Horeb as follows: "In speaking of God, Moses was capable of an unprecedented exercise in abstraction. He could envisage a God above nature, a God immune from human passion and natural vicissitudes." (p. 26)

Another step came from an inner voice defining God as I AM THAT I AM, or an incorporeal Divine Being who is the Ego and Source of each individual man or woman. Moses also recognized God as the same God of Abraham, Isaac, and Jacob, who were the forefathers of the people of Israel. God's "everlasting covenant" with Abraham included the provision to "walk before me [God], and be thou perfect." (Gen. 17: 1)

Finally, Moses' healing from leprosy was preceded by conquering the fear of a serpent transformed from a shepherd's rod. This impressive "first sign" possibly symbolized in some degree the capacity of a recognition of God's power to destroy the serpent thought or evil mind attached to the Adam account of creation. It was immediately followed by the very convincing proof that healing leprosy was the effect of obeying the inner voice of God. This "latter sign" was intended to assure Moses of God's protection in his mission to free the people of Israel from slavery, and to convince any of his doubting followers of his mandate to guide them to the promised land.

A crucial aspect of the healing process started by Moses in his first encounter with God at Mount Horeb is that the sole power in the restoration of health and wholeness comes from God. Healing, in brief, results from a correct understanding of man's relationship to his Creator. Moses' leadership in liberating his people from Egypt constituted a notable achievement of collective healing from foreign political oppression; his ability to restore his leprous hand to its normal healthy condition was an equally impressive demonstration of individual healing from internal mental oppression. Both forms of healing were accomplished not by the power of man, but by the sovereignty of God. Both healings were early evidence of man's inherent right to dignity and freedom.

Moses' role in inaugurating Biblical healing was supplemented by his receiving the Ten Commandments at a later time on the same mountain where he was told by God to lead the people of Israel from Egypt to the promised land. The Mosaic Decalogue includes both spiritual and moral precepts which are vital in preserving health and achieving healing. Obedience to God's commandments is part of His law upholding harmony and freedom for each individual man and woman as well as for the community.

The following readings from the book of Exodus relate Moses' role in beginning the practice of Biblical healing:

> •Now Moses kept the flock of Jethro his father in law, the priest of Midian: and he led the flock to the backside of the desert, and came to the mountain of God, even to Horeb. And the angel of the Lord appeared to him in a flame of fire out of the midst of a bush: and he looked, and, behold the bush burned with fire, and the bush was not consumed. And Moses said, I will now turn aside, and see this great

sight, why the bush is not burnt. And when the Lord saw that he turned aside to see, God called unto him out of the midst of the bush, and said, Moses, Moses. And he said, Here am I. And he said, Draw not nigh hither: put off thy shoes from off thy feet, for the place whereon thou standest is holy ground.

Moreover he said, I am the God of thy father, the God of Abraham, the God of Isaac, and the God of Jacob. And Moses hid his face; for he was afraid to look upon God. And the Lord said, I have surely seen the affliction of my people which are in Egypt, and have heard their cry by reason of their taskmasters; for I know their sorrows; And I am come down to deliver them out of the hand of the Egyptians, and to bring them up out of that land unto a good land and a large, unto a land flowing with milk and honey; unto the place of the Canaanites, and the Hittites, and the Amorites, and the Perizzites, and the Hivites, and the Jebusites. Now therefore, behold, the cry of the children of Israel is come unto me: and I have also seen the oppression wherewith the Egyptians oppress them. Come now therefore, And I will send thee unto Pharaoh, that thou mayest bring forth my people the children of Israel out of Egypt.

And Moses said unto God, Who am I, that I should go unto Pharaoh, and that I should bring forth the children of Israel out of Egypt? And he said, Certainly I will be with thee; and this shall be a token unto thee, that I have sent thee: When thou hast brought forth the people out of Egypt, ye shall serve God upon this mountain. And Moses said unto God, Behold, when I come unto the children of Israel, and shall say unto them, The God of your fathers hath sent me unto you; and they shall say to me, What is his name? what shall I say unto them? And God said unto Moses, I AM THAT I AM; and he said, Thus shalt thou say unto the children of Israel, I AM hath sent me unto you. And God said moreover unto Moses, Thus shalt thou say unto the children of

Israel, The Lord God of your fathers, the God of
Abraham, the God of Isaac, and the God of Jacob,
hath sent me unto you: this is my name for ever, and
this is my memorial unto all generations. (3: 1 - 15)

•And Moses answered and said, But, behold, they
will not believe me, nor hearken unto my voice: for
they will say, The Lord hath not appeared unto thee.
And the Lord said unto him, What is that in thine
hand? And he said, A rod. And he said, Cast it on
the ground. And he cast it on the ground, and it
became a serpent; and Moses fled from before it.
And the Lord said unto Moses, Put forth thine hand,
and take it by the tail. And he put forth his hand,
and caught it, and it became a rod in his hand: That
they may believe that the Lord God of their fathers,
the God of Abraham, the God of Isaac, and the God
of Jacob, hath appeared unto thee.

And the Lord said furthermore unto him, Put now
thine hand into thy bosom. And he put his hand into
his bosom: and when he took it out, behold, his
hand was leprous as snow. And he said, Put thine
hand into thy bosom again. And he put his hand into
his bosom again; and plucked it out of his bosom,
and, behold, it was turned again as his other flesh.
And it shall come to pass, if they will not believe
thee, neither hearken to the voice of the first sign,
that they will believe the voice of the latter sign. (4:
1 - 8)

The following selections from Exodus describe Moses' actions and
words in delivering the Ten Commandments.

•In the third month, when the children of Israel were
gone forth out of the land of Egypt, the same day
came they into the wilderness of Sinai. And Moses
came and called for the elders of the people, and
laid before their faces all these words which the
Lord commanded him. (19: 1, 7)

•And God spake all these words, saying, I am the
Lord thy God, which have brought thee out of the
land of Egypt, out of the house of bondage.

Thou shalt have no other gods before me.

Thou shalt not make unto thee any graven
image, or any likeness of any thing that is
in heaven above, or that is in the earth
beneath, or that is in the water under the
earth: Thou shalt not bow down thyself to
them, nor serve them: for I the Lord thy
God am a jealous God, visiting the iniquity
of the fathers upon the children unto the
third and fourth generation of them that
hate me; And shewing mercy unto thousands of them that love me, and keep my
commandments.

Thou shalt not take the name of the Lord
thy God in vain; for the Lord will not hold
him guiltless that taketh his name in vain.

Remember the sabbath day to keep it holy.
Six days shalt thou labour, and do all thy
work: But the seventh day is the sabbath of
the Lord thy God: in it thou shalt not do
any work, thou, nor thy son, nor thy daughter, thy manservant, nor thy maidservant,
nor thy cattle, nor the stranger that is within thy gates: For in six days the Lord made
heaven and earth, the sea, and all that in
them is, and rested the seventh day: wherefore the Lord blessed the sabbath day, and
hallowed it.

Honour thy father and thy mother: that thy
days may be long upon the land which the
Lord thy God giveth thee.

Thou shalt not kill.

Thou shalt not commit adultery.

Thou shalt not steal.

Thou shalt not bear false witness against
thy neighbor.

Thou shalt not covet thy neighbor's house,
thou shalt not covet thy neighbor's wife,
nor his manservant, nor his maidservant,
nor his ox, nor his ass, nor anything that is
thy neighbor's. (20: 1-17)

Moses also performed spiritual healing on other people. The healing of his sister, Miriam, involved a reversal of the Hebrew doctrine
that disease is caused only by sin. It is the first recorded Biblical healing made by an appeal to God on behalf of another person. It is the
only specific reference in the Old Testament to a physical healing of a
woman. Moses likewise used his healing ability to stop an epidemic
and to heal snake bites among his people on their trek to the promised
land.

The following readings which narrate these healings by Moses are
from the book of Numbers.

•And Miriam and Aaron spake against Moses
because of the Ethiopian woman whom he had married: for he had married an Ethiopian woman. And
they said, Hath the Lord indeed spoken only by
Moses? hath he not spoken also by us? And the
Lord heard it. . . .And the Lord spake suddenly unto
Moses, and unto Aaron, and unto Miriam, Come out
ye three unto the tabernacle of the congregation.
And they three came out.

And the Lord came down in the pillar of the cloud,
and stood in the door of the tabernacle, and called
Aaron and Miriam: and they both came forth. And
he said, Hear now my words: If there be a prophet
among you, I the Lord will make myself known
unto him in a vision, and will speak unto him in a
dream. My servant Moses is not so, who is faithful

in all mine house. With him will I speak mouth to mouth, even apparently, and not in dark speeches; and the similitude of the Lord shall he behold: wherefore then were ye not afraid to speak against my servant Moses?

And the anger of the Lord was kindled against them; and he departed. And the cloud departed from off the tabernacle; and, behold, Miriam became leprous, white as snow: and Aaron looked upon Miriam, and, behold she was leprous.

And Aaron said unto Moses, Alas, my lord, I beseech thee, lay not the sin upon us, wherein we have done foolishly, and wherein we have sinned. Let her not be as one dead, of whom the flesh is half consumed when he cometh out of his mother's womb. And Moses cried unto the Lord, saying, Heal her now, O God, I beseech thee.

And the Lord said unto Moses, If her father had but spit in her face, should she not be ashamed seven days? let her be shut out from the camp seven days, and after that let her be received in again. And Miriam was shut out from the camp seven days: and the people journeyed not till Miriam was brought in again. (12: 1 - 15)

•On the morrow all the congregation of the children of Israel murmured against Moses and against Aaron, saying, Ye have killed the people of the Lord. And it came to pass, when the congregation was gathered against Moses and against Aaron, that they looked toward the tabernacle of the congregation: and, behold, the cloud covered it, and the glory of the Lord appeared. And Moses and Aaron came before the tabernacle of the congregation.

And Moses said unto Aaron, Take a censer, and put fire therein from off the altar, and put on incense, and go quickly unto the congregation, and make an

atonement for them: for there is wrath gone out
from the Lord; the plague is begun. And Aaron took
as Moses commanded, and ran into the midst of the
congregation; and, behold, the plague was begun
among the people: and he put on incense, and made
an atonement for the people.

And he stood between the dead and the living; and
the plague was stayed. Now they that died in the
plague were fourteen thousand and seven hundred,
beside them that died about the matter of Korah.
And Aaron returned unto Moses unto the door of the
tabernacle of the congregation: and the plague was
stayed. (16: 41 - 43, 46 - 50)

•And they journeyed from mount Hor by the way of
the Red sea, to compass the land of Edom: and the
soul of the people was much discouraged because of
the way. And the people spake against God, and
against Moses, Wherefore have ye brought us up out
of Egypt to die in the wilderness? for there is no
bread, neither is there any water; and our soul loa-
theth this light bread. And the Lord sent fiery serpents among the people, and they bit the people; and
much people of Israel died.

Therefore the people came to Moses, and said, We
have sinned, for we have spoken against the Lord,
and against thee; pray unto the Lord, that he take
away the serpents from us.

And Moses prayed for the people. And the Lord
said unto Moses, Make thee a fiery serpent, and set
it upon a pole: and it shall come to pass, that every
one that is bitten, when he looketh upon it, shall
live. And Moses made a serpent of brass, and put it
upon a pole, and it came to pass, that if a serpent
had bitten any man, when he beheld the serpent of
brass, he lived. (21: 4 - 9)

ELIJAH RAISETH THE SON OF THE WIDOW OF ZAREPHATH

And Elijah took the child, and brought him down out of the chamber into the house,
and delivered him unto his mother: and Elijah said, See, thy son liveth . . .
(I Kings 17: 23)

CHAPTER 2

ELIJAH

(CIRCA 930 - 850 B. C.)

Elijah preserved and strengthened some of Moses' teachings about four centuries after the arduous journey of the people of Israel from Egypt to the promised land. This prophet from Gilead was surnamed "the Tishbite;" his name in Greek is transliterated as "Elias." In Hebrew his name means "My God is I AM."

Although historical data on his life are very limited and fragmentary, most Bible scholars rank Elijah second only to Moses as a great Hebrew religious leader. He helped preserve monotheism from the nature-worshippers of Baal, and he fought against the tyranny of despotic monarchs. In *The Abingdon Bible Commentary,* Professor A.C. Knudson has written: "There was. . .one important contribution made to the development of the idea of divine unity in the preprophetic period. . . .This came from Elijah. He seems to have identified Jehovah with deity in such an exclusive sense as to imply the non-existence of Baal and of other gods in general. . . .For his own people he regarded Jehovah alone as truly divine." (p.160)

Elijah, like Moses, often experienced deep despair and despondency in his effort to establish the worship of Jehovah, the God of Israel. Yet Elijah also received hope and inspiration from a pilgrimage to Mount Sinai, where he witnessed "a great and strong wind," an earthquake, and a fire followed by "a still small voice" similar to Moses' inner spiritual probing at the burning bush.

One of Elijah's major contributions to Hebrew theology was an inextricable linkage among religion, morality, and law. He passed along a "double portion" of his teachings and understanding to his follower, Elisha. Elijah was one of the four religious figures recorded in the Bible to ascend beyond mortal view and evade the experience of death.

Important aspects of Elijah's mission were continued in the life and works of Jesus. The New Testament cites five occasions when Jesus mentioned the name of Elijah (Elias). When Jesus once asked his disciples what the people thought of his words and works, they replied that many said he was Elijah. At the transfiguration, Moses and Elijah appeared with Jesus as a "voice out of the cloud" spoke approvingly of Jesus' mission. The book of Matthew relates that Jesus called for Elijah when he was first placed on the cross at his crucifixion.

Elijah performed several impressive miracles, including the provision of food at times of famine and the ignition of fire under a water-soaked sacrificial altar before 450 prophets of Baal. One of his most memorable achievements was the raising of the young son of a widow in Zarephath from death. This incident was the first recorded Biblical healing of a child. Like Moses' healing of Miriam, it counteracted the Hebrew belief that God sends sickness as punishment for sin. Elijah's healing reinforced the subdued yet powerful message of Old Testament theology that God is a loving Creator, and that part of man's heritage as His image includes health and wholeness.

The following reading from I Kings explains Elijah's role in healing the widow's son from death.

> •And Elijah the Tishbite, who was of the inhabitants of Gilead, said unto Ahab, As the Lord God of Israel liveth, before whom I stand, there shall not be dew nor rain these years, but according to my word.

> And the word of the Lord came unto him, saying, Arise, get thee to Zarephath, which belongeth to Zidon, and dwell there: behold, I have commanded a widow woman there to sustain thee.

> And it came to pass after these things, that the son of the woman, the mistress of the house, fell sick; and his sickness was so sore, that there was no breath left in him. And she said unto Elijah, What have I to do with thee, O thou man of God? art thou come unto me to call my sin to remembrance, and to slay my son?

> And he said unto her, Give me thy son. And he took him out of her bosom, and carried him up into a loft, where he abode, and laid him upon his own bed. And he cried unto the Lord, and said, O Lord my God, hast thou also brought evil upon the widow

with whom I sojourn, by slaying her son? And he stretched himself upon the child three times, and cried unto the Lord, and said, O Lord my God, I pray thee, let this child's soul come into him again.

And the Lord heard the voice of Elijah; and the soul of the child came into him again, and he revived. And Elijah took the child, and brought him down out of the chamber into the house, and delivered him unto his mother: and Elijah said, See, thy son liveth. And the woman said to Elijah, Now by this I know that thou art a man of God, and that the word of the Lord in thy mouth is truth. (17: 1, 8, 9, 17 - 24)

CHAPTER 3

ELISHA

(CIRCA 900 - 820 B.C.)

Elisha continued the struggle started by Elijah to preserve the worship of God from invading alien armies and the prophets of Baal. By the end of his life he succeeded in removing Baal worship from the land of Israel. His name is transliterated as "Eliseus" in Greek; it means "God has saved" in Hebrew. Elisha tended to be more gentle and moderate than Elijah, and at times he showed considerable mercy and good-will toward his foes.

Elisha, like Elijah, used his understanding of God to accomplish many impressive feats. His clairvoyance enabled him to warn the king of Israel of threatening military actions by the Syrian army, and he temporarily smote an encircling Syrian military force with blindness to relieve the siege of a major city. His prayer multiplied a modest supply of oil in the house of a poor widow so she could pay her deceased husband's debts and prevent her two sons from going into imprisonment and bondage.

Elisha repeated the example of Elijah in counteracting the physical forces of gravity. Following Elijah's ascension, he smote the waters of the Jordan river with his mantle and "they parted hither and thither and Elisha went over." When an axe head accidently fell into the river while men were cutting wood, Elisha thrust a stick into the water near the place where it fell "and the iron did swim."

Elisha continued Elijah's ability to heal. He raised the young son of a Shunammite woman from death, and he healed Naaman, a Syrian military officer, of leprosy. Elisha's healing capability is the first account in the Bible of this important skill being transferred from an inspired and learned religious leader to a devoted disciple. These experiences foretold Jesus bestowing his healing ability on his own disciples some nine centuries later. Elisha's healing of Naaman is the first healing of a Gentile recorded in the Old Testament. This impressive restoration of health revealed that God's law of life and love extended beyond the people of Israel. It likewise showed the need for humility and obedience in obtaining spiritual healing.

The following readings from II Kings relate Elisha's healing of an elderly Shunammite couple from barrenness and the restoration of their child from death several years later. They also describe the healing of Naaman, the Syrian army captain, from leprosy.

>•And it fell on a day, that Elisha passed to Shunem, where was a great woman; and she constrained him to eat bread. And so it was, that as oft as he passed by, he turned in thither to eat bread. And she said unto her husband, Behold now, I perceive that this is an holy man of God, which passeth by us continually. Let us make a little chamber, I pray thee, on the wall; and let us set for him there a bed, and a table, and a stool, and a candlestick: and it shall be, when he cometh to us, that he shall turn in thither.

>And it fell on a day, that he came thither, and he turned into the chamber, and lay there. And he said to Gehazi his servant, Call this Shunammite. And when he had called her, she stood before him. And he said unto him, Say now unto her, Behold, thou hast been careful for us with all this care; what is to be done for thee? wouldest thou be spoken for to the king, or to the captain of the host? And she answered, I dwell among mine own people.

>And he said, What then is to be done for her? And Gehazi answered, Verily she hath no child, and her husband is old. And he said, Call her. And when he had called her, she stood in the door. And he said, About this season, according to the time of life, thou shalt embrace a son. And she said, Nay, my lord, thou man of God, do not lie unto thine handmaid. And the woman conceived, and bare a son at that season that Elisha had said unto her, according to the time of life.

>And when the child was grown, it fell on a day, that he went out to his father to the reapers. And he said unto his father, My head, my head. And he said to a

lad, Carry him to his mother. And when he had taken him, and brought him to his mother, he sat on her knees till noon, and then died.

And she went up, and laid him on the bed of the man of God, and shut the door upon him, and went out. And she called unto her husband, and said, Send me, I pray thee, one of the young men, and one of the asses, that I may run to the man of God, and come again.

So she went and came unto the man of God to mount Carmel. And it came to pass, when the man of God saw her afar off, that he said to Gehazi his servant, Behold, yonder is that Shunammite: Run now, I pray thee, to meet her, and say unto her, Is it well with thee? is it well with thy husband? is it well with the child? And she answered, It is well.

And when she came to the man of God to the hill, she caught him by the feet: but Gehazi came near to thrust her away. And the man of God said, Let her alone; for her soul is vexed within her: and the Lord hath hid it from me, and hath not told me. Then she said, Did I desire a son of my lord? did I not say, Do not deceive me? Then he said to Gehazi, Gird up thy loins, and take my staff in thine hand, and go thy way: if thou meet any man, salute him not; and if any salute thee, answer him not again: and lay my staff upon the face of the child.

And the mother of the child said, As the Lord liveth, and as thy soul liveth, I will not leave thee. And he arose, and followed her. And Gehazi passed on before them, and laid the staff upon the face of the child; but there was neither voice, nor hearing. Wherefore he went again to meet him, and told him, saying, The child is not awaked.

And when Elisha was come into the house, behold, the child was dead, and laid upon his bed. He went in therefore, and shut the door upon them, and prayed unto the Lord. And he went up, and lay upon the child, and put his mouth upon his mouth, and his eyes upon his eyes, and his hands upon his hands: and he stretched himself upon the child; and the flesh of the child waxed warm.

Then he returned, and walked in the house to and fro; and went up, and stretched himself upon him: and the child sneezed seven times, and the child opened his eyes. And he called Gehazi, and said, Call this Shunammite. So he called her. And when she was come in unto him, he said, Take up thy son. Then she went in, and fell at his feet, and bowed herself to the ground, and took up her son, and went out. (4: 8 - 23, 25 - 37)

•Now Naaman, captain of the host of the king of Syria, was a great man with his master, and honourable, because by him the Lord had given deliverance unto Syria: he was also a mighty man in valour, but he was a leper. And the Syrians had gone out by companies, and had brought away captive out of the land of Israel a little maid; and she waited on Naaman's wife. And she said unto her mistress, Would God my lord were with the prophet that is in Samaria! for he would recover him of his leprosy. And one went in, and told his lord saying, Thus and thus said the maid that is of the land of Israel.

So Naaman came with his horses and with his chariot, and stood at the door of the house of Elisha. And Elisha sent a messenger unto him, saying, Go and wash in Jordan seven times, and thy flesh shall come again to thee, and thou shalt be clean. But Naaman was wroth, and went away, and said, Behold, I thought, He will surely come out to me, and stand, and call on the name of the Lord his God, and strike his hand over the place, and recover the leper. Are not Abana and Pharpar, rivers of Damascus, better than all the waters of Israel? may I not wash in them, and be clean? So he turned and went away in a rage.

And his servants came near, and spake unto him, and said, My father, if the prophet had bid thee do some great thing, wouldest thou not have done it? how much rather then, when he saith to thee, Wash, and be clean? Then went he down, and dipped himself seven times in Jordan, according to the saying of the man of God: and his flesh came again like unto the flesh of a little child, and he was clean. (5: 1 - 4, 9 - 14)

CHAPTER 4

JOB

(?)

The book of Job, like some other parts of the Old Testament, is an allegory. It comprises a legendary drama of a heroic man rather than a biographical account of real-life religious leaders such as Moses, Elijah, and Elisha. Bible scholars are uncertain of the time depicted by Job's life or the time when this epic was written. Some scholars claim it dates back to the pre-Mosaic period. Others believe this book may have been written during the time of Moses or the reign of Solomon. Recent research places the writing most likely between the sixth and fourth centuries B.C. The author or authors of the book are unknown, and it was almost certainly the work of several writers. In his essay on Job in *The Interpreter's Dictionary of the Bible,* M. H. Pope states that except for Hosea, "Job remains textually the most difficult book of the Old Testament." (p. 912)

Despite its eclectic and legendary character, many scholars and laymen alike believe the book of Job is one of the most penetrating and significant writings in the Bible. It deals with a classic problem of all ages: why do good people suffer?

This book is relevant in a survey of the literature on Biblical healing since it consists largely of a protest against the traditional Hebrew teaching that God sends disease in an effort to make man repent for his sins. Job rigorously rejected this orthodox doctrine because he had not sinned. The arguments with his three friends and a youthful idealist comprise a strong defense of freedom of thought in seeking an understanding of the nature of God and the rights of individual man.

In many respects, Job was an early "radical" or "free thinker." He was an advocate of divine and human rights. He also challenged some of the most inveterate teachings of Hebrew theology. In her book, *The Search for God,* Marchette Chute has stated: "The story of the *Book of Job* is the story of the fierce and unorthodox *Why?* that its hero sent thundering against the very gates of heaven; and the philosophic value of the story lies in the fact that the gates of heaven

opened to let his question in. . . .It is primarily this quality of intellectual freedom that makes the *Book of Job* so important. . . .It is its vin-
dication of the right of mankind to free inquiry." (pp. 15 - 16)

Job's appeal depicts one of the most moving struggles for justice
and individual freedom recorded in the entire Bible. The long period
of time involved in writing this book indicates that some opposition
existed during much of the Old Testament period to the orthodox view
of a punitive God and man as a sinning mortal. It also shows that
important writers over many years adhered to the second strand of
Hebrew thought upholding God as a loving Creator capable of restoring man's health and wholeness. The search for a higher concept of
God and a better understanding of the meaning of life in the story of
Job presaged some aspects of the rebellion against traditional religious
doctrine staged by Jesus.

In the end of the book, Job did not receive final answers to his questions. Yet in some degree he discovered the dignity and freedom of
man conceived as God's image and likeness. He also disproved the
Hebrew teaching that God imposes sickness and suffering on man for
sins he does not commit. As a reward, a family and fortune were
restored. Equally important, God "turned the captivity of Job" and
healed him of the severe skin disease which had covered his body.

The book of Job consists of an integrated epic, and it does not readily lend itself to the use of selected passages to portray a specific
theme. The entire work should be read to obtain a clear view of Job's
struggle and the results of his quest for more spiritual understanding.
The following passages attempt to depict the portions of Job that
relate most closely to the elevation of thought about God and a higher
concept of individual freedom capable of achieving physical healing.

The first selections explain the contest between God and Satan for
the loyalty of Job as well as the adversities inflicted on him. He is visited by three friends, Eliphaz, Bildad, and Zophar, who seek to comfort him by stressing orthodox Hebrew teachings. At times these com-
panions stress God's grandeur and power, but they never depart from
the view that God sends sickness and adversity to mankind to punish
sin.

> •There was a man in the land of Uz, whose name
> was Job; and that man was perfect and upright, and
> one that feared God, and eschewed evil. And there
> were born unto him seven sons and three daughters.
> His substance also was seven thousand sheep, and

three thousand camels, and five hundred yoke of oxen, and five hundred she asses, and a very great household; so that this man was the greatest of all the men of the east.

Now there was a day when the sons of God came to present themselves before the Lord, and Satan came also among them. And the Lord said unto Satan, Whence comest thou? Then Satan answered the Lord, and said, From going to and fro in the earth, and from walking up and down in it.

And the Lord said unto Satan, Hast thou considered my servant Job, that there is none like him in the earth, a perfect and an upright man, one that feareth God, and escheweth evil? Then Satan answered the Lord, and said, Doth Job fear God for nought? Hast not thou made an hedge about him, and about his house, and about all that he hath on every side? thou hast blessed the work of his hands, and his substance is increased in the land. But put forth thine hand now, and touch all that he hath, and he will curse thee to thy face. And the Lord said unto Satan, Behold, all that he hath is in thy power; only upon himself put not forth thine hand. So Satan went forth from the presence of the Lord.

And there was a day when his sons and his daughters were eating and drinking wine in their eldest brother's house: And there came a messenger unto Job, and said, The oxen were plowing, and the asses feeding beside them: And the Sabeans fell upon them, and took them away; yea, they have slain the servants with the edge of the sword; and I only am escaped alone to tell thee.

While he was yet speaking, there came also another, and said, The fire of God is fallen from heaven, and hath burned up the sheep, and the servants, and consumed them; and I only am escaped alone to tell thee. While he was yet speaking, there came also another, and said, The Chaldeans made out three bands, and fell upon the camels, and have carried them away, yea, and slain the servants with the edge of the sword; and I only am escaped alone to tell thee.

While he was yet speaking, there came also another, and said, Thy sons and thy daughters were eating and drinking wine in their eldest brother's house: And, behold, there came a great wind from the wilderness, and smote the four corners of the house, and it fell upon the young men, and they are dead; and I only am escaped alone to tell thee.

Then Job arose, and rent his mantle, and shaved his head, and fell down upon the ground, and worshipped, And said, Naked came I out of my mother's womb, and naked shall I return thither: the Lord gave, and the Lord hath taken away; blessed be the name of the Lord. In all this Job sinned not, nor charged God foolishly. (1: 1 - 3, 6 - 22)

•So went Satan forth from the presence of the Lord, and smote Job with sore boils from the sole of his foot unto his crown. Then said his wife unto him, Dost thou still retain thine integrity? curse God, and die. But he said unto her, Thou speakest as one of the foolish women speaketh. What? shall we receive good at the hand of God, and shall we not receive evil? In all this did not Job sin with his lips.

Now when Job's three friends heard of all this evil that was come upon him, they came every one from his own place; Eliphaz the Temanite, and Bildad the Shuhite, and Zophar the Naamathite: for they had made an appointment together to come to mourn with him and to comfort him. And when they lifted up their eyes afar off, and knew him not, they lifted up their voice, and wept; and they rent every one his mantle, and sprinkled dust upon their heads toward heaven. So they sat down with him upon the ground

seven days and seven nights, and none spake a word
unto him: for they saw that his grief was very great.
(2: 7, 9 - 13)

•After this opened Job his mouth, and cursed his
day. And Job spake, and said, Let the day perish
wherein I was born, and the night in which it was
said, There is a man child conceived. Let that day be
darkness; let not God regard it from above, neither
let the light shine upon it. For the thing which I
greatly feared is come upon me, and that which I
was afraid of is come unto me. (3: 1 - 4, 25)

Among the three friends Eliphaz speaks first and relates the many
good and kind things Job has done to less fortunate people. Yet he also
affirms the orthodox doctrine that although God is good and righteous,
He punishes the evil doer with affliction.

•Then Eliphaz the Temanite answered and said, If
we assay to commune with thee, wilt thou be
grieved? but who can withhold himself from speaking? Behold, thou hast instructed many, and thou
hast strengthened the weak hands. Thy words have
upholden him that was falling, and thou hast
strengthened the feeble knees.

But now it is come upon thee, and thou faintest; it
toucheth thee, and thou art troubled. Is not this thy
fear, thy confidence, thy hope, and the uprightness
of thy ways? Remember, I pray thee, who ever perished, being innocent? or where were the righteous
cut off? Even as I have seen, they that plow iniquity,
and sow wickedness, reap the same. By the blast of
God they perish, and by the breath of his nostrils are
they consumed.

Shall mortal man be more just than God? shall a
man be more pure than his maker? Behold, he put
no trust in his servants; and his angels he charged
with folly: How much less in them that dwell in
houses of clay, whose foundation is in the dust,

which are crushed before the moth? They are destroyed from morning to evening: they perish for ever without any regarding it. Doth not their excellence which is in them go away? they die, even without wisdom. (4: 1 - 9, 17 - 21)

•Although affliction cometh not forth of the dust, neither doth trouble spring out of the ground; Yet man is born unto trouble, as the sparks fly upward. He disappointeth the devices of the crafty, so that their hands cannot perform their enterprise. He taketh the wise in their own craftiness: and the counsel of the froward is carried headlong. Behold, happy is the man whom God correcteth: therefore despise not thou the chastening of the Almighty. (5: 6, 7, 12, 13, 17)

Job replies to Eliphaz.

•But Job answered and said, Oh that my grief were throughly weighed, and my calamity laid in the balances together! For now it would be heavier than the sand of the sea: therefore my words are swallowed up. For the arrows of the Almighty are within me, the poison whereof drinketh up my spirit: the terrors of God do set themselves in array against me. (6: 1 - 4)

•Is there not an appointed time to man upon earth? are not his days also like the days of an hireling? As a servant earnestly desireth the shadow, and as an hireling looketh for the reward for his work: So am I made to possess months of vanity, and wearisome nights are appointed to me. When I lie down, I say, When shall I arise, and the night be gone? and I am full of tossings to and fro unto the dawning of the day. (7: 1- 4)

Bildad speaks next and talks of God's justice.

•Then answered Bildad the Shuhite, and said, How long wilt thou speak these things? and how long shall the words of thy mouth be like a strong wind? Doth God pervert judgment? or doth the Almighty pervert justice? If thy children have sinned against him, and he have cast them away for their transgressions; If thou wouldest seek unto God betimes, and make thy supplication to the Almighty; If thou wert pure and upright; surely now he would awake for thee, and make the habitation of thy righteousness prosperous.

Though thy beginning was small, yet thy latter end should greatly increase. For enquire, I pray thee, of the former age, and prepare thyself to the search of their fathers; Shall not they teach thee, and tell thee, and utter words out of their heart?

Behold, God will not cast away a perfect man, neither will he help the evil doers: Till he fill thy mouth with laughing, and thy lips with rejoicing. They that hate thee shall be clothed with shame; and the dwelling place of the wicked shall come to nought. (8: 1 - 8, 10, 20 - 22)

Job replies to the second friend.

•Then Job answered and said, I know it is so of a truth: but how should man be just with God? If he will contend with him, he cannot answer him one of a thousand. He is wise in heart, and mighty in strength: who hath hardened himself against him, and hath prospered? Which removeth the mountains, and they know not: which overturneth them in his anger. Which shaketh the earth out of her place, and the pillars thereof tremble. Which commandeth the sun, and it riseth not; and sealeth up the stars. Which alone spreadeth out the heavens, and treadeth upon the waves of the sea. (9: 1 - 8)

•My soul is weary of my life; I will leave my complaint upon myself; I will speak in the bitterness of my soul. I will say unto God, Do not condemn me;

shew me wherefore thou contendest with me. Is it
good unto thee that thou shouldest oppress, that thou
shouldest despise the work of thine hands, and shine
upon the counsel of the wicked? Thine hands have
made me and fashioned me together round about;
yet thou dost destroy me. Wherefore then hast thou
brought me forth out of the womb? Oh that I had
given up the ghost, and no eye had seen me! (10: 1
- 3, 8, 18)

Zophar rebukes Job's refusal to attribute his suffering to his sins.

•Then answered Zophar the Naamathite, and said,
Should not the multitude of words be answered? and
should a man full of talk be justified? Should thy
lies make men hold their peace? and when thou
mockest, shall no man make thee ashamed? For
thou hast said, My doctrine is pure, and I am clean
in thine eyes.

But oh that God would speak, and open his lips
against thee; And that he would shew thee the
secrets of wisdom, that they are double to that
which is! Know therefore that God exacteth of thee
less than thine iniquity deserveth. Canst thou by
searching find out God? canst thou find out the
Almighty unto perfection?

It is as high as heaven; what canst thou do? deeper
than hell; what canst thou know? The measure
thereof is longer than the earth, and broader than the
sea. If he cut off, and shut up, or gather together,
then who can hinder him? For he knoweth vain
men: he seeth wickedness also; will he not then consider it? (11: 1 - 11)

Job defends his own understanding of God and increases his confidence in God's law. He expresses a sense of humility and reaffirms a
desire to seek God.

•And Job answered and said, No doubt but ye are the people, and wisdom shall die with you. But I have understanding as well as you; I am not inferior to you: yea, who knoweth not such things as these? I am as one mocked of his neighbour, who calleth upon God, and he answereth him: the just upright man is laughed to scorn. (12: 1 - 4)

•Lo, mine eye hath seen all this, mine ear hath heard and understood it. What ye know, the same do I know also: I am not inferior unto you. Surely I would speak to the Almighty, and I desire to reason with God. But ye are forgers of lies, ye are all physicians of no value. O that ye would altogether hold your peace! and it should be your wisdom. (13: 1 - 5)

•Man that is born of a woman is of few days, and full of trouble. He cometh forth like a flower, and is cut down: he fleeth also as a shadow, and continueth not. (14: 1, 2)

•For I know that my redeemer liveth, and that he shall stand at the latter day upon the earth: And though after my skin worms destroy this body, yet in my flesh shall I see God. (19: 25, 26)

•Oh that I knew where I might find him! that I might come even to his seat! But he knoweth the way that I take: when he hath tried me, I shall come forth as gold. My foot hath held his steps, his way have I kept, and not declined. Neither have I gone back from the commandment of his lips; I have esteemed the words of his mouth more than my necessary food. But he is in one mind, and who can turn him? and what his soul desireth, even that he doeth. For he performeth the thing that is appointed for me: and many such things are with him. (23: 3, 10 - 14)

The conversation is joined by Elihu, a young idealist, who rebukes Job and talks of God's wisdom and power.

•So these three men ceased to answer Job, because he was righteous in his own eyes. Then was kindled the wrath of Elihu the son of Barachel the Buzite, of the kindred of Ram: against Job was his wrath kindled, because he justified himself rather than God. Also against his three friends was his wrath kindled, because they had found no answer, and yet had condemned Job.

Now Elihu had waited till Job had spoken, because they were elder than he. When Elihu saw that there was no answer in the mouth of these three men, then his wrath was kindled. And Elihu the son of Barachel the Buzite answered and said, I am young, and ye are very old; wherefore I was afraid, and durst not shew you mine opinion. I said, Days should speak, and multitude of years should teach wisdom. But there is a spirit in man: and the inspiration of the Almighty giveth them understanding. Great men are not always wise: neither do the aged understand judgment. (32: 1 - 9)

•Wherefore, Job, I pray thee, hear my speeches, and hearken to all my words. Behold, now I have opened my mouth, my tongue hath spoken in my mouth. My words shall be of the uprightness of my heart: and my lips shall utter knowledge clearly. Behold, in this thou art not just: I will answer thee, that God is greater than man. Why dost thou strive against him? for he giveth not account of his matters. For God speaketh once, yea twice, yet man perceiveth it not. He keepeth back his soul from the pit, and his life from perishing by the sword.

Yea, his soul draweth near unto the grave, and his life to the destroyers. If there be a messenger with him, an interpreter, one among a thousand, to shew unto man his uprightness: Then he is gracious unto him, and saith, Deliver him from going down to the pit: I have found a ransom. His flesh shall be fresher than a child's: he shall return to the days of his

youth: He shall pray unto God, and he will be
favourable unto him: and he shall see his face with
joy: for he will render unto man his righteousness.

He will deliver his soul from going into the pit, and
his life shall see the light. Lo, all these things worketh God oftentimes with man. To bring back his
soul from the pit, to be enlightened with the light of
the living. Mark well, O Job, hearken unto me: hold
they peace, and I will speak. (33: 1 - 3, 12 - 14, 18,
22 - 26, 28 - 31)

•Behold, God is mighty, and despiseth not any: he is
mighty in strength and wisdom. He preserveth not
the life of the wicked: but giveth right to the poor.
He openeth also their ear to discipline, and commandeth that they return from iniquity. If they obey
and serve him, they shall spend their days in prosperity, and their years in pleasures. But if they obey
not, they shall perish by the sword, and they shall
die without knowledge. (36: 5, 6, 10 - 12)

Job does not reply to Elihu. Instead God speaks directly to Job out
of a whirlwind in a manner similar to God's inner voice to Moses at
the burning bush and His "still small voice" to Elijah before a great
and strong wind.

•Then the Lord answered Job out of the whirlwind,
and said, Who is this that darkeneth counsel by
words without knowledge? Gird up now thy loins
like a man; for I will demand of thee, and answer
thou me. Where wast thou when I laid the foundations of the earth? declare, if thou hast understanding. Who hath laid the measures thereof, if thou
knowest? or who hath stretched the line upon it?
Whereupon are the foundations thereof fastened? or
who laid the corner stone thereof; When the morning stars sang together, and all the sons of God
shouted for joy? (38: 1 - 7)

•Gird up thy loins now like a man: I will demand of
thee, and declare thou unto me. Wilt thou also disan-
nul my judgment? wilt thou condemn me, that thou
mayest be righteous? Hast thou an arm like God? or
canst thou thunder with a voice like him? Deck thyself now with majesty and excellency; and array
thyself with glory and beauty. Cast abroad the rage
of thy wrath: and behold every one that is proud,
and abase him. Look on every one that is proud, and
bring him low; and tread down the wicked in their
place. Hide them in the dust together; and bind their
faces in secret. Then will I confess unto thee that
thine own right hand can save thee. (40: 7 - 14)

Job replies to God who in turn rebukes the three friends who sought
to convince Job of his sin and the need for his suffering. Afterward
Job is healed of his skin disease, and a family and fortune are restored.

•Then Job answered the Lord, and said, I know that
thou canst do every thing, and that no thought can
be withholden from thee. Who is he that hideth
counsel without knowledge? therefore have I uttered
that I understood not; things too wonderful for me,
which I knew not. Hear, I beseech thee, and I will
speak: I will demand of thee, and declare thou unto
me. I have heard of thee by the hearing of the ear:
but now mine eye seeth thee. Wherefore I abhor
myself, and repent in dust and ashes.

And it was so, that after the Lord had spoken these
words unto Job, the Lord said to Eliphaz the Temanite, My wrath is kindled against thee, and against
thy two friends: for ye have not spoken of me the
thing that is right, as my servant Job hath. Therefore
take unto you now seven bullocks and seven rams,
and go to my servant Job, and offer up for yourselves a burnt offering; and my servant Job shall
pray for you: for him will I accept: lest I deal with
you after your folly, in that ye have not spoken of
me the thing which is right, like my servant Job.

So Eliphaz the Temanite and Bildad the Shuhite and Zophar the Naamathite went, and did according as the Lord commanded them: the Lord also accepted Job. And the Lord turned the captivity of Job, when he prayed for his friends: also the Lord gave Job twice as much as he had before.

Then came there unto him all his brethren, and all his sisters, and all they that had been of his acquaintance before, and did eat bread with him in his house: and they bemoaned him, and comforted him over all the evil that the Lord had brought upon him: every man also gave him a piece of money, and every one an earring of gold.

So the Lord blessed the latter end of Job more than his beginning: for he had fourteen thousand sheep, six thousand camels, and a thousand yoke of oxen, and a thousand she asses. He had also seven sons and three daughters. And in all the land were no women found so fair as the daughters of Job: and their father gave them inheritance among their brethren. After this lived Job an hundred and forty years, and saw his sons, and his sons' sons, even four generations. So Job died, being old and full of days. (42: 1 - 13, 15 - 17)

CHAPTER 5

THE PROMISE OF HEALING

IN THE OLD TESTAMENT

The Old Testament contains numerous references to God's healing power which are not related to specific incidents of personal healing. These statements extend from Genesis to Malachi. Some of the books of Psalms and Isaiah are especially lucid in portraying the power of God to heal physical and mental illnesses. Many Psalms, like the book of Job, were written for the inspiration of the individual rather than the collective group, race, or nation. They stress an inner worship and sense of peace. They are also directed toward the spiritual enlightenment of all mankind rather than a single ethnic community.

In varying degree, these readings show a growing recognition of the concept of God and man included in the second strand of Hebrew thought. As previously discussed, this view perceived of God as a loving and benevolent Creator, and man as His image and likeness. These writings reject the doctrine that God inflicts sickness or other adversity on mortals who are sometimes inclined to sin. Instead they tell of healing and health achieved by an understanding of a spiritual relationship or a divine law in which God is never really separated from man and His own creation.

These references constitute the promise of healing in the Old Testament. They are affirmations providing us with insights into an important part of Hebrew thought which has enabled people of all generations to overcome suffering from sickness and sin. At times these passages closely link healing to God's covenant and law. In some places they prophesied the coming of the Messiah or Anointed One who would firmly establish the Biblical practice of healing and regeneration.

The first readings refer to God's healing power embodied in His covenant with the people of Israel.

> •And when Abram was ninety years old and nine,
> the Lord appeared to Abram, and said unto him, I

am the Almighty God; walk before me, and be thou perfect. And I will make my covenant between me and thee, and will multiply thee exceedingly.

And Abram fell on his face: and God talked with him saying, As for me, behold, my covenant is with thee, and thou shalt be a father of many nations. Neither shall thy name any more be called Abram, but thy name shall be Abraham; for a father of many nations have I made thee. And I will make thee exceeding fruitful, and I will make nations of thee, and kings shall come out of thee. And I will establish my covenant between me and thee and thy seed after thee in their generations for an everlasting covenant, to be a God unto thee, and to thy seed after thee. (Gen. 17: 1 - 7)

•Know therefore that the Lord thy God, he is God, the faithful God, which keepeth covenant and mercy with them that love him and keep his commandments to a thousand generations; Thou shalt therefore keep the commandments, and the statutes, and the judgments, which I command thee this day, to do them.

Wherefore it shall come to pass, if ye hearken to these judgments, and keep, and do them, that the Lord thy God shall keep unto thee the covenant and the mercy which he sware unto thy fathers: And he will love thee, and bless thee, and multiply thee: he will also bless the fruit of thy womb, and the fruit of the land, thy corn, and thy wine, and thine oil, the increase of thy kine, and the flocks of thy sheep, in the land which he sware unto thy fathers to give thee.

Thou shalt be blessed above all people: there shall not be male or female barren among you, or among your cattle. And the Lord will take away from thee all sickness, and will put none of the evil diseases of Egypt, which thou knowest, upon thee; . . .(Deut. 7: 9, 11 - 15)

•Thou shalt be perfect with the Lord thy God.
(Deut. 18: 13)

•And Solomon stood before the altar of the Lord in
the presence of all the congregation of Israel, and
spread forth his hands toward heaven: And he said,
Lord God of Israel, there is no God like thee, in
heaven above, or on earth beneath, who keepest
covenant and mercy with thy servants that walk
before thee with all their heart:

If there be in the land famine, if there be pestilence,
blasting, mildew, locust, or if there be caterpiller; if
their enemy besiege them in the land of their cities;
whatsoever plague, whatsoever sickness there be;
What prayer and supplication soever be made by
any man, or by all thy people Israel, which shall
know every man the plague of his own heart and
spread forth his hands toward this house:

Then hear thou in heaven thy dwelling place, and
forgive, and do, and give to every man according to
his ways, whose heart thou knowest; (for thou, even
thou only, knowest the hearts of all the children of
men;) That they may fear thee all the days that they
live in the land which thou gavest unto our fathers.

Blessed be the Lord, that hath given rest unto his
people Israel, according to all that he promised:
there hath not failed one word of all his good
promise, which he promised by the hand of Moses
his servant. Let your heart therefore be perfect with
the Lord our God, to walk in his statutes, and to
keep his commandments, as at this day. (I Kings 8:
22, 23, 37 - 40, 56, 61)

The following readings describe the close relationship between
healing and God's law, a law viewed in some of the latter parts of the
Old Testament as a source of health and freedom for the people of all
nations.

•The law of the Lord is perfect, converting the soul:
the testimony of the Lord is sure, making wise the
simple. The statutes of the Lord are right, rejoicing

the heart: the commandment of the Lord is pure, enlightening the eyes. The fear of the Lord is clean , enduring for ever: the judgments of the Lord are true and righteous altogether.

More to be desired are they than gold, yea, than much fine gold: sweeter also than honey and the honeycomb. Moreover by them is thy servant warned: and in keeping of them there is great reward.

Keep back thy servant also from presumptuous sins; let them not have dominion over me: then shall I be upright, and I shall be innocent from the great transgression. Let the words of my mouth, and the meditation of my heart, be acceptable in thy sight, O Lord, my strength, and my redeemer. (Psalm 19: 7 - 11, 13, 14)

•Happy is he that hath the God of Jacob for his help, whose hope is in the Lord his God; which made heaven, and earth, the sea, and all that therein is: which keepeth truth for ever: Which executeth judgment for the oppressed: which giveth food to the hungry. The Lord looseth the prisoners. The Lord openeth the eyes of the blind: the Lord raiseth them that are bowed down: the Lord loveth the righteous: The Lord shall reign for ever, even thy God, O Zion, unto all generations. (Psalm 146: 5 - 8, 10)

•My son, forget not my law; but let thine heart keep my commandments; For length of days, and long life, and peace, shall they add to thee. Trust in the Lord with all thine heart; and lean not unto thine own understanding. In all thy ways acknowledge him, and he shall direct thy paths. Be not wise in thine own eyes: fear the Lord, and depart from evil. It shall be health to thy navel, and marrow to thy bones. (Prov. 3: 1, 2, 5 - 8)

•Thus saith God the Lord, he that created the heavens, and stretched them out; he that spread forth the earth, and that which cometh out of it; he that giveth breath unto the people upon it, and spirit to them that walk therein: I the Lord have called thee in righteousness, and will hold thine hand, and will keep thee, and give thee for a covenant of the people, for a light of the Gentiles; To open the blind eyes, to bring the prisoners from the prison, and them that sit in darkness out of the prison house.

And I will bring the blind by a way that they knew not; I will lead them in paths that they have not known: I will make darkness light before them, and crooked things straight. These things will I do unto them, and not forsake them. (Isaiah 42: 5 - 7, 16)

•Now thus saith the Lord that created thee, O Jacob, and he that formed thee, O Israel, Fear not: for I have redeemed thee, I have called thee by thy name, thou art mine. When thou passest through the waters, I will be with thee; and through the rivers, they shall not overflow thee: when thou walkest through the fire, thou shalt not be burned; neither shall the flame kindle upon thee.

Fear not: for I am with thee: I will bring thy seed from the east, and gather thee from west; I will say to the north, Give up; and to the south, Keep not back: bring my sons from far, and my daughters from the ends of the earth; Even every one that is called by my name: for I have created him for my glory, I have formed him; yea, I have made him. Bring forth the blind people that have eyes, and the deaf that have ears. I, even I, am the Lord; and beside me there is no savior. (Isaiah 43: 1, 2, 5 - 8, 11)

•Unto you that fear my name shall the Sun of righteousness arise with healing in his wings; . . . Remember ye the law of Moses my servant, which I commanded him in Horeb for all Israel, with the statutes and judgments. (Malachi 4: 2, 4)

The following passages describe God as a healing Comforter.

•Comfort ye, comfort ye my people, saith your God. Speak ye comfortably to Jerusalem, and cry unto her, that her warfare is accomplished, that her iniquity is pardoned: for she hath received of the Lord's hand double for all her sins. The voice of him that crieth in the wilderness, Prepare ye the way of the Lord, make straight in the desert a highway for our God.

Every valley shall be exalted, and every mountain and hill shall be made low: and the crooked shall be made straight, and the rough places plain: And the glory of the Lord shall be revealed, and all flesh shall see it together: for the mouth of the Lord hath spoken it.

Hast thou not known? hast thou not heard, that the everlasting God, the Lord, the Creator of the ends of the earth, fainteth not, neither is weary? there is no searching of his understanding. He giveth power to the faint; and to them that have no might he increaseth strength. . . .[T]hey that wait upon the Lord shall renew their strength; they shall mount up with wings as eagles; they shall run, and not be weary; and they shall walk, and not faint. (Isaiah 40: 1 - 5, 28, 29, 31)

•For the Lord shall comfort Zion: he will comfort all her waste places; and he will make her wilderness like Eden, and her desert like the garden of the Lord; joy and gladness shall be found therein, thanksgiving, and the voice of melody. Hearken unto me, my people; and give ear unto me, O my nation: for a law shall proceed from me, and I will make my judgment to rest for a light of the people.

Therefore the redeemed of the Lord shall return, and come with singing unto Zion; and everlasting joy shall be upon their head: they shall obtain gladness and joy; and sorrow and mourning shall flee away. I, even I, am he that comforteth you. (Isaiah 51: 3, 4, 11, 12)

•As one whom his mother comforteth, so will I
comfort you; and ye shall be comforted in
Jerusalem. (Isaiah 66: 13)

Some passages in the Old Testament are general statements relevant
to healing. They stress God's preservation of man, and the strength
and protection inherently bestowed on His creation.

•Give ear, O ye heavens, and I will speak; and hear,
O earth, the words of my mouth. My doctrine shall
drop as the rain, my speech shall distil as the dew, as
the small rain upon the tender herb, and as the
showers upon the grass; Because I will publish the
name of the Lord: ascribe ye greatness unto our
God. He is the Rock, his work is perfect: for all his
ways are judgment: a God of truth and without iniquity, just and right is he. (Deut. 32: 1 - 4)

•Preserve me, O God: for in thee do I put my trust. . .
The Lord is the portion of mine inheritance and of
my cup: thou maintainest my lot. The lines are fall-
en unto me in pleasant places; yea, I have a goodly
heritage. I will bless the Lord, who hath given me
counsel: my reins also instruct me in the night seasons.

I have set the Lord always before me: because he is
at my right hand, I shall not be moved. Therefore
my heart is glad, and my glory rejoiceth: my flesh
also shall rest in hope. For thou wilt not leave my
soul in hell; neither wilt thou suffer thine Holy One
to see corruption. Thou wilt shew me the path of
life: in thy presence is fulness of joy; at thy right
hand there are pleasures for evermore. (Psalm 16: 1,
5 - 11)

•As for God, his way is perfect: the word of the
Lord is tried: he is a buckler to all those that trust in
him. For who is God save the Lord? or who is a
rock save our God? It is God that girdeth me with
strength, and maketh my way perfect. (Psalm 18: 30
- 32)

•The Lord is my shepherd; I shall not want. He maketh me to lie down in green pastures: he leadeth me beside the still waters. He restoreth my soul: he leadeth me in the paths of righteousness for his name's sake. Yea, though I walk through the valley of the shadow of death, I will fear no evil: for thou art with me; thy rod and thy staff they comfort me. Thou preparest a table before me in the presence of mine enemies: thou anointest my head with oil; my cup runneth over. Surely goodness and mercy shall follow me all the days of my life: and I will dwell in the house of the Lord for ever. (Psalm 23: 1 - 6)

•Mark the perfect man, and behold the upright: for the end of that man is peace. (Psalm 37: 37)

•He that dwelleth in the secret place of the most High shall abide under the shadow of the Almighty. I will say of the Lord, He is my refuge and my fortress: my God; in him will I trust. Surely he shall deliver thee from the snare of the fowler, and from the noisome pestilence. He shall cover thee with his feathers, and under his wings shalt thou trust: his truth shall be thy shield and buckler.

Because thou hast made the Lord, which is my refuge, even the most High, thy habitation; there shall no evil befall thee, neither shall any plague come nigh thy dwelling. For he shall give his angels charge over thee, to keep thee in all thy ways. They shall bear thee up in their hands, lest thou dash thy foot against a stone. . . .With long life will I satisfy him, and shew him my salvation. (Psalm 91: 1 - 4, 9 - 12, 16)

•I will praise thee; for I am fearfully and wonderfully made: marvellous are thy works; and that my soul knoweth right well. (Psalm 139: 14)

A large number of passages in the Old Testament consist of explicit declarations of God's healing power and His care for the health of mankind.

•Then sang Moses and the children of Israel this
song unto the Lord, and spake, saying, I will sing
unto the Lord, for he hath triumphed gloriously: . . .
The Lord is my strength and song, and he is become
my salvation: he is my God, and I will prepare him
an habitation; my father's God, and I will exalt him.
So Moses brought Israel from the Red sea, and they
went out into the wilderness of Shur; and they went
three days in the wilderness and found no water.

And when they came to Marah, they could not drink
of the waters of Marah, for they were bitter: . . .And
the people murmured against Moses, saying, What
shall we drink? And he cried unto the Lord; and the
Lord shewed him a tree which when he had cast into
the waters, the waters were made sweet: there he
made for them a statute and an ordinance, and there
he proved them, And said, If thou wilt diligently
hearken to the voice of the Lord thy God, and wilt
do that which is right in his sight, and wilt give ear
to his commandments, and keep all his statutes, I
will put none of these diseases upon thee, which I
have brought upon the Egyptians: for I am the Lord
that healeth thee. (Ex. 15: 1, 2, 22 - 26)

•Behold, I send an Angel before thee, to keep thee
in the way, and to bring thee into the place which I
have prepared. . . .But if thou shalt indeed obey his
voice, and do all that I speak; then I will be an
enemy unto thine enemy, and an adversary unto
thine adversaries. . . .And ye shall serve the Lord
your God, and he shall bless thy bread, and thy
water; and I will take sickness away from the midst
of thee. (Ex. 23: 20, 22, 25)

•O Lord my God, I cried unto thee, and thou hast
healed me. O Lord, thou hast brought up my soul
from the grave: thou hast kept me alive, that I
should not go down to the pit. (Psalm 30: 2, 3)

•The eyes of the Lord are upon the righteous, and
his ears are open unto their cry. The righteous cry,
and the Lord heareth, and delivereth them out of all

their troubles. The Lord is nigh unto them that are of a broken heart; and saveth such as be of a contrite spirit. Many are the afflictions of the righteous: but the Lord delivereth him out of them all. He keepeth all his bones: not one of them is broken. . . .The Lord redeemeth the soul of his servants: and none of them that trust in him shall be desolate. (Psalm 34: 15, 17 - 20, 22)

•Why art thou cast down, O my soul? and why art thou disquieted within me? hope thou in God: for I shall yet praise him, who is the health of my countenance, and my God. (Psalm 42: 11)

•God be merciful unto us, and bless us; and cause his face to shine upon us; That thy way may be known upon earth, thy saving health among all nations. (Psalm 67: 1, 2)

•Bless the Lord, O my soul: and all that is within me, bless his holy name. Bless the Lord, O my soul, and forget not all his benefits: Who forgiveth all thine iniquities; who healeth all thy diseases; who redeemeth thy life from destruction; who crowneth thee with lovingkindness and tender mercies; Who satisfieth thy mouth with good things; so that thy youth is renewed like the eagle's. (Psalm 103: 1 - 5)

•Oh that men would praise the Lord for his goodness, and for his wonderful works to the children of men! . . .He sent his word, and healed them, and delivered them from their destructions. (Psalm 107: 15, 20)

•Happy is he that hath the God of Jacob for his help, whose hope is in the Lord his God: Which made heaven, and earth, the sea, and all that therein is: which keepeth truth for ever: Which executeth judgment for the oppressed: which giveth food to the hungry. The Lord looseth the prisoners: The Lord openeth the eyes of the blind: the Lord raiseth them that are bowed down: the Lord loveth the righteous. (Psalm 146: 5 - 8)

•My son, attend to my words; incline thine ear unto my sayings. Let them not depart from thine eyes; keep them in the midst of thine heart. For they are life unto those that find them, and health to all their flesh. (Prov. 4: 20 - 22)

•Strengthen ye the weak hands, and confirm the feeble knees. Say to them that are of a fearful heart, Be strong, fear not: behold, your God will come with vengeance, even God with a recompence; he will come and save you. Then the eyes of the blind shall be opened, and the ears of the deaf shall be unstopped. Then shall the lame man leap as an hart, and the tongue of the dumb sing: for in the wilderness shall waters break out, and streams in the desert. (Isaiah 35: 3 - 6)

•For thus saith the high and lofty One that inhabiteth eternity, whose name is Holy; I dwell in the high and holy place, with him also that is of a contrite and humble spirit, to revive the spirit of the humble, and to revive the heart of the contrite ones. . . .I have seen his ways, and will heal him: I will lead him also, and restore comforts unto him and to his mourners. I create the fruit of the lips; Peace, peace to him that is far off, and to him that is near, saith the Lord; and I will heal him. (Isaiah 57: 15, 18, 19)

•Blessed is the man that trusteth in the Lord, and whose hope the Lord is. For he shall be as a tree planted by the waters, and that spreadeth out her roots by the river, and shall not see when heat cometh, but her leaf shall be green; and shall not be careful in the year of drought, neither shall cease from yielding fruit. . . .Heal me, O Lord, and I shall be healed; save me, and I shall be saved: for thou art my praise. (Jer. 17: 7, 8, 14)

PART TWO

PRIMITIVE CHRISTIANTY

Jesus appeared among his people as a *physician.*
"The healthy need not a physician, but the sick."
(Mark ii. 17, Luke v. 31). The first three gospels
depict him as the physician of soul and body, as the
Savior or healer of men. Jesus says very little about
sickness; he cures it. He does not explain that sickness is health; he calls it by its proper name, and is
sorry for the sick person. There is nothing sentimen-
tal or subtle about Jesus; he draws no fine distinctions, he utters no sophistries about healthy people
being really sick and sick people healthy. He sees
himself surrounded by crowds of sick folk; he
attracts them, and his one impulse is to help them.
Jesus does not distinguish rigidly between sicknesses of the body and of the soul; he takes them both as
different expressions of the *one* supreme ailment of
humanity.

Adolf Harnack
The Mission and Expansion
of Christianity in the First
Three Centuries

PART TWO

PRIMITIVE CHRISTIANITY

The achievements of Biblical healing took much deeper root in Western civilization during the period of Primitive Christianity. This era began with the life and mission of Jesus; it started to decline around 325 A.D.when Constantine convened the Council of Nicea and initiated an imperial policy which made Christianity the official religion of the Roman empire. This three-hundred year period is one of the most significant epochs in human history. It cast a deep imprint on Western thought by revising the religious concepts of God, man, and law beyond the narrow racism and legalism of the Judaic religion. It also provided new spiritual and moral values at a time when Greek philosophy and Roman jurisprudence were becoming more deeply entrenched in Western culture.

Biblical healing reached its pinnacle during the early years of Primitive Christianity. In three years Jesus accomplished more healings than did the followers of Hebrew theology during the preceding thirteen centuries. Within a very brief period of time, he expanded spiritual healing far beyond its previous limited basis into the new form of Christian healing.

Jesus was the first and only religious leader in history to make healing a distinct and vital part of his teachings. This aspect of his mission is well defined in the book of Matthew: "And Jesus went about all Galilee, teaching in their synagogues, and preaching the gospel of the kingdom, and healing all manner of sickness and all manner of disease among the people." (4: 23) The patriarchs and prophets of the Old Testament as well as the founders of major religions elsewhere in the Near East and the Orient were often great teachers and great preachers. Jesus was the only religious leader who was also a great healer.

From the beginning of his religious career, Jesus acknowledged some elements of Hebrew theology that included the foretelling of his own life and mission. He spoke often of Moses' words and works, and he was likely aware of Moses' prophecy to the people of Israel: "The Lord thy God will raise up unto thee a Prophet from the midst of thee, of thy brethren, like unto me; unto him ye shall hearken." (Deut. 18: 15) As already cited, Jesus referred at times to Elijah and Elisha. Perhaps his most poignant referral to Old Testament prophecy and the meaning of his own mission occurred when he entered a synagogue in Nazareth early in his ministry and read from the book of Esaias (Isaiah) the following passage:

> The Spirit of the Lord is upon me, because he hath anointed me to preach the gospel to the poor; he hath sent me to heal the brokenhearted, to preach deliverance to the captives, and recovering of the sight to the blind, to set at liberty them that are bruised, to preach the acceptable year of the Lord. (Luke 4: 18, 19)

This narrative continues:

> And he [Jesus] closed the book, and he gave it again to the minister, and sat down. And the eyes of all them that were in the synagogue were fastened on him. And he began to say unto them, This day is this scripture fulfilled in your ears. And all bare him witness, and wondered as the gracious words which proceeded out of his mouth. (Luke 4: 20 - 22)

On this occasion, Jesus also cited the proverb: "Physician, heal thyself."

Jesus placed much greater emphasis on the well-being of the human body than did the Hebrew religious thinkers who preceded him. He perceived health and wholeness as an expression by each individual man and woman of an unseen eternal and perfect life derived from God. He established health completely on a spiritual, rather than a material, basis. This divine source was the power which accomplished all of his remarkable healings. In his book *Health and Healing: Studies in New Testament Principles and Practice*, Reverend John Wilkinson has stated: "The New Testament presupposes the Old Testament concept of health and accepts its expression in terms of wholeness, obedience, righteousness, and life. However, the content of these terms was transformed by the fuller revelation given in Jesus Christ. . . . [H]e changed the concept of life. In Old Testament terms this had meant life measured by the quantity of time and the quality of this world, but Jesus came to bring eternal life, life measured by the quality of eternity where quantity and duration have no relevance." (p. 16)

The Christian idea of the human body was later explained very clearly by Paul when he wrote: "Know ye not that your body is the temple of the Holy Ghost which is in you, which ye have of God, and ye are not your own. . . .[T]herefore glorify God in your body, and in your spirit, which are God's." (I Cor. 6: 19, 20) In Jesus' view, God created man to partake of a life of health and comfort. He gave little credence to religious rituals, ceremonies, and dietary rules. His chief concern was the quality of individual thought and progress toward a higher understanding of man's spiritual being and his rights as a child of God.

According to Jesus, healing the body was not the only purpose of Christianity. Nor was it the major purpose. Yet the destruction of physical and mental disease was an important step in proving his teachings about the relationship between God and man. Healing supplied necessary evidence to validate the higher goal of Christianity to overcome sin and aid in the spiritual regeneration of mankind. Healing, in brief, provided an important step to a clearer understanding of God and the true nature of man.

When the Pharisees criticized Jesus and his disciples for sitting among publicans and sinners, he replied that his mission was directed specifically toward those who suffered from sickness and sin. He said: "They that are whole need not a physician; but they that are sick. I am not come to call the righteous, but sinners to repentance." (Luke 5: 31, 32) When sending the twelve disciples among the people of Israel, he took special care to prepare them to heal all kinds of diseases. Even their preaching, he said, was to support the work of healing. As written in Matthew:

> And when he had called unto him his twelve disciples, he gave them power against unclean spirits, to cast them out, and to heal all manner of sickness and all manner of disease. . . . These twelve Jesus sent forth, and commanded them, saying, Go not into the way of the Gentiles, and into any city of the Samaritans enter ye not. But go rather to the lost sheep of the house of Israel. And as ye go, preach, saying, The kingdom of heaven is at hand. Heal the sick, cleanse the lepers, raise the dead, cast out devils: freely ye have received, freely give. (10: 5 - 8)

At a later time Jesus sent an additional seventy of his followers to go in pairs to spread his teachings in places "whither he himself would come." As these "labourers" went into cities and villages, he instructed them to "heal the sick that are therein, and say unto them, The kingdom of God is come nigh unto you." (Luke 10: 9)

Jesus' healing mission was further emphasized when John the Baptist sent two of his own disciples asking if he was the Messiah "or do we look for another?" Jesus' reply was very clear:

> Go and shew John again those things which ye do hear and see. The blind receive their sight, and the lame walk, the lepers are cleansed, and the deaf hear, the dead are raised up, and the poor have the gospel preached to them. And blessed is he, whosoever shall not be offended in me. (Matt. 11: 4 - 6)

As previously cited, Jesus was aware of his Hebrew heritage; yet he spoke frequently of the many differences between his own teachings and the orthodox doctrines of the Old Testament. He upheld the validity of the Old Testament view that sin often causes disease and that the overcoming of sin is conducive to physical and mental healing. At the same time he vehemently denounced the Hebrew teachings that God inflicts disease on man as a means of punishing sin; his message to the scribes and Pharisees on this issue was very blunt. He said: "Ye are of your father the devil, and the lusts of your father ye will do. He was a murderer from the beginning, and abode not in the truth, because there is no truth in him. When he speaketh a lie; he speaketh of his own: for he is a liar and the father of it." (John 8: 44)

This "blasphemy" of orthodox doctrine combined with his healing works as proof of a living, loving, and perfect God led eventually to Jesus' condemnation and crucifixion. Yet he overruled this injustice by the greatest healing of all time in his resurrection from the grave.

In a historical period of widespread tyranny, Jesus' healing works raised the level of one area of individual freedom and the rule of law to an unprecedented height. While many people touched by his mission lived under oppressive laws which restricted their political, economic, and social freedom, they did obtain a degree of freedom from sin, disease, and death as well as a freedom to enjoy their God-given health and wholeness. These physical and mental healings achieved by a higher spiritual law provided a model of freedom and liberty for future generations.

JESUS HEALING THE SICK

And great multitudes came unto him, having with them those that were lame, blind, dumb, maimed, and many others, and cast them down at Jesus' feet; and he healed them...(Matthew 15: 30)

CHAPTER 6

JESUS

(CIRCA 6 B. C. - 27 A.D.)

The healing words and works of Jesus are recorded in the first four books of the New Testament. The founder of Christianity did not leave any written record of his own life and mission. The gospels of Matthew, Mark, Luke, and John devote slightly more than one-third of their narrative space to Jesus' healings. They cite forty different incidents of healing, many of which are described in considerable detail. Many of those healed were women and children. Jesus also performed many healings that are not recorded in the New Testament. Their number is almost certainly in the thousands. According to the concluding words of the book of John: "And there are also many other things which Jesus did, the which, if they should be written every one, I suppose even the world itself could not contain the books that should be written." (21: 25)

Many Bible scholars explain the term for healing most commonly used in the New Testament is *therapeuō*. This Greek word means "to serve" or "to attend to" the needs of another person. It denotes a close relationship between the person rendering the service and the person receiving the service. Its use in the four Gospels refers to healing done without the use of medicine or to healing performed by persons who were not members of the medical profession of the time. Many people healed by Jesus were suffering from organic diseases which these physicians had failed to heal. These diseases included demon possession, leprosy, palsy, fever, blindness, deafness, lameness, dropsy, arthritis, hemorrhage, and epilepsy. Before his own resurrection, he also raised three other persons from death.

The following readings illustrate different methods used by Jesus in healing disease. Many of these healings also reveal important aspects of his teachings.

The first group shows the use of touching combined with healing words, the use of only a healing command, and the use of distant healing where the sick person was absent from Jesus' presence.

•When he was come down from the mountain, great
multitudes followed him. And, behold, there came a
leper and worshipped him, saying, Lord, if thou
wilt, thou canst make me clean. And Jesus put forth
his hand, and touched him, saying, I will; be thou
clean. And immediately his leprosy was cleansed.
(Matt. 8: 1 - 3)

•And it came to pass also on another sabbath, that he
entered into the synagogue and taught: and there
was a man whose right hand was withered. And the
scribes and Pharisees watched him, whether he
would heal on the sabbath day; that they might find
an accusation against him.

But he knew their thoughts, and said to the man
which had the withered hand, Rise up, and stand
forth in the midst. And he arose and stood forth.
Then said Jesus unto them, I will ask you one thing;
Is it lawful on the sabbath days to do good or to do
evil? to save life, or to destroy it? And looking
round about upon them all, he said unto the man,
Stretch forth thy hand. And he did so: and his hand
was restored whole as the other. (Luke 6: 6 - 10)

•Now when he had ended all his sayings in the audience of the people, he entered into Capernaum. And
a certain centurion's servant, who was dear unto
him, was sick, and ready to die. And when he heard
of Jesus, he sent unto him the elders of the Jews,
beseeching him that he would come and heal his
servant.

And when they came to Jesus, they besought him
instantly, saying, That he was worthy for whom he
should do this: For he loveth our nation, and he hath
built us a synagogue.

Then Jesus went with them. And when he was now
not far from the house, the centurion sent friends to

him, saying unto him, Lord, trouble not thyself: for I
am not worthy that thou shouldest enter under my
roof: Therefore neither thought I myself worthy to
come unto thee: but say in a word, and my servant
shall be healed. For I also am a man set under
authority, having under me soldiers, and I say unto
one, Go, and he goeth; and to another, Come, and he
cometh; and to my servant, Do this, and he doeth it.

When Jesus heard these things, he marvelled at him,
and turned him about, and said unto the people that
followed him, I say unto you, I have not found so
great faith, no, not in Israel. And they that were
sent, returning to the house, found the servant whole
that had been sick. (Luke 7: 1 - 10)

Some people were healed by touching Jesus' clothing. On one occasion a woman suffering from hemorrhaging was instantly healed by
merely touching his garment while he was on his way to raise Jairus'
daughter from death.

•And, behold, there came a man named Jairus, and
he was a ruler of the synagogue: and he fell down at
Jesus' feet, and besought him that he would come
into his house, For he had one only daughter, about
twelve years of age, and she lay a dying. But as he
went the people thronged him.

And a woman having an issue of blood twelve
years, which had spent all her living upon physicians, neither could be healed of any, Came behind
him, and touched the border of his garment: and
immediately her issue of blood stanched. And Jesus
said, Who touched me? When all denied, Peter and
they that were with him said, Master, the multitude
throng thee and press thee, and sayest thou, Who
toucheth me?

And Jesus said, Somebody hath touched me: for I
perceive that virtue is gone out of me. And when the

woman saw that she was not hid, she came trem-
bling, and falling down before him, she declared
unto him before all the people for what cause she
had touched him, and how she was healed immediately. And he said unto her, Daughter, be of good
comfort: thy faith hath made thee whole; go in
peace. (Luke 8: 41 - 48)

Occasionally Jesus healed individual cases involving both sickness
and sin.

•And he entered into a ship, and passed over, and
came into his own city. And, behold, they brought to
him a man sick of the palsy, lying on a bed: and
Jesus seeing their faith said unto the sick of the
palsy; Son, be of good cheer; thy sins be forgiven
thee. And, behold, certain of the scribes said within
themselves, This man blasphemeth.

And Jesus knowing their thoughts said, Wherefore
think ye evil in your hearts? For whether is easier to
say, Thy sins be forgiven thee; or to say, Arise, and
walk? But that ye may know that the Son of man
hath power on earth to forgive sins, (then saith he to
the sick of the palsy,) Arise, take up thy bed, and go
unto thine house.

And he arose, and departed to his house. But when
the multitude saw it, they marvelled, and glorified
God, which had given such power unto men. (Matt.
9: 1 - 8)

At times Jesus healed people who resisted healing.

•And in the synagogue there was a man, which had
a spirit of an unclean devil, and cried out with a
loud voice, Saying, Let us alone; what have we to
do with thee, thou Jesus of Nazareth? art thou come
to destroy us? I know thee who thou art; the Holy
One of God.

And Jesus rebuked him, saying, Hold thy peace, and come out of him. And when the devil had thrown him in the midst, he came out of him, and hurt him not.

And they were all amazed, and spake among themselves, saying, What a word is this! for with authority and power he commandeth the unclean spirits, and they come out. And the fame of him went out into every place of the country round about. (Luke 4: 33 - 37)

The healing of the widow's son at Nain was the second occasion where Jesus overcame death.

•And it came to pass the day after, that he went into a city called Nain; and many of his disciples went with him, and much people. Now when he came nigh to the gate of the city, behold, there was a dead man carried out, the only son of his mother, and she was a widow: and much people of the city was with her.

And when the Lord saw her, he had compassion on her, and said unto her, Weep not. And he came and touched the bier: and they that bare him stood still. And he said, Young man, I say unto thee, Arise.

And he that was dead sat up, and began to speak. And he delivered him to his mother. And there came a fear on all: and they glorified God, saying, That a great prophet is risen up among us; and, That God hath visited his people. (Luke 7: 11 - 16)

Jesus' healings revealed a deep compassion for mankind. They illustrated that healing is one of the highest means of exemplifying a God who is Love. One of the most vivid accounts of Jesus' tenderness and kindness is the healing of an arthritic woman. This incident indicates the importance he placed on the health and comfort of the human body. It also shows his strong opposition to many Jewish customs, including the traditional use of the sabbath, which ignored the dignity and well-being of individual men and women.

•And, behold, there was a woman which had a spirit of infirmity eighteen years, and was bowed together, and could in no wise lift up herself. And when Jesus saw her, he called her to him, and said unto her, Woman, thou art loosed from thine infirmity. And he laid his hands on her: and immediately she was made straight, and glorified God.

And the ruler of the synagogue answered with indignation, because that Jesus had healed on the sabbath day, and said unto the people, There are six days in which men ought to work: in them therefore come and be healed, and not on the sabbath day.

The Lord then answered him, and said, Thou hypocrite, doth not each one of you on the sabbath loose his ox or his ass from the stall, and lead him away to watering? And ought not this woman, being a daughter of Abraham, whom Satan hath bound, lo, these eighteen years, be loosed from this bond on the sabbath day?

And when he had said these things, all his adversaries were ashamed: and all the people rejoiced for all the glorious things that were done by him. (Luke 13: 11 - 17)

Like Elisha, Jesus demonstrated the universality of God's power by healing Gentiles. One of these incidents, the healing of the centurion's servant, has already been cited as an illustration of distant healing. Jesus healed a second Gentile, the daughter of a Greek woman from Syrophenicia, after he was convinced of her devout faith.

•Then Jesus went thence, and departed into the coasts of Tyre and Sidon. And, behold, a woman of Canaan came out of the same coasts, and cried unto him, saying, Have mercy on me, O Lord, thou son of David; my daughter is grievously vexed with a devil.

But he answered her not a word. And his disciples
came and besought him, saying, Send her away; for
she crieth after us. But he answered and said, I am
not sent but unto the lost sheep of the house of
Israel.

Then came she and worshipped him, saying, Lord,
help me. But he answered and said, It is not meet to
take the children's bread, and to cast it to dogs. And
she said, Truth, Lord: yet the dogs eat of the crumbs
which fall from their master's table.

Then Jesus answered and said unto her, O woman,
great is thy faith: be it unto thee even as thou wilt.
And her daughter was made whole in that very hour.
(Matt. 15: 21 - 28)

Jesus readily proved the fallacy of the Hebrew doctrine that God
inflicts disease on people to punish them for their sins. One of the
most graphic accounts of this part of his mission is the healing of a
man who had been blind from his birth. This incident is described in
more detail than any of Jesus' other healings recorded in the New Testament. It illustrates in some degree the vast difference regarding
man's right to health and wholeness according to Hebrew orthodox
theology and the rights of man according to the new teachings of
Christianity.

•And as Jesus passed by, he saw a man which was
blind from his birth. And his disciples asked him,
saying, Master, who did sin, this man, or his parents,
that he was born blind? Jesus answered, Neither
hath this man sinned, nor his parents: but that the
works of God should be made manifest in him. I
must work the works of him that sent me, while it is
day: the night cometh, when no man can work. As
long as I am in the world, I am the light of the
world.

When he had thus spoken, he spat on the ground,
and made clay of the spittle, and he anointed the

eyes of the blind man with the clay, And said unto him, Go, wash in the pool of Siloam, (which is by interpretation, Sent.) He went his way therefore, and washed, and came seeing.

The neighbours therefore, and they which before had seen him that he was blind, said, Is not this he that sat and begged? Some said, This is he: others said, He is like him: but he said, I am he. Therefore said they unto him, How were thine eyes opened?

He answered and said, A man that is called Jesus made clay, and anointed mine eyes, and said unto me, Go to the pool of Siloam, and wash: and I went and washed, and I received sight. Then said they unto him, Where is he? He said, I know not.

They brought to the Pharisees him that aforetime was blind. And it was the sabbath day when Jesus made the clay, and opened his eyes. Then again the Pharisees also asked him how he had received his sight. He said unto them, He put clay upon mine eyes, and I washed, and do see.

Therefore said some of the Pharisees, This man is not of God, because he keepeth not the sabbath day. Others said, How can a man that is a sinner do such miracles? And there was a division among them. They say unto the blind man again, What sayest thou of him, that he hath opened thine eyes? He said, He is a prophet.

But the Jews did not believe concerning him, that he had been blind, and received his sight, until they called the parents of him that had received his sight. And they asked them, saying, Is this your son, who ye say was born blind? how then doth he now see?

His parents answered them and said, We know that this is our son, and that he was born blind: But by what means he now seeth, we know not; or who

hath opened his eyes, we know not: he is of age; ask
him: he shall speak for himself. These words spake
his parents, because they feared the Jews: for the
Jews had agreed already, that if any man did confess
that he was Christ, he should be put out of the synagogue. Therefore said his parents, He is of age; ask
him.

Then again called they the man that was blind, and
said unto him, Give God the praise: we know that
this man is a sinner. He answered and said, Whether
he is a sinner or no, I know not: one thing I know,
that, whereas I was blind, now I see. Then said they
to him again, What did he to thee? how opened he
thine eyes? He answered them, I have told you
already, and ye did not hear: wherefore would ye
hear it again? will ye also be his disciples?

Then they reviled him, and said, Thou art his disciple; but we are Moses' disciples. We know that God
spake unto Moses: as for this fellow, we know not
from whence he is. The man answered and said unto
them, Why herein is a marvelous thing, that ye
know not from whence he is, and yet he hath opened
mine eyes. Now we know that God hearest not sinners: but if any man be a worshipper of God, and
doeth his will, him he heareth. Since the world
began was it not heard that any man opened the eyes
of one that was born blind. If this man were not of
God, he could do nothing.

They answered and said unto him, Thou wast altogether born in sins, and dost thou teach us? And
they cast him out. Jesus heard that they had cast him
out; and when he had found him, he said unto him,
Dost thou believe on the Son of God? He answered
and said, Who is he, Lord, that I might believe on
him?

And Jesus said unto him, Thou hast both seen him,
and it is he that talketh with thee. And he said, Lord,
I believe. And he worshipped him. (John 9: 1 - 38)

Jesus' teachings were based on the healing power which accompanied the spiritual and moral maxims first enunciated by Moses in the Ten Commandments. The founder of Christianity likewise declared spiritual and moral precepts relevant to the healing of sin, disease, and death in his Sermon on the Mount.

> •And seeing the multitudes, he went up into a mountain: and when he was set, his disciples came unto him: And he opened his mouth, and taught them, saying,
>
> Blessed are the poor in spirit: for their's is the kingdom of heaven.
>
> Blessed are they that mourn: for they shall be comforted.
>
> Blessed are the meek: for they shall inherit the earth.
>
> Blessed are they which do hunger and thirst after righteousness: for they shall be filled.
>
> Blessed are the merciful: for they shall obtain mercy.
>
> Blessed are the pure in heart: for they shall see God.
>
> Blessed are the peacemakers: for they shall be called the children of God.
>
> Blessed are they which are persecuted for righteousness' sake: for their's is the kingdom of heaven.
>
> Blessed are ye, when men shall revile you, and persecute you, and shall say all manner of evil against you falsely, for my sake.
>
> Rejoice, and be exceeding glad: for great is your reward in heaven: for so persecuted they the prophets which were before you. (Matt. 5: 1 - 12)

•Thou, when thou prayest, enter into thy closet, and when thou hast shut thy door, pray to thy Father which is in secret; and thy Father which seeth in secret shall reward thee openly. But when ye pray, use not vain repetitions, as the heathen do: for they think that they shall be heard for their much speaking. Be not ye therefore like unto them: for your Father knoweth what things ye have need of, before ye ask him.

After this manner therefore pray ye: Our Father which art in heaven, Hallowed by thy name. Thy kingdom come. Thy will be done in earth, as it is in heaven. Give us this day our daily bread. And forgive us our debts, as we forgive our debtors. And lead us not into temptation, but deliver us from evil: For thine is the kingdom, and the power, and the glory, for ever. (Matt. 6: 6 - 13)

•Ask, and it shall be given you; seek, and ye shall find; knock, and it shall be opened unto you: For every one that asketh receiveth; and he that seeketh findeth; and to him that knocketh it shall be opened.

Or what man is there of you, whom if his son ask bread, will he give him a stone? Or if he ask a fish, will he give him a serpent? If ye then, being evil, know how to give good gifts unto your children, how much more shall your Father which is in heaven give good things to them that ask him? Therefore all things whatsoever ye would that men should do to you, do ye even so to them: for this is the law and the prophets.

Enter ye in at the strait gate: for wide is the gate, and broad is the way, that leadeth to destruction, and many there be which go in thereat: Because strait is the gate, and narrow is the way, which leadeth unto life, and few there be that find it.

Beware of false prophets, which come to you in sheep's clothing, but inwardly they are ravening wolves. Ye shall know them by their fruits. Do men gather grapes of thorns, or figs of thistles? Even so every good tree bringeth forth good fruit: but a corrupt tree bring forth evil fruit. A good tree cannot bring forth evil fruit, neither can a corrupt tree bring forth good fruit. Every tree that bringeth not forth good fruit is hewn down, and cast into the fire. Wherefore by their fruits ye shall know them. (Matt. 7: 7 - 20)

ST. PETER AND ST. JOHN AT THE BEAUTIFUL GATE
Then Peter said, Silver and gold have I none; but such as I have give I thee: In the
name of Jesus Christ of Nazareth rise up and walk. . . . (Acts 3: 6)

CHAPTER 7

THE APOSTLES

(CIRCA 24 -100 A.D.)

Jesus' disciples received many instructions during his ministry to heal the sick. Just before his ascension, he gave them a special commission regarding healing. He said:

> Go ye into all the world, and preach the gospel to every creature. . . . And these signs shall follow them that believe; In my name shall they cast out devils; they shall speak with new tongues; They shall take up serpents; and if they drink any deadly thing, it shall not hurt them; they shall lay hands on the sick, and they shall recover. (Mark 16: 15, 17, 18)

In this transfer of authority to his disciples, Jesus used the word "signs" to designate healing in the continuation of his mission. Healing had been an important part of his own ministry; he expected his followers to perform healing as a major part of the work of his new church. In the view of some Christian writers, Jesus' commission to heal was the only sign or wonder he expected his disciples to perform. They do not believe he gave them the ability to achieve other signs or wonders which he had done himself, such as walking on the water, feeding five thousand people with a few loaves and fishes, and stilling the violent waves of the sea. In his book *Body and Soul,* the English scholar Percy Dearmer has emphasized this point as follows:

> There is. . .no doubt that the miracles usually denoted as "works" are the ordinary works of healing, which indeed form so enormously large a proportion of our Lord's signs that the nature-miracles may be considered as quite exceptional occurrences. We may, I think, safely assume that it was not such exceptional miracles as these that Christ was here

referring; for in his commission to the Twelve he
confined their powers to the works of healing, and
we find no trace of anything like the "cosmic" miracles in the Acts of the Apostles: it must have been
clearly understood that Christ did not commission
his disciples to exercise authority over the powers of
nature. (p. 183)

Other Christians maintain that Jesus placed no limits on the mira-
cle-works to be performed by his followers. They cite his declaration
in John 14: 12, where he said that they who believed on him would do
the same works which he did and even "greater works than these shall
he do."

Jesus' commission to heal was bequeathed to eleven of his original
disciples who continued using the title of apostle after their master's
ascension. The word "apostle" means a "commissioned messenger or
ambassador" or "one sent forth." In addition to the first disciples, the
apostles also included Matthias, Barnabas, and James, the brother of
Jesus. Paul likewise declared himself an apostle in his writings
because of his dramatic conversion and encounter with the voice of
Jesus on the road to Damascus. Other followers of Jesus cited in the
New Testament who performed healing works were Stephen, Philip,
and Ananias.

The four Gospels and the book of Acts relate seventeen incidents of
healing by the apostles and other followers of Jesus. More than half of
these cases refer to healings among multitudes of people. They
describe several healings of children. The apostles healed many of the
same diseases as Jesus did, including demon possession, lameness,
blindness, palsy, fever, dysentery, and death. On one occasion Paul
healed himself of a poisonous viper bite; he also raised himself from
death after being stoned by a mob. He likewise performed many healings among Gentiles in his missionary journeys.

The methods of healing most commonly used by the apostles were
similar to those used by Jesus, including the laying on of hands, a
healing command, and touching. At times they healed by anointing
sick persons with oil. On one occasion healing was accomplished by
Peter as his shadow was cast on diseased people lying on beds and
couches in a street. Some healings occurred by touching clothing
taken from Paul as he was preaching at Ephesus.

In all these healing works, the apostles stated clearly that the
destruction of disease and death was achieved by the power of God

and an understanding of Jesus' teachings. Never did they claim any healing power of their own. Many of their healings were performed "in the name of Jesus Christ." (Acts 4: 10 and Acts 9: 34) This impersonal healing authority became an important part of the foundation of the emerging Christian church. In the presence of Jewish priests and elders, Peter affirmed that Jesus' healing mission was "the stone rejected by the builders which has become the keystone - and you are the builders. There is no salvation in anyone else at all, for there is no name under heaven granted to me, by which we may receive salvation." (New English Bible, Acts 4: 11, 12)

At times the healing work of the apostles and other followers of Jesus confronted a problem which has concerned the healing mission of the Christian church for almost two thousand years. In spite of their impressive healing ability, they encountered some situations where they were unable to achieve a healing. One case of this kind occurred during Jesus' ministry when a father brought his lunatic son whom the disciples had failed to heal. Jesus promptly cured the child and counseled his disciples on the need for a stronger faith as well as "prayer and fasting." (Matt. 17: 14 - 21)

The apostles later accomplished similar instantaneous healings of mental disease in their own healing work, yet they intermittently faced some cases which they were unable to heal. At one time Paul sent a fellow worker named Epaphroditus to the Christian community at Philippi because he had been seriously ill. On another journey Paul left a companion named Trophimus at the city of Miletum because he was sick. Paul does not explain why he did not heal these two men since he had performed more impressive healings on himself and on other people.

Perhaps the most notable physical malady which was not healed by the apostles was Paul's own "thorn in the flesh." Bible scholars have debated the nature of this affliction for many years, and most scholars believe it was periodic bouts of rheumatism or malaria. Three times he prayed to God to be healed of this ailment, but the physical disorder remained. Yet instead of becoming discouraged, Paul used this infirmity to remind himself of the need to increase his understanding of Jesus' teachings. It did not deter him from making his arduous missionary journeys where he continued to preach and to heal.

Paul's example encouraged the Christian church to continue with the healing ministry in spite of some failures. The number of healings far exceeded the few failures, and they inspired early Christian healers to strive more assiduously for a stronger faith and deeper spiritual understanding. Their healing works conveyed a sense of hope and conviction that future generations of Christians would some day attain a higher level of thought as encouraged by Jesus and do the same kinds of healings that he did without any failures.

The writings of the apostles give us only a fragmentary view of their healing ministry. Much of their correspondence and written works has not survived the ravages of time and turmoil. Portions of the four Gospels and the book of Acts provide the major source of information about their healings. The epistles of the New Testament make only a few specific references to healing. Yet from these writings we do receive convincing proof that the healing mission which comprised a vital part of Jesus' life and teachings was continued by his disciples and the early Christian church.

The first two selections in Luke relate healings achieved by the apostles and other followers of Jesus during his lifetime and ministry.

> •Then he called his twelve disciples together, and gave them power and authority over all devils, and to cure diseases. And he sent them to preach the kingdom of God, and to heal the sick. And he said unto them, Take nothing for your journey, neither staves, nor scrip, neither bread, neither money; neither have two coats apiece.

> And whatsoever house ye enter into, there abide, and thence depart. And whosoever will not receive you, when ye go out of that city, shake off the very dust from your feet for a testimony against them.

> And they departed, and went through the towns, preaching the gospel, and healing every where. (9: 1 - 6)

> •After these things the Lord appointed other seventy also, and sent them two and two before his face into every city and place, whither he himself would come.

> And the seventy returned again with joy, saying, Lord, even the devils are subject unto us through thy name. And he said unto them, I beheld Satan as lightning fall from heaven. Behold, I give unto you

power to tread on serpents and scorpions, and over
all the power of the enemy: and nothing shall by any
means hurt you. Notwithstanding in this rejoice not,
that the spirits are subject unto you; but rather
rejoice, because your names are written in heaven.
(10: 1, 17 - 20)

Two references are made in Acts to healings done by all the apostles after Jesus' ascension.

•Then they that gladly received his word were baptized: and the same day there were added unto them
about three thousand souls. And they continued
stedfastly in the apostles' doctrine and fellowship,
and in breaking of bread, and in prayers. And fear
came upon every soul: and many wonders and signs
were done by the apostles. (2: 41 - 43)

•And by the hands of the apostles were many signs
and wonders wrought among the people; . . .There
came also a multitude out of the cities round about
unto Jerusalem, bringing sick folks, and them which
were vexed with unclean spirits: and they were
healed every one. (5: 12, 16)

Several specific references in Acts relate healings performed by
Peter, who was one of the apostles most frequently queried by Jesus
regarding his mission and teachings. The first healing cited here was
done in the company of John, who was one of the most spiritually
minded of Jesus' apostles. The other healings were done by Peter
alone, including raising a woman from death.

•Now Peter and John went up together into the temple at the hour of prayer, being the ninth hour. And a
certain man lame from his mother's womb was carried, whom they laid daily at the gate of the temple
which is called Beautiful, to ask alms of them that
entered into the temple; Who seeing Peter and John
about to go into the temple asked an alms.

And Peter, fastening his eyes upon him with John, said, Look on us. And he gave heed unto them, expecting to receive something of them. Then Peter said, Silver and gold have I none; but such as I have give I thee: In the name of Jesus Christ of Nazareth rise up and walk.

And he took him by the right hand, and lifted him up: and immediately his feet and ankle bones received strength. And he leaping up stood, and walked, and entered with them into the temple, walking, and leaping, and praising God. And all the people saw him walking and praising God: And they knew that it was he which sat for alms at the Beautiful gate of the temple: and they were filled with wonder and amazement at that which had happened unto him. (3: 1 - 10)

•And it came to pass, as Peter passed throughout all quarters, he came down also to the saints which dwelt at Lydda. And there he found a certain man named Aeneas, which had kept his bed eight years, and was sick of the palsy. And Peter said unto him, Aeneas, Jesus Christ maketh thee whole: arise, and make thy bed. And he arose immediately. And all that dwelt at Lydda and Saron saw him, and turned to the Lord. (9: 32 - 35)

•Now there was at Joppa a certain disciple named Tabitha, which by interpretation is called Dorcas: and this woman was full of good works and almsdeeds which she did. And it came to pass in those days, that she was sick, and died: whom when they had washed, they laid her in an upper chamber.

And forasmuch as Lydda was nigh to Joppa, and the disciples had heard that Peter was there, they sent unto him two men, desiring him that he would not delay to come to them. Then Peter arose and went with them. When he was come, they brought him into the upper chamber: and all the widows stood by

him weeping, and shewing the coats and garments
which Dorcas made, while she was with them.

And Peter put them all forth, and kneeled down, and
prayed; and turning him to the body said, Tabitha,
arise. And she opened her eyes: and when she saw
Peter, she sat up. And he gave her his hand, and lifted her up, and when he had called the saints and
widows, presented her alive. And it was known
throughout all Joppa; and many believed in the
Lord. (9: 36 - 42)

Paul performed the largest number of healings recorded in the book
of Acts. His healing works were of special interest and inspiration to
future Christians, since he had no personal contact with Jesus. Instead
he had persecuted the early Christian churches until his conversion to
Christianity on the road to Damascus. Thereafter he played a significant role in spreading Christianity to Gentile communities in Asia
Minor, Macedonia, and Rome. His healing works vividly illustrated
the impersonal power and ability to heal by using Jesus' teachings.
Paul is considered by theologians and historians alike as second only
to Jesus in establishing Christianity as a world religion. His missionary journeys were important in making the Christian church a vital
force in the evolution of Western civilization.

•And there sat a certain man at Lystra, impotent in
his feet, being a cripple from his mother's womb,
who never had walked: The same heard Paul speak:
who stedfastly beholding him, and perceiving that
he had faith to be healed, Said with a loud voice,
Stand upright on thy feet. And he leaped and
walked. (14: 8 - 10)

•And a certain woman named Lydia, a seller of pur-
ple, of the city of Thyatira, which worshipped God,
heard us: whose heart the Lord opened, that she
attended unto the things which were spoken of Paul.
And when she was baptized, and her household, she
besought us, saying, If ye have judged me to be
faithful to the Lord, come into my house, and abide
there. And she constrained us.

And it came to pass, as we went to prayer, a certain
damsel possessed with a spirit of divination met us,
which brought her masters much gain by soothsay-
ing: The same followed Paul and us, and cried, saying, These men are the servants of the most high
God, which shew unto us the way of salvation.

And this did she many days. But Paul, being
grieved, turned and said to the spirit, I command
thee in the name of Jesus Christ to come out of her.
And he came out the same hour. (16: 14 - 18)

•And upon the first day of the week, when the disciples came together to break bread, Paul preached
unto them, ready to depart on the morrow; and continued his speech until midnight. And there were
many lights in the upper chamber, where they were
gathered together.

And there sat in a window a certain young man
named Eutychus, being fallen into a deep sleep: and
as Paul was long preaching, he sunk down with
sleep, and fell down from the third loft, and was
taken up dead. And Paul went down, and fell on
him, and embracing him said, Trouble not yourselves; for his life is in him.

When he therefore was come up again, and had broken bread, and eaten, and talked a long while, even
till break of day, so he departed. And they brought
the young man alive, and were not a little comforted. (20: 7 - 12)

•And when they were escaped, then they knew that
the island was called Melita. And the barbarous people shewed us no little kindness: for they kindled a
fire, and received us every one, because of the present rain, and because of the cold.

And when Paul had gathered a bundle of sticks, and
laid them on the fire, there came a viper out of the

heat, and fastened on his hand. And when the barbarians saw the venomous beast hang on his hand, they said among themselves, No doubt this man is a murderer, whom, though he hath escaped the sea, yet vengeance suffereth not to live.

And he shook off the beast into the fire, and felt no harm. Howbeit they looked when he should have swollen, or fallen down dead suddenly: but after they had looked a great while, and saw no harm come to him, they changed their minds, and said that he was a god.

In the same quarters were possessions of the chief man of the island, whose name was Publius; who received us, and lodged us three days courteously. And it came to pass, that the father of Publius lay sick of a fever and of a bloody flux: to whom Paul entered in, and prayed, and laid his hands on him, and healed him. So when this was done, others also, which had diseases in the island, came, and were healed. (28: 1 - 9)

One of the most vivid and powerful statements relevant to healing in the epistles of the New Testament was written by James. He said:

•Is any among you afflicted? Let him pray. Is any merry? let him sing psalms. Is any sick among you? let him call for the elders of the church; and let them pray over him, anointing him with oil in the name of the Lord: And the prayer of faith shall save the sick, and the Lord shall raise him up; and if he have committed sins, they shall be forgiven him. Confess your faults one to another, and pray for one another, that ye may be healed. The effectual fervent prayer of a righteous man availeth much. (5: 13 - 16)

These words written by the brother of Jesus added another method to the practice of Christian healing. They explained the healing efficacy of individual prayer by "a righteous man" as well as the power of collective prayer by the elders or representatives of a church. The early Christian churches quickly adopted prayer "for one another" in healing the sick in their communities. James' passage was also used to facilitate healing by urging Christians to confess their faults and uncover their sins. The anointing of the sick with oil "in the name of the Lord" served a sacramental role in symbolizing an influx of God's love and power as well as a purification of thought capable of achieving healing.

CHAPTER 8

THE PROMISE OF HEALING
IN THE NEW TESTAMENT

Like the Old Testament, the New Testament contains many passages which are unrelated to specific incidents of individual or group healing. These statements consist primarily of general affirmations of God's healing power. They uphold a promise of healing for both present and future generations. Some promises of healing were made by Jesus; some were made by the apostles.

The promise of healing in the New Testament is based on the strand of Old Testament thought which conceived of God as a loving and caring Creator and man as His image and likeness. Jesus' words and the writings of the apostles maintained that an understanding of man's godlike selfhood was capable of destroying sin, sickness, and death. They elevated the concept of law established in primitive Hebrew teachings. The promise of New Testament healing is also founded on a "new covenant" and a higher universal law upholding the rights of individual men and women to a life of health, wholeness, and freedom. As in the Old Testament, some readings in the New Testament refer explicitly to healing; some are more general in describing the healing nature of God.

The first group of readings consists of promises of healing made by Jesus.

•Be ye therefore perfect, even as your Father which is in heaven is perfect. (Matt. 5: 48)

•Come unto me, all ye that labour and are heavy laden, and I will give you rest. Take my yoke upon you, and learn of me; for I am meek and lowly in heart: and ye shall find rest unto your souls. For my yoke is easy, and my burden is light. (Matt. 11: 28 - 30)

•And these signs shall follow them that believe; In
my name shall they cast out devils; they shall speak
with new tongues; They shall take up serpents; and
if they drink any deadly thing, it shall not hurt them;
they shall lay hands on the sick, and they shall
recover. (Mark 16: 17, 18)

•And ye shall know the truth, and the truth shall
make you free. (John 8: 32)

•Verily, verily, I say unto you, He that believeth on
me, the works that I do shall he do also; and greater
works than these shall he do; because I go unto my
Father. And whatsoever ye shall ask in my name,
that will I do, that the Father may be glorified in the
Son. If ye shall ask any thing in my name, I will do
it. (John 14: 12 - 14)

The following selections from the epistles also relate the promise of
healing recorded in the New Testament.

•For the word of God is quick, and powerful, and
sharper than any two-edged sword, piercing even to
the dividing asunder of soul and spirit, and of the
joints and marrow, and is a discerner of the thoughts
and intents of the heart. (Hebrews 4: 12)

•The God of all grace, who hath called us unto his
eternal glory by Christ Jesus, after that ye have suffered a while, make you perfect, stablish, strength-
en, settle you. To him be glory and dominion for
ever and ever. (I Peter 5: 10, 11)

•Behold, what manner of love the Father hath
bestowed upon us, that we should be called the sons
of God: therefore the world knoweth us not, because
it knew him not. Beloved, now are we the sons of
God, and it doth not yet appear what we shall be:
but we know that, when he shall appear, we shall be
like him; for we shall see him as he is. And every
man that hath this hope in him purifieth himself,
even as he is pure. (I John 3: 1- 3)

•Continue thou in the things which thou hast learned and hast been assured of, knowing of whom thou hast learned them; And that from a child thou hast known the holy scriptures, which are able to make thee wise unto salvation through faith which is in Christ Jesus. All scripture is given by inspiration of God, and is profitable for doctrine, for reproof, for correction, for instruction in righteousness: That the man of God may be perfect, throughly furnished unto all good works. (II Tim. 3: 14 - 17)

•For we know that if our earthly house of this tabernacle were dissolved, we have a building of God, an house not made with hands, eternal in the heavens. For in this we groan, earnestly desiring to be clothed upon with our house which is from heaven: If so that being clothed we shall not be found naked.

For we that are in this tabernacle do groan, being burdened: not for that we would be unclothed, but clothed upon, that mortality might be swallowed up of life. Now he that hath wrought us for the selfsame thing is God, who also hath given unto us the earnest of the Spirit.

Therefore we are always confident, knowing that, whilst we are at home in the body, we are absent from the Lord: (For we walk by faith, not by sight:) We are confident, I say, and willing rather to be absent from the body, and to be present with the Lord.

Wherefore henceforth know we no man after the flesh: yea, though we have known Christ after the flesh, yet now henceforth know we him no more. Therefore if any man be in Christ, he is a new creature: Old things are passed away; behold, all things are become new. (II Cor. 5: 1 - 8, 16, 17)

•Brethren, I count not myself to have apprehended: but this one thing I do, forgetting those things which are behind, and reaching forth unto those things which are before, I press toward the mark for the prize of the high calling of God in Christ Jesus. Let us therefore, as many as be perfect, be thus minded: and if in any thing ye be otherwise minded, God shall reveal even this unto you.

For our conversation is in heaven; from whence also we look for the Savior, the Lord Jesus Christ: Who shall change our vile body, that it may be fashioned like unto his glorious body, according to the working whereby he is able even to subdue all things unto himself. (Phil. 3: 13 - 15, 20, 21)

•Wherefore seeing we also are compassed about with so great a cloud of witnesses, let us lay aside every weight, and the sin which doth so easily beset us, and let us run with patience the race that is set before us, Looking unto Jesus the author and finisher of our faith; who for the joy that was set before him endured the cross, despising the shame, and is set down at the right hand of the throne of God.

Wherefore lift up the hands which hang down, and the feeble knees; And make straight paths for your feet, lest that which is lame be turned out of the way; but let it rather be healed. (Hebrews 12: 1, 2, 12, 13)

•Beloved, I wish above all things that thou mayest prosper and be in health, even as thy soul prospereth. (III John: 2)

The next group of readings cites the nature of liberty and freedom under a new covenant and a new law. This covenant and law imply a mandate as well as a promise for healing.

•In the beginning was the Word, and the Word was with God, and the Word was God. All things were made by him; and without him was not any thing

made that was made. In him was life; and the life
was the light of men. And the light shineth in darkness; and the darkness comprehended it not.

And the Word was made flesh, and dwelt among us,
(and we beheld his glory, the glory as of the only
begotten of the Father,) full of grace and truth. And
of his fulness have all we received, and grace for
grace. For the law was given by Moses, but grace
and truth came by Jesus Christ. (John 1: 1, 3 - 5, 14,
16, 17)

•I was free born. (Acts 22: 28)

•There is therefore now no condemnation to them
which are in Christ Jesus, who walk not after the
flesh, but after the Spirit. For the law of the Spirit of
life in Christ Jesus hath made me free from the law
of sin and death. For what the law could not do, in
that it was weak through the flesh, God sending his
own Son in the likeness of sinful flesh, and for sin,
condemned sin in the flesh: That the righteousness
of the law might be fulfilled in us, who walk not
after the flesh, but after the Spirit.

For they that are after the flesh do mind the things
of the flesh; but they that are after the Spirit the
things of the Spirit. For to be carnally minded is
death; but to be spiritually minded is life and peace.
Because the carnal mind is enmity against God: for
it is not subject to the law of God, neither indeed
can be.

So then they that are in the flesh cannot please God.
But ye are not in the flesh, but in the Spirit, if so be
that the Spirit of God dwell in you. Now if any man
have not the Spirit of Christ, he is none of his. And
if Christ be in you, the body is dead because of sin;
but the Spirit is life because of righteousness. But if
the Spirit of him that raised up Jesus from the dead
dwell in you, he that raised up Christ from the dead

shall also quicken your mortal bodies by his Spirit that dwelleth in you.

Therefore, brethren, we are debtors, not to the flesh, to live after the flesh. For if ye live after the flesh, ye shall die: but if ye through the Spirit do mortify the deeds of the body, ye shall live. For as many as are led by the Spirit of God, they are the sons of God. For ye have not received the spirit of bondage again to fear; but ye have received the Spirit of adoption, whereby we cry, Abba, Father.

The Spirit itself beareth witness with our spirit, that we are the children of God: And if children, then heirs; heirs of God, and joint-heirs with Christ; if so be that we suffer with him, that we may be also glorified together. For I reckon that the sufferings of this present time are not worthy to be compared with the glory which shall be revealed in us.

And we know that all things work together for good to them that love God, to them who are the called according to his purpose.

If God be for us, who can be against us?

Who shall separate us from the love of Christ? shall tribulation, or distress, or persecution, or famine, or nakedness, or peril, or sword? Nay, in all these things we are more than conquerors through him that loved us. For I am persuaded, that neither death, nor life, nor angels, nor principalities, nor powers, nor things present, nor things to come, Nor height, nor depth, nor any other creature, shall be able to separate us from the love of God, which is in Christ Jesus our Lord. (Romans 8: 1 - 18, 28, 31, 35 - 39)

•Ye are our epistle written in our hearts, known and read of all men: Forasmuch as ye are manifestly declared to be the epistle of Christ ministered by us, written not with ink, but with the Spirit of the living

God; not in tables of stone, but in fleshy tables of the heart.

And such trust have we through Christ to God-ward: Not that we are sufficient of ourselves to think any thing as of ourselves; but our sufficiency is of God; Who also hath made us able ministers of the new testament; not of the letter, but of the spirit: for the letter killeth, but the spirit giveth life.

Now the Lord is that Spirit: and where the Spirit of the Lord is, there is liberty. But we all, with open face beholding as in a glass the glory of the Lord, are changed into the same image from glory to glory even as by the Spirit of the Lord. (II Cor. 3: 2 - 6, 17, 18)

•Stand fast therefore in the liberty wherewith Christ hath made us free, and be not entangled again with the yoke of bondage. . . .For, brethren, ye have been called unto liberty; only use not liberty for an occasion to the flesh, but by love serve one another. For all the law is fulfilled in one word, even in this; Thou shalt love thy neighbour as thyself.

This I say then, Walk in the Spirit, and ye shall not fulfil the lust of the flesh. For the flesh lusteth against the Spirit, and the Spirit against the flesh: and these are contrary the one to the other: so that ye cannot do the things that ye would. But if ye be led of the Spirit, ye are not under the law.

Now the works of the flesh are manifest which are these; Adultery, fornication, uncleanness, lasciviousness, Idolatry, witchcraft, hatred, variance, emulations, wrath, strife, seditions, heresies, Envyings, murders, drunkenness, revellings, and such like: of the which I tell you before, as I have also told you in time past, that they which do such things shall not inherit the kingdom of God.

But the fruit of the Spirit is love, joy, peace, long-suffering, gentleness, goodness, faith, Meekness, temperance: against such there is no law. . . .If we live in the Spirit, let us also walk in the Spirit. (Gal. 5: 1, 13, 14, 16 - 23, 25)

•This is the covenant that I will make with the house of Israel after those days, saith the Lord; I will put my laws into their mind, and write them in their hearts: and I will be to them a God, and they shall be to me a people: And they shall not teach every man his neighbour, and every man his brother, saying, Know the Lord: for all shall know me, from the least to the greatest. (Heb. 8: 10, 11)

As in the book of Isaiah, some passages in the New Testament refer to God as a Comforter and a source of healing. The first statement recorded here is by Jesus; the other declarations are by Paul.

•And I will pray the Father, and he shall give you another Comforter, that he may abide with you for ever; Even the Spirit of truth; whom the world cannot receive, because it seeth him not, neither knoweth him: but ye know him; for he dwelleth with you, and shall be in you. I will not leave you comfortless: I will come to you.

These things have I spoken unto you, being yet present with you. But the Comforter, which is the Holy Ghost, whom the Father will send in my name, he shall teach you all things, and bring all things to your remembrance, whatsoever I have said unto you.

Peace I leave with you, my peace I give unto you: not as the world giveth, give I unto you. Let not your heart be troubled, neither let it be afraid. (John 14: 16 - 18, 25 - 27)

•Blessed be God, even the Father of our Lord Jesus Christ, the Father of mercies, and the God of all

comfort; Who comforteth us in all our tribulation,
that we may be able to comfort them which are in
any trouble, by the comfort wherewith we ourselves
are comforted of God. (II Cor. 1: 3, 4)

•Be perfect, be of good comfort, be of one mind,
live in peace; and the God of love and peace shall be
with you. (II Cor. 13: 11)

•Now our Lord Jesus Christ himself, and God, even
our Father, which hath loved us, and hath given us
everlasting consolation and good hope through
grace, Comfort your hearts, and stablish you in
every good word and work. (II Thes. 2: 16, 17)

The promise of healing in the New Testament makes it clear that a
time in human history will come when mankind's understanding of
God and His creation will be sufficient to overcome death. The first
promise cited here is by Jesus; the second is by Paul, and the third is
by John.

•If a man keep my saying, he shall never see death.
(John 8: 51)

•Now if Christ be preached that he rose from the
dead, how say some among you that there is no resurrection of the dead? But if there be no resurrection
of the dead, then is Christ not risen: And if Christ be
not risen, then is our preaching vain, and your faith
is also vain.

If in this life only we have hope in Christ, we are of
all men most miserable. But now is Christ risen
from the dead, and become the firstfruits of them
that slept. For since by man came death, by man
came also the resurrection of the dead. For as in
Adam all die, even so in Christ shall all be made
alive.

The last enemy that shall be destroyed is death.

And so it is written, The first man Adam was made a living soul; the last Adam was made a quickening spirit. Howbeit that was not first which is spiritual, but that which is natural; and afterward that which is spiritual. The first man is of the earth earthy: the second man is the Lord from heaven.

As is the earthy, such are they also that are earthy: and as is the heavenly, such are they also that are heavenly. And as we have borne the image of the earthy, we shall also bear the image of the heavenly. Now this I say, brethren, that flesh and blood cannot inherit the kingdom of God; neither doth corruption inherit incorruption.

For this corruptible must put on incorruption, and this mortal must put on immortality. So when this corruptible shall have put on incorruption, and this mortal shall have put on immortality, then shall be brought to pass the saying that is written, Death is swallowed up in victory.

O death, where is thy sting? O grave, where is thy victory? The sting of death is sin; and the strength of sin is the law. But thanks be to God, which giveth us the victory through our Lord Jesus Christ. Therefore, my beloved brethren, be ye stedfast, unmoveable, always abounding in the work of the Lord, forasmuch as ye know that your labour is not in vain in the Lord. (I Cor. 15: 12 - 14, 19 - 22, 26, 45 - 50, 53 - 58)

•And this is the record, that God hath given to us eternal life, and this life is in his Son. He that hath the Son hath life; and he that hath not the Son of God hath not life. These things have I written unto you that believe on the name of the Son of God; that ye may know that ye have eternal life, and that ye may believe on the name of the Son of God.

And we know that the Son of God is come, and hath
given us an understanding, that we may know him
that is true, and we are in him that is true, even in
his Son Jesus Christ. This is the true God, and eternal life. (I John 5: 11 - 13, 20)

In the book of Revelation, the apostle John prophesies a "new heav-
en and a new earth" in which there will be no more suffering or disease. This is one of the most powerful and hopeful promises of healing recorded in the entire Bible.

•And I saw a new heaven and a new earth: for the
first heaven and the first earth were passed away;
and there was no more sea. And I John saw the holy
city, new Jerusalem, coming down from God out of
heaven, prepared as a bride adorned for her husband.

And I heard a great voice out of heaven saying,
Behold, the tabernacle of God is with men, and he
will dwell with them, and they shall be his people,
and God himself shall be with them, and be their
God. And God shall wipe away all tears from their
eyes; and there shall be no more death, neither sorrow, nor crying, neither shall there be any more
pain: for the former things are passed away.

And he that sat upon the throne said, Behold, I make
all things new. And he said unto me, Write: for these
words are true and faithful. And he said unto me, It
is done. I am Alpha and Omega, the beginning and
the end. I will give unto him that is athirst of the
fountain of the water of life freely. He that over-
cometh shall inherit all things; and I will be his God,
and he shall be my son.

And I saw no temple therein: for the Lord God
Almighty and the Lamb are the temple of it. And the
city had no need of the sun, neither of the moon, to
shine in it: for the glory of God did lighten it, and
the Lamb is the light thereof.

And the nations of them which are saved shall walk in the light of it: and the kings of the earth do bring their glory and honour into it. And the gates of it shall not be shut at all by day: for there shall be no night there.

And they shall bring the glory and honour of the nations into it. And there shall in no wise enter into it any thing that defileth, neither whatsoever worketh abomination, or maketh a lie: but they which are written in the Lamb's book of life. (Rev. 21: 1 - 7, 22 - 27)

•And he shewed me a pure river of water of life, clear as crystal, proceeding out of the throne of God and of the Lamb. In the midst of the street of it, and on either side of the river, was there the tree of life, which bare twelve manner of fruits, and yielded her fruit every month: and the leaves of the tree were for the healing of the nations. (Rev. 22: 1, 2)

CHAPTER 9

THE ANTE-NICENE FATHERS

(100 - 325 A.D.)

The Ante-Nicene Fathers lived from the beginning of the second century until the time of the Council of Nicea (325). For slightly more than two hundred years these early leaders and writers sought to preserve the teachings of Jesus and to strengthen the fledgling Christian church. They formulated early Christian doctrine and defended their interpretations from attacks both inside and outside the ranks of the growing Christian movement.

We know relatively little about the lives of the Ante-Nicene Fathers. Many of their writings have been lost, and in most cases the historical records which have survived are fragmentary and incomplete. We have only limited knowledge about their places of birth, their childhood, and their participation in the Christian church. We do know that most were from Greek parentage, with the remainder coming from Roman families. Most were born and reared as pagans and became converts to Christianity. Only a few (such as Irenaeus and Origen) were born into Christian families. Most became bishops of the church. Almost all were martyred by Roman authorities for their Christian faith.

These early church fathers were not of the same spiritual stature as Jesus' apostles. Many scholars have labeled their era as "the sub-apostolic age" in the development of the Christian church. Yet the Ante-Nicene leaders were highly inspired and learned men. In some cases the quantity of their writings on Christian teachings greatly surpassed that of the apostles. Most were from upper class families and studied at major learning centers in the classical world. At times their writings exerted considerable influence in non-Christian educated circles. They displayed enormous courage and resolution in defending their religious convictions in a political environment that became increasingly hostile as the stability of the Roman empire began to wane.

In an introductory note in the first volume of *The Ante-Nicene Fathers*, Dr. A. Cleveland Coxe describes this new group of church leaders and their writings as follows:

Those were times of heroism, not of words; an age,
not of writers, but of soldiers; not of talkers, but of
sufferers. Curiosity is baffled, but faith and love are
fed by these scanty relics of primitive antiquity. Yet
may we well be grateful for what we have. These
writings come down to us as the earliest response of
converted nations to the testimony of Jesus. They
are primary evidences of the Canon and the credibility of the New Testament. Disappointment may be
the first emotion of the student who comes down
from the mount where he has dwelt in the taberna-
cles of evangelists and apostles: for these disciples
are confessedly inferior to the masters; they speak
with voices of infirm and fallible men, and not like
the New Testament writers, with the fiery tongues of
the Holy Ghost. Yet the thoughtful and loving spirit
soon learns their exceeding value. For who does not
close the records of St. Luke with longings to get at
least a glimpse of the further history of the progress
of the Gospel? What of the Church when its
founders were fallen asleep? Was the Good Shepherd "always" with His little flock, according to His
promise? Was the Blessed Comforter felt in His
presence amid the fires of persecution? Was the
Spirit of Truth really able to guide the faithful into
all truth, and to keep them in the truth? (p. vii)

The writings of the Ante-Nicene Fathers provide the major source
of information about Christian healing in the period immediately following the lives of Jesus and the apostles. Their written works that
have survived contain only limited accounts of the healing of the early
church, and none of these church leaders has left a detailed description
of their own healing ministry. Their expositions about healing are
clearly subordinate to their apologies defending Christian teachings
and opposing theological attacks from pagans and heretics. Some of
their writing about healing is quite general and includes few references to specific persons, since the early Christians were often forced
to organize clandestinely as an underground church. Their discussions
of healing at times appear almost offhand as the cure of disease
became a normal and accepted activity of the church.

The writings of the early church fathers on healing consist primarily of explanations of cures done by other Christians as well as discussions of the healing works done by Jesus and the apostles. There is no clear indication that these leaders performed healings themselves. They give little or no information about the Christians who actually did the healing works. These men were not trained historians writing for future generations. Instead much of their writing about healing and church doctrine was for the internal readership of the Christian movement.

Yet from their written works we know that healing was a vital part of the early Christian church which was perceived as the "body" of Christ Jesus and the embodiment of his teachings. Christian churches were active centers for individual and group healing. This practice fostered unity and fellowship in the Christian communities. The elimination of sickness and suffering was a potent force in expanding the ranks of Christianity. Deep convictions instilled by witnessing physical healings enabled Christians to withstand the intermittent persecutions ordered by Roman emperors. Many Christians perished in these pogroms. Many survived severe torture and pain through their religious faith. And the church continued to grow.

The Ante-Nicene period produced about thirty leaders whose writings in various forms have survived. A smaller number of "minor writers" have bequeathed a more modest body of literature. The readings included in this survey consist of relevant portions of the writings of seven of these early church fathers. These readings are from the works of four Greek leaders: Justin Martyr, Irenaeus, Origen, and Arnobius; and three Latin leaders: Tertullian, Cyprian, and Lactantius.

The lives and writings of these seven Ante-Nicene Fathers span the entire sub-apostolic era. At times they did not agree with each other in their explanations of Christian theology, and often they argued over the relationship between the teachings of Jesus and elements of Greek philosophy. In some places they made historical errors and occasionally they came close to accusing other church fathers of heresy.

In considerable degree their theological differences were caused by the fact that they were writing prior to the time when church councils began approving important parts of church doctrine. Differences in interpretation were also caused by the absence of the final compilation of the New Testament as the authorized scripture of Christian theology. The writings of the Ante-Nicene Fathers were based almost entirely on the Old Testament and on individual books written by the apostles as well as their own experiences as leaders in the Christian church. Yet in spite of many differences, their common purpose in expounding church doctrine, including their explanations of spiritual healing, was based on the Judeo-Christian writings which were combined in the fourth century in the form of the Bible.

The writings of the Ante-Nicene Fathers may seem somewhat verbose and discursive to first-time readers. Usually their prose is not as lucid and cogent as the passages in many parts of the Bible. Much of it is not as inspiring as familiar verses from the Old and New Testaments. At times their writings are also fragmentary and repetitious since they consist of initial probings into basic issues of early Christian doctrine, including the controversy over the nature and role of Jesus. In some places they raise the question whether or not God was incarnate in the human Jesus. Some of them declare that in certain aspects Jesus was God. Also, their style of writing was almost always influenced by the need to refute numerous pointed and bitter attacks against Christian teachings. The need to defend Christianity from its many determined enemies often encouraged the writing of lengthy and detailed treatises.

It is likewise important to remind ourselves as we read the works of these lesser known church leaders that their original works were written in Greek or Latin, and many of their writings now available to us are translations into nineteenth century English. The style of some Victorian writers, especially theolgians, often tended to be somewhat pedantic and prolix.

Yet in spite of their shortcomings, the written works we do have of the Ante-Nicene Fathers give us an important perspective on the evolution of healing in the Christian church between the historical period covered by the New Testament and the beginning of the Middle Ages. They explain another development of Christianity as this new religion grew from its Jewish background into Greek and Roman cultures. They describe the second expansion of Christian healing as it took deeper root in Western civilization.

CHAPTER 10

JUSTIN MARTYR

(100 - 165)

Justin Martyr was born at Flavia Neapolis in Samaria, now the city of Nablus in Jordan. His parents were pagan Greeks, yet his youth was greatly influenced by Jewish culture. He studied Greek philosophy, including the writings of Plato, Aristotle, Pythagoras, and the Stoics in a search for an acceptable system of thought and a satisfactory way of life. Justin was converted to Christianity in 132 at Ephesus after discussions with an elderly man convinced him that truth was not to be found in philosophy, but in the teachings and miracles of the Old Testament and in the life and works of Jesus. He was also impressed by Christian morality and the sacrifices of Christian martyrs.

Like the apostle Paul, Justin traveled extensively in Asia Minor, Greece, and Rome, where he preached the teachings of Christianity. He continued to wear the cloak of a philosopher, while declaring Jesus as the Son of God and the message of the Bible above the doctrines of philosophy. Justin upheld the concept of the "spermatic Logos" explaining that the Hebrew prophets and some Greek philosophers prior to Jesus demonstrated parts of the Logos or Word of God. The whole Logos, he declared, appeared with the life of Jesus, who was the full expression of the Word. Justin's approach to Christianity combined a search for more knowledge about God and a desire to apply Christian teachings in daily life. In his book *The Fathers of the Greek Church,* the German scholar Hans von Campenhausen has stated:

> Justin's Christianity is marked by an urge to give practical expression to his faith and by the absolute certainty of his ultimate convictions. Christians possess the truth on which to base their lives; this is proved by the high moral standards of their conduct. The sources from which they derive their knowledge of God are, furthermore, undoubtedly reliable. To that extent their teaching fulfills the real mission

of philosophy, which, according to Justin, is above
all to explore the Divine. (p.14)

Justin sought to convert pagan audiences to the Christian church by
claiming Christianity as the highest form of reason which was one of
the chief goals of Greek philosophy. He voiced admiration for
Socrates, who had denounced the worship of pagan gods. In 165 he
was accused of disloyalty to the Roman emperor. He was martyred
after refusing to renounce his Christian faith and offer sacrifices to the
Roman gods.

The only surviving major works of Justin are his *First Apologia,
Second Apologia,* and the *Dialogue with Trypho.* He probably wrote
several shorter treatises, which include an address specifically directed
to the Greeks and a discussion of the resurrection. These writings
established him as the leading apologist of his time. The *First Apologia* was written about 150 and consisted of a defense of Christian
teachings addressed to the Roman emperor Antoninus Pius. The second apology was a brief supplement to his first apology and addressed
to the Roman Senate.

In the *Dialogue* Justin recorded a lengthy debate with a Jew he had
met at Ephesus. In this work, he explained how the new covenant
taught by Jesus had superseded the earlier covenant and law of the
Old Testament. Justin's writing exerted considerable influence on
other Greek Christians, especially Irenaeus, Clement of Alexandria,
and Origen. Some Christian writers disagreed with his explanations
that linked certain elements of Greek thought with Christianity.

The first group of readings is from the *Second Apologia* and presents Justin's explanation of the nature of God, the Word, Christ Jesus,
and healing.

> •But to the Father of all, who is unbegotten, there is
> no name given. For by whatever name He be called,
> He has as His elder the person who gives him the
> name. But these words, Father, and God, and Cre-
> ator, and Lord, and Master, are not names, but
> appellations derived from His good deeds and func-
> tions. And His Son, who alone is properly called
> Son, the Word, who also was with Him and was
> begotten before the works, when at first he created
> and arranged all things by Him, is called Christ, in
> reference to His being anointed and God's ordering

all things through Him; this name itself also containing an unknown significance; as also the appellation "God" is not a name, but an opinion implanted in the nature of men of a thing that can hardly be explained. But "Jesus," His name as man and Savior, has also significance. For He was made man also, as we before said, having been conceived according to the will of God the Father, for the sake of believing men, and for the destruction of the demons.

And now you can learn this from what is under your own observation. For numberless demoniacs throughout the whole world, and in your city, many of our Christian men exorcising them in the name of Jesus Christ, who was crucified under Pontius Pilate, have healed and do heal, rendering helpless and driving the possessing devils out of the men, though they could not be cured by all the other exorcists, and those who used incantations and drugs. (Chap. VI)

•For I myself, when I discovered the wicked disguise which the evil spirits had thrown around the divine doctrines of the Christians, to turn aside others from joining them, laughed both at those who framed these falsehoods, and at the disguise itself, and at popular opinion; and I confess that I both boast and with all my strength strive to be found a Christian; not because the teachings of Plato are different from those of Christ, but because they are not in all respects similar, as neither are those of the others, Stoics, and poets, and historians. For each man spoke well in proportion to the share he had of the spermatic word, seeing what was related to it. But they who contradict themselves on the more important points appear not to have possessed the heavenly wisdom, and the knowledge which cannot be spoken against.

Whatever things were rightly said among all men, are the property of us Christians. For next to God,

we worship and love the Word who is from the
unbegotten and ineffable God, since also He became
man for our sakes, that, becoming a partaker of our
sufferings, He might also bring us healing. For all
the writers were able to see realities darkly through
the sowing of the implanted word that was in them.
For the seed and imitation imparted according to
capacity is one thing, and quite another is the thing
itself, of which there is the participation and imitation according to the grace which is from Him.
(Chap. XIII)

The following passages are from a short work entitled *On the Resurrection*. They contain Justin's explanation of "the word of truth" in
proving God's power and in overcoming "the adversary" who "uses
many and divers arts to ensnare them [mankind]." These excerpts also
explain the early Christian emphasis on the role of the body in
expressing qualities of the soul as well as the importance of Jesus'
healing works.

•The word of truth is free, and carries its own
authority, disdaining to fall under any skillful argument, or to endure the logical scrutiny of its hearers.
But it would be believed for its own nobility, and for
the confidence due to Him who sends it. Now the
word of truth is sent from God; wherefore the freedom claimed by the truth is not arrogant. For being
sent with authority, it were not fit that it should be
required to produce proof of what is said; since neither is there any proof beyond itself, which is God.
For every proof is more powerful and trustworthy
than that which it proves; since what is disbelieved,
until proof is produced, gets credit when such proof
is produced, and is recognized as being what it was
stated to be.

But nothing is either more powerful or more trustworthy than the truth; so that he who requires proof
of this, is like one who wishes it demonstrated why
the things that appear to the senses do appear. For

the test of those things which are received through
the reason, is sense; but of sense itself there is no
test beyond itself.

And the Word, being His Son, came to us, having
put on flesh, revealing both Himself and the Father,
giving to us in Himself resurrection from the dead,
and eternal life afterwards. And this is Jesus Christ,
our Savior and Lord. He, therefore, is Himself both
the faith and the proof of Himself and of all things.
Wherefore those who follow Him, and know Him,
having faith in Him as their proof, shall rest in Him.
But since the adversary does not cease to resist
many, and uses many and divers arts to ensnare
them, that he may seduce the faithful from their
faith, and that he may prevent the faithless from
believing, it seems to me necessary that we also,
being armed with the invulnerable doctrines of the
faith, do battle against him in behalf of the weak.
(Chap. I)

•All things which the Savior did, He did in the first
place in order that what was spoken concerning Him
in the prophets might be fulfilled, "that the blind
should receive sight, and the deaf hear," and so on;
but also to induce the belief that in the resurrection
the flesh shall rise entire. For if on earth He healed
the sicknesses of the flesh, and made the body
whole, much more will He do this in the resurrection, so that the flesh shall rise perfect and entire. In
this manner, then, shall those dreaded difficulties of
theirs be healed. (Chap. IV)

•Considering, therefore, even such arguments as are
suited to his world, and finding that, even according
to them it is not impossible that the flesh be regener-
ated; and that, besides all these proofs, the Savior in
the whole Gospel shows that there is salvation for
the flesh, why do we any longer endure those unbelieving and dangerous arguments, and fail to see that
we are retrograding when we listen to such an argu-

ment as this: that the soul is immortal, but the body
mortal, and incapable of being revived?

But if the flesh did not rise, why is it also guarded,
and why do we not rather suffer it to indulge its
desires? Why do we not imitate physicians, who, it
is said, when they get a patient that is despaired of
and incurable, allow him to indulge his desires?

But if our physician Christ, God, having rescued us
from our desires, regulates our flesh with His own
wise and temperate rule, it is evident that He guards
it from sins because it possesses a hope of salvation,
as physicians do not suffer men whom they hope to
save to indulge in what pleasures they please.
(Chap. X)

The *Dialogue with Trypho* has a brief commentary repeating the
message of the New Testament that God bestows different gifts on the
followers of Christ Jesus, including the gift of healing. In this writing,
Justin likewise exhorts the Jews to accept the teachings of Jesus and
learn to heal.

•"Now it is not surprising," I continued, "that you
hate us who hold these opinions, and convict you of
a continual hardness of heart. For indeed Elijah,
conversing with God concerning you, speaks thus:
'Lord, they have slain Thy prophets, and digged
down Thine altars: and I am left alone, and they
seek my life.' And he answers him: 'I have still
seven thousand men who have not bowed the knee
to Baal.'

Therefore, just as God did not inflict His anger on
account of those seven thousand men, even so He
has now neither yet inflicted judgment, nor does
inflict it, knowing that daily some [of you] are
becoming disciples in the name of Christ, and quit-
ting the path of error; who are also receiving gifts,
each as he is worthy, illumined through the name of
this Christ. For one receives the spirit of understand-

ing, another of counsel, another of strength, another
of healing, another of foreknowledge, another of
teaching, and another of the fear of God." (Chap.
XXXIX)

•Moreover, it is also manifest to all, that we who
believe in Him pray to be kept by Him from strange,
i.e. from wicked and deceitful, spirits; as the word
of prophecy, personating one of those who believe
in Him, figuratively declares. For we do continually
beseech God by Jesus Christ to preserve us from the
demons which are hostile to the worship of God,
and whom we of old time served, in order that, after
our conversion by Him to God, we may be blameless.

For we call Him Helper and Redeemer, the power of
whose name even the demons do fear; and at this
day, when they are exorcised in the name of Jesus
Christ, crucified under Pontius Pilate, governor of
Judea, they are overcome. And thus it is manifest to
all, that His Father has given Him so great power,
by virtue of which demons are subdued to His
name, and to the dispensation of His suffering.
(Chap. XXX)

•For every demon, when exorcised in the name of
this very Son of God — who is the Firstborn of
every creature, who became man by the Virgin, who
suffered, and was crucified under Pontius by your
nation, and died, who rose from the dead, and
ascended into heaven — is overcome and subdued.
(Chap. LXXXV)

CHAPTER 11

IRENAEUS

(120 - 200)

Irenaeus was born near Smyrna in Asia Minor in 120. He was a generation younger than Justin Martyr, and he was more directly exposed in his youth to early Christian teachings. His parents were Greek Christians, and he received religious instruction from Polycarp, the bishop of Smyrna, who had been a disciple of the apostle John. He moved to Lugdunum in southern Gaul near the modern French city of Lyons, where he served as a missionary and presbyter of the church.

In 177 Irenaeus became the bishop of Lyons, and he played a major role in converting the surrounding region to Christianity. On one occasion he visited the bishop of Rome to appeal for more unity and tolerance in the church. At another time he wrote letters to the church in Rome urging stronger measures against internal and external threats of heresy. During this time the Christian missions in Gaul were in direct and frequent contact with the church in Asia Minor. Irenaeus believed that the church in Rome was too susceptible to heretical influences, especially Gnosticism and paganism. For the rest of his life he became a leading opponent of heretical threats to early Christian doctrine. In this struggle the Bible was his primary source of information and inspiration. The English writer, John Lawson, has described this deep commitment by Irenaeus in his book *The Biblical Theology of Saint Irenaeus* as follows:

> With him [Irenaeus] it is fundamental that the Scriptures provide complete proof for all Christian doctrine. 'But our faith is steadfast, unfeigned, and the only true one, having clear proof from these Scriptures, which were interpreted in the way I have related.' They are an independent authority, an authority that speaks for itself. A witness to this is the constant habit of quoting Biblical texts in final settlement of matters of all kinds. Irenaeus plainly

believes himself to be founding everything upon
'the Book of God'. The church's bulwark against
error is the Bible. (p. 23)

From 182 to 188 Irenaeus wrote his major work titled *A Refutation
and Overthrow of Knowledge Falsely So-Called,* more commonly
known by its shorter title *Against Heresies.* A second work, *The
Demonstration of the Apostolic Teaching,* has been available only
since the early twentieth century when a translation in Armenian was
discovered. Several brief fragments of his written works have also
been preserved. In considerable degree, his writings were influenced
by Justin Martyr, and they served as a link between Greek Christianity
and Latin Christianity. Irenaeus accepted some elements of Greek philosophy and quoted occasionally from Plato and Greek poets such as
Homer, Hesiod, and Pindar. His written works helped in preparing the
way for Latin writers such as Tertullian and Cyprian. Yet unlike the
apologists, who wrote largely for non-Christian audiences, Irenaeus
directed his writings primarily at readers within the Christian church.
His style was that of an experienced preacher — poised, confident,
and instructive.

The bulk of *Against Heresies* consists of a detailed and pointed
refutation of Gnosticism. It also contains a forceful exposition of
Christian teachings as well as much useful information on the activi-
ties of the early church. It likewise includes valuable observations on
early Christian healing. Irenaeus was the first of the Ante-Nicene
Fathers to declare there should be only four gospels in the New Testa-
ment which he helped to elevate to the same theological stature as the
Old Testament. His major contribution to the development of the
Christian church was the victory of Christianity over the threat of
Gnosticism.

Irenaeus died in 200. Some sources report that he perished in a mas-
sacre of Christians in southern Gaul, but most historians maintain that
there is no reliable evidence he was martyred.

The first reading is from *Fragments from the Lost Writings of Irenaeus,* which explains the nature and role of Jesus, including his
power to heal.

•The sacred books acknowledge with regard to
Christ, that as He is the Son of man, so is the same
Being not a [mere] man; and as He is flesh, so is He
also spirit, and the Word of God, and God. And as

He was born of Mary in the last times, so did He
also proceed from God as the First-begotten of
every creature; and as He hungered, so did He satisfy [others]; and as He thirsted, so did He of old
cause the Jews to drink, for the "Rock was Christ"
Himself: thus does Jesus now give to His believing
people power to drink spiritual waters, which spring
up to life eternal.

And as He was the son of David, so was He also the
Lord of David. And as He was from Abraham, so
did He also exist before Abraham. And as He was
the servant of God, so is He the Son of God, and
Lord of the universe. . . . And as He was saddened,
so also did He give joy to His people. And as He
was capable of being handled and touched, so again
did He, in a non-apprehensible form, pass through
the midst of those who sought to injure Him, and
entered without impediment through closed doors.
And as He slept, so did He also rule the sea, the
winds, and the storms. And as He suffered, so also
is He alive, and life-giving, and healing all our infirmity. (LII)

The remainder of these writings by Irenaeus are from *Against
Heresies*. The first group explains the nature of God and man, and the
power of God in healing the human body.

•It is proper, then, that I should begin with the first
and most important head, that is, God the Creator,
who made the heaven and the earth, and all things
that are therein. . . and to demonstrate that there is
nothing either above Him or after Him; nor that,
influenced by any one, but of His own free will, He
created all things, since He is the only God, the only
Lord, the only Creator, the only Father, alone containing all things, and Himself commanding all
things into existence.

For how can there be any other Fulness, or Principle, or Power, or God, above Him, since it is matter

of necessity that God, the Pleroma (Fulness) of all
these, should contain all things in His immensity,
and should be contained by no one? But if there *is*
anything beyond Him, He is not then the Pleroma of
all, nor does He contain all. For that which they
declare to be beyond Him will be wanting to the
Pleroma, or, [in other words,] to that God who is
above all things. . . .But then that which is greater is
also stronger, and in a greater degree Lord; and that
which is greater, and stronger, and in a greater
degree Lord — must be God. (Book II, Chap. I, 1,
2)

•For the Maker of all things, the Word of God, who
did also from the beginning form man, when He
found His handiwork impaired by wickedness, performed upon it all kinds of healing. At one time [He
did so], as regards each separate member, as it is
found in His own handiwork; and at another time
He did once for all restore man sound and whole at
all points, preparing him perfect for Himself unto
the resurrection.

For what was His object in healing [different] portions of the flesh, and restoring them to their original condition, if those parts which had been healed
by Him were not in a position to obtain salvation?
For if it was [merely] a temporary benefit which He
conferred, He granted nothing of importance to
those who were the subjects of His healing. Or how
can they maintain that the flesh is incapable of
receiving the life which flows from Him, when it
received healing from Him? For life is brought
about through healing, and incorruption through
life. He, therefore, who confers healing, the same
does also confer life; and He [who gives] life, also
surrounds His own handiwork with incorruption.
(Book V, Chap XII, 6)

The following statement by Irenaeus is a denunciation of the Gnos-
tics who maintained that they could also perform miracles and heal-

ings by the use of magic. In this passage Irenaeus cites the healings
done by the apostles based on the power of God. He also tells of some
of the healings in the Christian church, here called "the brotherhood,"
including the raising of a man from death.

> •Moreover, those also will be thus confuted who
> belong to Simon and Carpocrates, and if there be
> any others who are said to perform miracles — who
> do not perform what they do either through the
> power of God, or in connection with the truth, nor
> for the well-being of men, but for the sake of
> destroying and misleading mankind, by means of
> magical deceptions, and with universal deceit, thus
> entailing greater harm than good on those who
> believe them, with respect to the point on which
> they lead them astray.
>
> For they can neither confer sight on the blind, nor
> hearing on the deaf, nor chase away all sorts of
> demons — [none, indeed,] except those that are sent
> into others by themselves, if they can even do so
> much as this. Nor can they cure the weak, or the
> lame, or the paralytic, or those who are distressed in
> any other part of the body, as has often been done in
> regard to bodily infirmity. Nor can they furnish
> effective remedies for those external accidents
> which may occur. And so far are they from being
> able to raise the dead, as the Lord raised them, and
> the apostles did by means of prayer, and as has been
> frequently done in the brotherhood on account of
> some necessity — the entire Church in that particu-
> lar locality entreating [the boon] with much fasting
> and prayer, the spirit of the dead man has returned,
> and he has been bestowed in answer to the prayers
> of the saints — that they do not even believe this
> can possibly be done, [and hold] that the resurrec-
> tion from the dead is simply an acquaintance with
> that truth which they proclaim.
>
> Since, therefore, there exist among them error and
> misleading influences, and magical illusions are

impiously wrought in the sight of men; but in the
Church, sympathy, and compassion, and stedfast-
ness, and truth, for the aid and encouragement of
mankind, are not only displayed without fee or
reward, but we ourselves lay out for the benefit of
others our own means; and inasmuch as those who
are cured very frequently do not possess the things
which they require, they receive them from us;
[since such is the case,] these men are in this way
undoubtedly proved to be utter aliens from the
divine nature, the beneficence of God, and all spiritual excellence. (Book II, Chap. XXXI, 2, 3)

The next passage relates in considerable detail the healing done in
the early Christian church.

•Again, while they [the Gnostics] possess souls
from the same sphere as Jesus, and that they are like
to Him, sometimes even maintaining that they are
superior; while [they affirm that they were] produced, like Him, for the performance of works tend-
ing to the benefit and establishment of mankind,
they are found doing nothing of the same or a like
kind [with His actions], nor what can in any respect
be brought into comparison with them. And if they
have in truth accomplished anything [remarkable]
by means of magic, they strive [in this way] deceit-
fully to lead foolish people astray, since they confer
no real benefit or blessing on those over whom they
declare that they exert [supernatural] power; but,
bringing forward mere boys [as subjects on whom
they practise], and deceiving their sight, while they
exhibit phantasms that instantly cease, and do not
endure even a moment of time, they are proved to
be like, not Jesus our Lord, but Simon the magician.

It is certain, too, from the fact that the Lord rose
from the dead on the third day, and manifested Himself to His disciples, and was in their sight received
up into heaven, that, inasmuch as these men die, and
do not rise again, nor manifest themselves to any,

they are proved as possessing souls in no respect similar to that of Jesus.

If, however, they maintain that the Lord, too, performed such works simply in appearance, we shall refer them to the prophetical writings, and prove from these both that all things were thus predicted regarding Him, and did take place undoubtedly, and that He is the only Son of God. Wherefore, also, those who are in truth His disciples, receiving grace from Him, do in His name perform [miracles], so as to promote the welfare of other men, according to the gift which each one has received from Him.

For some do certainly and truly drive out devils, so that those who have thus been cleansed from evil spirits frequently both believe [in Christ], and join themselves to the Church. Others have foreknowledge to things to come: they see visions, and utter prophetic expressions. Others still, heal the sick by laying their hands upon them, and they are made whole. Yea, moreover, as I have said, the dead even have been raised up, and remained among us for many years.

And what shall I more say? It is not possible to name the number of gifts which the Church, [scattered] throughout the whole world, has received from God, in the name of Jesus Christ, who was crucified under Pontius Pilate, and which she exerts day by day for the benefit of the Gentiles, neither practising deception upon any, nor taking any reward from them [on account of such miraculous interpositions]. For as she has received freely from God, freely also does she minister [to others].

Nor does she perform anything by means of angelic invocations, or by incantations, or by any other wicked curious art; but, directing her prayers to the Lord, who made all things, in a pure, sincere, and straightforward spirit, and calling upon the name of

our Lord Jesus Christ, she has been accustomed to
work miracles for the advantage of mankind, and
not to lead them into error.

If, therefore, the name of our Lord Jesus Christ even
now confers benefits [upon men], and cures thoroughly and effectively all who anywhere believe on
Him, but not that of Simon, or Menander, or Car-
pocrates, or of any other man whatever, it is manifest that, when He was made man, He held fellowship with His own creation, and did all things truly
through the power of God, according to the will of
the Father of all, as the prophets had foretold. But
what these things were, shall be described in dealing
with the proofs to be found in the prophetical writings. (Book II, Chap. XXXII, 3, 4, 5)

The final reading by Irenaeus discusses the healing done by Jesus
and the apostles without any fraud, deception, or hypocrisy.

•Since, therefore, the tradition from the apostles
does thus exist in the Church, and is permanent
among us, let us revert to the Scriptures proof furnished by those apostles who did also write the
Gospel, in which they recorded the doctrine regarding God, pointing out that our Lord Jesus Christ is
the truth, and that no lie is in Him. As also David
says, prophesying His birth from a virgin, and the
resurrection from the dead, "Truth has sprung out of
the earth." The apostles, likewise, being disciples of
the truth, are above all falsehood; for a lie has no
fellowship with the truth, just as darkness has none
with light, but the presence of the one shuts out that
of the other. . . .

Such [a line of conduct] belongs not to those who
heal, or who give life: it is rather that of those bringing on diseases, and increasing ignorance; and much
more true than these men shall the law be found,
which pronounces every one accursed who sends
the blind man astray in the way. For the apostles,

who were commissioned to find out the wanderers, and to be for sight to those who saw not, and medicine to the weak, certainly did not address them in accordance with their opinion at the time, but according to revealed truth.

For no persons of any kind would act properly, if they should advise blind men, just about to fall over a precipice, to continue their most dangerous path, as if it were the right one, and as if they might go on in safety. Or what medical man, anxious to heal a sick person, would prescribe in accordance with the patient's whims, and not according to the requisite medicine? But that the Lord came as the physician of the sick, He does Himself declare, saying, "They that are whole need not a physician, but they that are sick; I came not to call the righteous, but sinners to repentance."

How then shall the sick be strengthened, or how shall sinners come to repentance? Is it by persevering in the very same courses? or, on the contrary, is it by undergoing a great change and reversal of their former mode of living, by which they have brought upon themselves no slight amount of sickness, and many sins? But ignorance, the mother of all these, is driven out by knowledge. Wherefore the Lord used to impart knowledge to His disciples, by which also it was His practice to heal those who were suffering, and to keep back sinners from sin. He therefore did not address them in accordance with their pristine notions, nor did He reply to them in harmony with the opinion of His questioners, but according to the doctrine leading to salvation, without hypocrisy or respect of person. (Book III, Chap. V, 1, 2)

CHAPTER 12

TERTULLIAN

(145 - 220)

Quintus Septimius Florens Tertullianus was born into a pagan family around 145 at Carthage in north Africa. His father was a Roman army officer who imparted to his son a strong sense of discipline and order. Tertullian was educated in philosophy, science, literature, rhetoric, and law. He was also exposed at an early age to the surrounding Christian influence in an area which was becoming a major center of the Church. For a time he lived in Rome, where he practiced law.

Tertullian was converted to Christianity sometime between 185 and 195, probably as a result of his observations of the heroism of Christian martyrs. Some sources also state that he was attracted to Christianity after watching Christian exorcists expel demons. Tertullian received no formal theological training, but he became an avid student of the Bible. Soon he began using his legal skills in defending Christianity. Like Justin and Irenaeus, he wrote numerous apologies opposing heresy and wayward Christians.

As a Latin Christian, Tertullian tended to be more militant, polemical, and uncompromising than many Greek Christian writers in expounding Christianity. He was more an advocate than a scholar of his newly found religion. In his book *The Fathers of the Latin Church,* von Campenhausen has described Tertullian as follows:

> Everything Tertullian thought, said, and did was directed toward the real world and pressed for a practical decision. This was the determinative factor also in his intellectual and spiritual life. Tertullian was impetuous, hot-blooded, at times intentionally reckless; he himself complained that he could never learn the precious virtue of patience. Jerome, who had in many respects a similar nature, once called him a man always afire (*vir ardens*). Yet his manner was not primitive; he never lost control of his tem-

per. On the contrary, the more he spoke in anger,
and the more passionately and personally he threw
his weight behind what he thought was right, the
more polished were his thoughts and his style, the
more subtle his tactics and the more sparkling his
cruelly biting wit. Roman restraint, legal clarity, and
military discipline were transmuted into an intellectual and moral force in the ardent, aspiring mind and
heart of Tertullian. (pp. 5 - 6)

Tertullian rejected Greek philosophy and opposed the claim that
Greek thought had prepared the Western mind for Christianity. He
called Greek philosophers the "patriarchs of heretics." He opposed the
tendency of the Church to move toward worldly power and influence
at the turn of the third century. For a time he embraced some aspects
of Montanism, an extremist Christian movement which upheld the
imminent end of the world as well as celibacy, several forms of asceti-
cism, and a readiness to experience martyrdom.

Tertullian has been labeled "the Father of Latin Christianity." He
was the first major Christian writer to write in Latin, and along with
Origen he was one of the most influential Christian leaders of the second and third century. He was also one of the most polished, brilliant,
and persuasive writers. Tertullian wrote more than thirty major works,
most of which have survived. His writings made him a leader in counteracting the strong one-way flow of Greek Christian thought toward
the West. He placed greater emphasis on law and the application of
Christianity to mundane affairs than did many of his Greek predecessors, a tendency which aided in bringing more vigor and independence
to Latin Christianity.

The Latin language began replacing Greek in Western churches
during Tertullian's lifetime. His writings influenced other Latin theologians such as Cyprian and Lactantius. They also helped in opening
the way for an era called "the Golden Age of Theology" which was
led by Augustine and shaped much of Western thought throughout the
Middle Ages. Like Justin Marytyr and Irenaeus, Tertullian devoted the
bulk of his writings to major aspects of Christian doctrine. He also
explained Christian healing and reported on the healing mission of the
early church.

The first reading is from Tertullian's work titled *Against Marcion*.
In this treatise he explains God's Word and His creation of good
things, including man made in His likeness.

•Look at the total result: how fruitful was the Word!
God issued His *fiat,* and it was done: God also saw
that it was good; not as if He were ignorant of the
good until He saw it; but because it was good, He
therefore saw it, and honoured it, and set His seal
upon it; and consummated the goodness of His
works by His vouchsafing to them that contempla-
tion. Thus God blessed what He made good, in
order that He might commend Himself to you as
whole and perfect, good both in word and act. . . .

Meanwhile the world consisted of all things good,
plainly foreshowing how much good was preparing
for him for whom all this was provided. Who indeed
was so worthy of dwelling amongst the works of
God, as he who was His own image and likeness?
That image was wrought out by a goodness even
more operative than its wont, with no imperious
word, but with friendly hand preceded by an almost
affable utterance: "Let us make man in our image,
after our likeness." (Chap. IV)

In a lengthy work titled *On the Resurrection of the Flesh,* Tertullian
explains Jesus' teaching regarding the promise of eternal life and the
power of God in healing the whole man, including the ills and injuries
of the flesh. He replies to critics of Christianity who maintain that God
saves only our souls and has no effect on our bodies.

•The Lord explains to us the meaning of the thing
when He says: "I came not to do my own will, but
the Father's, who hath sent me." What, I ask, is that
will? "That of all which He hath given me I should
lose nothing, but should raise it up again at the last
day." Now, what had Christ received of the Father
but that which He had Himself put on? Man, of
course, in his texture of flesh and soul. Neither,
therefore, of those parts which He has received will
He allow to perish; nay, no considerable portion —
nay, not the least fraction, of either.

If the flesh be, *as our opponent slightingly think,* but a poor fraction, then the flesh is safe, because not a fraction *of man is to perish;* and no longer a portion is in danger, because every portion of man is in equally safe keeping with Him. If, however, He will not raise the flesh also up at the last day, then He will permit not only a fraction of man to perish, but (as I will venture to say, in consideration of so important a part) almost the whole of him. But when He repeats His words with increased emphasis, "And this is the Father's will, that every one which seeth the Son, and believeth on Him, may have eternal life: and I will raise him up at the last day," — He asserts the full extent of the resurrection. (Chap. XXXIV)

•Now, if the dominion of death operates only in the dissolution of the flesh, in like manner death's contrary, life, ought to produce the contrary effect, even the restoration of the flesh; so that, just as death had swallowed it up in its strength, it also, after this mortal was swallowed up of immortality, may hear the challenge pronounced against it: "O death, where is thy sting? O grave, where is thy victory?" For in this way "grace shall there much more abound, where sin once abounded."

In this way also "shall strength be made perfect in weakness," — saving what is lost, reviving what is dead, healing what is stricken, curing what is faint, redeeming what is lost, freeing what is enslaved, recalling what has strayed, raising what has fallen; and this from earth to heaven, where, as the apostle teaches the Philippians, "we have our citizenship, from whence also we look for our Savior Jesus Christ, who shall change our body of humiliation, that it may be fashioned like unto His glorious body" — of course after the resurrection, because Christ Himself was not glorified before He suffered. These must be "the bodies" which he "beseeches" the Romans to "present" as "a living sacrifice, holy, acceptable unto God."

But how a *living* sacrifice, if these bodies are to perish? How a *holy* one, if they are profanely soiled? How *acceptable to God,* if they are condemned? Come, now, tell me how that passage (in the Epistle) to the Thessalonians — which, because of its clearness, I should suppose to have been written with a sunbeam — is understood by our heretics, who shun the light of Scripture: "And the very God of peace sanctify you wholly." And as if this were not plain enough, it goes on to say: "And may your whole body, and soul, and spirit be preserved blameless unto the coming of the Lord." Here you have the entire substance of man destined to salvation, and *that* at no other time than at the coming of the Lord, which is the key of the resurrection. (Chap. XLVII)

In spite of his somewhat impetuous nature, Tertullian wrote a beautiful and powerful piece called *On Patience.* In this brief work he explains the virtues of patience and the qualities of health, comfort, and strength which come from man's relationship to God.

•So amply sufficient a Depositary of patience is God. If it be a wrong which you deposit in his care, He is an Avenger; if a loss, He is a Restorer; if pain, He is a Healer; if death, He is a Reviver. What honour is granted to Patience, to have God as her Debtor! And not without reason: for she keeps all His decrees; she has to do with all His mandates. She fortifies faith; is the pilot of peace; assists charity; establishes humility; waits long for repentance; sets her seal on confession; rules the flesh; preserves the spirit; bridles the tongue; restrains the hand; tramples temptations under foot; drives away scandals; gives their crowning grace to martyrdom; consoles the poor; teaches the rich moderation; overstrains not the weak; exhausts not the strong; is the delight of the believer; invites the Gentile; commends the servant to his lord, and his lord to God;

adorns the woman; makes the man approved; is
loved in childhood, praised in youth, looked up to in
age; is beauteous in either sex, in every time of life.
(Chap. XV)

In his *Apology* Tertullian explains more about the nature of God and
the mission of Jesus. He denounces the rigidity of the Jews in reject-
ing the ministry of Jesus, and defends the works of Christian exorcists
in casting out demons. He condemns the trickery and magic of pagan
sorcerers who fail to permanently heal this prevalent mental malady
during the classical period.

> •And we, in like manner, hold that the Word, and
> Reason, and Power, by which we have said God
> made all, have spirit as their proper and essential
> *substratum,* in which the Word has in being to give
> forth utterances, and reason abides to dispose and
> arrange, and power is over all to execute. We have
> been taught that He proceeds forth from God, and in
> that procession He is generated; so that He is the
> Son of God, and is called God from unity of sub-
> stance with God. For God, too, is a Spirit. Even
> when the ray is shot from the sun, it is still part of
> the parent mass; the sun will still be in a ray,
> because it is a ray of the sun — there is no division
> of substance, but merely an extension.

> Thus Christ is Spirit of Spirit, and God of God, as
> light of light is kindled. The material matrix remains
> entire and unimpaired, though you derive from it
> any number of shoots possessed of its qualities; so,
> too, that which has come forth out of God is at once
> God and the Son of God, and the two are one. In
> this way also, as He is Spirit of Spirit and God of
> God, He is made a second in manner of existence —
> in position, not in nature; and He did not withdraw
> from the original source, but went forth. This ray of
> God, then, as it was always foretold in ancient
> times, descending into a certain virgin, and made
> flesh in her womb, is in His birth God and man unit-
> ed. The flesh formed by the Spirit is nourished,

grows up to manhood, speaks, teaches, works, and
is the Christ. . . .

As, then, under the force of their pre-judgment, they
had convinced themselves from His lowly guise that
Christ was no more than man, it followed from that,
as a necessary consequence, that they should hold
Him a magician from the powers which He displayed, — expelling devils from men by a word,
restoring vision to the blind, cleansing the leprous,
reinvigorating the paralytic, summoning the dead to
life again, making the very elements of nature obey
Him, stilling the storms and walking on the sea;
proving that He was the Logos of God, that primor-
dial first-begotten Word, accompanied by power and
reason, and based on Spirit, — that He who was
now doing all things by His word, and He who had
done that of old, were one and the same.

But the Jews were so exasperated by His teaching,
by which their rulers and chiefs were convicted of
the truth, chiefly because so many turned aside to
Him, that at last they brought Him before Pontius
Pilate, at that time Roman governor of Syria; and,
by the violence of their outcries against Him, extort-
ed a sentence giving Him up to them to be crucified.
(Chap. XXI)

•Thus far we have been dealing only in words: we
now proceed to a proof of facts, in which we shall
show that under different names you have real iden-
tity. Let a person be brought before your tribunals,
who is plainly under demoniacal possession. The
wicked spirit, bidden to speak by a follower of
Christ, will as readily make the truthful confession
that he is a demon, as elsewhere he has falsely
asserted that he is a god. Or, if you will, let there be
produced one of the god-possessed, as they are supposed, who, inhaling at the altar, conceive divinity
from the fumes, who are delivered of it by retching,
who vent it forth in agonies of gasping.

Let that same Virgin Caelestis herself the rain-
promiser, let Aesculapius discoverer of medicines,
ready to prolong the life of Socordius, and Tenatius,
and Asclepiodotus, now in the last extremity, if they
would not confess, in their fear of lying to a Christian, that they were demons, then and there shed the
blood of that most impudent follower of Christ.
What clearer than a word like that? what more trustworthy than such a proof? The simplicity of truth is
thus set forth; its own worth sustains it; no ground
remains for the least suspicion. Do you say that it is
done by magic, or some trick of that sort? You will
not say anything of the sort, if you have been
allowed the use of your ears and eyes. For what
argument can you bring against a thing that is exhibited to the eye in its naked reality? (Chap. XXIII)

•For, though the whole power of demons and kindred spirits is subject to us, yet still, as ill-disposed
slaves sometimes conjoin contumacy with fear, and
delight to injure those of whom they at the same
time stand in awe, so is it here, For fear also inspires
hatred. Besides, in their desperate condition, as
already under condemnation, it gives them some
comfort, while punishment delays, to have the
usufruct of their malignant dispositions.

And yet, when hands are laid on them, they are subdued at once, and submit to their lot; and those
whom at a distance they oppose, in close quarters
they supplicate for mercy. So when, like insurrec-
tionary workhouses, or prisons, or mines, or any
such penal slaveries, they break forth against us
their masters, they know all the while that they are
not a match for us, and just on that account, indeed,
rush the more recklessly to destruction. We resist
them unwillingly, as though they were equals, and
contend against them by persevering in that which
they assail; and our triumph over them is never
more complete than when we are condemned for
resolute adherence to our faith. (Chap. XXVII)

The next passage is from Tertullian's work called *The Shows, or De Spectaculis*. Here he cites the gratitude, freedom, and pleasure which accompanies a Christian life as well as the ability to exorcise evil and heal the sick.

•Even as things are, if your thought is to spend this period of existence in enjoyments, how are you so ungrateful as to reckon insufficient, as not thankfully to recognize the many and exquisite pleasures God has bestowed upon you? For what more delightful than to have God the Father and our Lord at peace with us, than revelation of the truth, than confession of our errors, than pardon of the innumerable sins of our past life? What greater pleasure than distaste of pleasure itself, contempt for all that the world can give, true liberty, a pure conscience, a contented life, and freedom from all fear of death? What nobler than to tread under foot the gods of the nations — to exorcise evil spirits — to perform cures — to seek divine revealings — to live to God? These are the pleasures, these the spectacles that befit Christian men — holy, everlasting, free. (Chap. XXIX)

The final reading is from *To Scapula* in which Tertullian appeals to a local Roman official for protection of the rights of Christians against false accusations from opponents of Christianity. His entreaty constitutes a courageous and brilliant defense of religious freedom during a time of frequent religious persecution. Tertullian relates numerous healings by Christians of high-ranking Roman officials, including a healing of Severus, the father of the Roman emperor Antonine. He also tells how the prayers of Christian soldiers brought rain and ended a drought during a military expedition by the emperor Marcus Aurelius in Germany.

•We who are without fear ourselves are not seeking to frighten you, but we would save all men if possible by warning them not to fight with God. You may perform the duties of your charge, and yet remember the claims of humanity; if on no other ground than that you are liable to punishment yourself, (You

ought to do so). For is not your commission simply
to condemn those who confess their guilt, and to
give over to the torture those who deny? You see,
then, how you trespass yourselves against your
instructions to wring from the confessing a denial. It
is, in fact, an acknowledgement of our innocence
that you refuse to condemn us at once when we confess.

In doing your utmost to extirpate us, if that is your
object, it is innocence you assail. But how many
rulers, men more resolute and more cruel than you
are, have contrived to get quit of such causes altogether, — as Cincius Severus, who himself suggest-
ed the remedy at Thysdris, pointing out how the
Christians should answer that they might secure an
acquittal. . . .

All this might be officially brought under your
notice, and by the very advocates, who are themselves also under obligations to us, although in court
they give their voice as it suits them. The clerk of
one of them who was liable to be thrown upon the
ground by an evil spirit, was set free from his affliction; as was also the relative of another, and the little
boy of a third. How many men of rank (to say nothing of common people) have been delivered from
devils, and healed of diseases! Even Severus himself, the father of Antonine, was graciously mindful
of the Christians; for he sought out the Christian
Proculus, surnamed Torpacion, the steward of Euho-
dias, and in gratitude for his having once cured him
by anointing, he kept him in his palace till the day
of his death.

Antonine, too, brought up as he was on Christian
milk, was intimately acquainted with this man. Both
women and men of highest rank, whom Severus
knew well to be Christians, were not merely permitted by him to remain uninjured; but he even bore
distinguished testimony in their favour, and gave

them publicly back to us from the hands of a raging populace.

Marcus Aurelius also, in his expedition to Germany, by the prayers his Christian soldiers offered to God, got rain in that well-known thirst. When, indeed, have not droughts been put away by our kneelings and our fastings? At times like these, moreover, the people crying to "the God of gods, the alone Omnipotent," under the name of Jupiter, have borne witness to our God. (Chap. IV)

CHAPTER 13

ORIGEN

(185 - 254)

Origen was born of Greek Christian parents in Alexandria about 185. He received his early education from his father (Leonides), who was a prominent teacher of mathematics, rhetoric, and Greek literature. Leonides was imprisoned during a persecution of Christianity when Origen was seventeen years old. The son wrote his father in prison encouraging him to adhere to his Christian faith regardless of the hardship imposed on their large family. Origen was prevented from joining his father in martyrdom only because his mother hid his clothes. In 202 Leonides was executed.

Origen supported himself and assisted his family by teaching Christianity. For a time he was a student of Clement of Alexandria, the director of the catechetical school in this large Egyptian city. When Clement was forced to flee because of renewed persecution, Origen took his place in this center of Christian learning at the age of eighteen. He soon assumed a life of selfless dedication to the Church. He became a eunuch, as he believed it was a way to remove all worldly temptations and devote his whole thought and effort to the teaching of Christianity.

In addition to his Christian learning, Origen studied Greek philosophy with pagan teachers; and, unlike Tertullian, he adapted some elements of Greek thought to his explanations of Christian doctrine. Yet throughout his life, he was a devout student of the Bible which served as the dominant source of his theology. Professor Harry Y. Gamble in his book *The New Testament Canon: Its Making and Meaning* has stated that Origen was "the greatest scripture scholar of the ancient church." (p. 50) And in a scholarly book titled *Origen,* Jean Danielou has written:

> With the study of the part played by the Bible in Origen's life and thinking, we come to the core of his writings. . . . Scripture was the centre of his life. If he studied philosophy, it was only because that would help him to a better understanding of God's word and enable him to explain it to his contempo-

raries. But the only master he ever acknowledged
was the Logos speaking through the Scriptures. We
have seen, too, that in his description of the Christian life, he gave the place of honour to the
didaskalos, i.e. to the man who explained Scripture.
The *didaskalos* was at the centre of the spiritual
worship proper to the New Testament. He was the
high priest, whose function it was to cut up the vic-
tim — the Logos — in such a way as to reveal its
inner meaning, and then to share it out on the spiritual altar, the souls of the faithful. This concept is
the unifying factor in Origen's mental world. (p.
131)

Following a dispute with the bishop of Alexandria, Origen moved
to Caesarea, where he lived most of his adult life. He established a
library and devoted himself largely to research and writing. He was
ordained a priest in 228 and soon acquired an international reputation
that enabled him to speak before religious councils in many parts of
the Roman empire. He likewise became a popular teacher of Christian
doctrine. Many of his students became leaders in the church, including
Eusebius, who became the first church historian, and Gregory Thau-
maturgus (the Wonder-Worker), who became a bishop and missionary
in Asia Minor.

Origen was imprisoned and tortured at Tyre during the Decian persecution (249 - 251). Extreme measures were taken by his captors to
force the sixty-five-year-old church leader to renounce his Christian
faith. This effort proved abortive and he was eventually released. Yet
he died shortly thereafter from his injuries and mistreatment.

With the help of wealthy supporters throughout much of his lifetime, Origen became one of the most prolific Christian writers. At one
time he employed seven clerks, seven transcribers, and a sizeable
number of young women skilled in calligraphy who assisted him in
his research and writing. He wrote thousands of manuscripts, many of
which have been lost. Some of his writings reappeared later in library
collections of the church, yet often they had been edited to delete his
unorthodox ideas.

Most of Origen's writings consisted of explanations of the Old Testament and the books written by the apostles. They affirmed that the
Hebrew scriptures combined with some aspects of Greek philosophy
had prepared mankind for Christianity. Origen often used allegories to

show how certain portions of the Bible were related to Greek philosophy. For a time his concept of salvation was closer to Greek and Gnostic thought than to the teachings of early Christianity. He emphasized the distinctions among the three elements of the Trinity rather than accepting their unity as formally approved as church doctrine at the Council of Nicea (325) and the Council of Constantinople (381). Many Christian leaders labeled him a heretic. Yet throughout his life, Origen insisted that he was an orthodox Christian.

In spite of the controversy surrounding his writing and teaching, Origen was probably the most influential of the Ante-Nicene Fathers. He was the first writer to provide a systematic order to Christian theology. He was the first to probe for new meanings in the Bible, even though this led to certain theological inconsistencies. His life and example exerted a strong influence on the eastern Greek church and many of the major Christian thinkers of the Middle Ages.

Origen's major written work is entitled *Contra Celsum* or *Against Celsus*. It comprises a detailed defense of Christianity in reply to Celsus, an articulate pagan critic of Christian teachings who wrote a widely read treatise in the 170's entitled *True Word*. Origen wrote his rebuttal in his old age and considered it an exposition of orthodox Christian doctrine. *Against Celsus* is generally regarded as the major classic of apologetical writing by the Ante-Nicene Fathers. It is one of the most relevant and interesting writings of the early Christian church for the modern reader.

Origen's writings are of special significance in the history of Biblical healing, as they provide organized and in-depth definitions of the nature of God, Christ Jesus, the Holy Spirit, and the relationship between God and man on which spiritual healing is based. Origen also describes how the Word of God embraces the flesh. His writings contain an extensive account of the healings performed by Jesus and an explanation of the failure of Greek philosophers to heal sin and disease. His reports on healing focus almost entirely on the exorcism of demons by Christians.

The first readings are from a relatively short treatise entitled *Origen De Principiis* , which contains his basic concepts of God, Christ Jesus, the Holy Spirit, and other precepts of Christian theology. These writings also show some aspects of the Greek influence on Origen's thought regarding the "intellectual" and "rational" nature of man. Yet a strong emphasis is on man's spiritual nature as the image and likeness of God.

•The particular points clearly delivered in the teaching of the apostles are as follows: -

First, That there is one God, who created and arranged all things, and who, when nothing existed, called all things into being — God from the first creation and foundation of the world — the God of all just men. . . .and that this God in the last days, as He had announced beforehand by His prophets, sent our Lord Jesus Christ to call in the first place Israel to Himself, and in the second place the Gentiles, after the unfaithfulness of the people of Israel. This just and good God, the Father of our Lord Jesus Christ, Himself gave the law, and the prophets, and the Gospels, being also the God of the apostles and of the Old and New Testaments.

Secondly, That Jesus Christ Himself, who came (into the world), was born of the Father before all creatures; that, after He had been the servant of the Father in the creation of all things — "For by Him were all things made" — He in the last times, divesting Himself (of His glory), became a man, and was incarnate although God, and while made a man remained the God which He was; that He assumed a body like to our own, differing in this respect only, that it was born of a virgin and of the Holy Spirit: that this Jesus Christ was truly born, and did truly suffer, and did not endure this death common (to man) in appearance only, but did truly die; that He did truly rise from the dead; and that after His resurrection He conversed with His disciples, and was taken up (into heaven).

Then, *Thirdly,* the apostles related that the Holy Spirit was associated in honour and dignity with the Father and the Son. But in His case it is not clearly distinguished whether He is to be regarded as born or innate, or also as a Son of God or not: for these are points which have to be inquired into out of sacred Scripture according to the best of our ability,

and which demand careful investigation. And that
this Spirit inspired each one of the saints, whether
prophets or apostles; and that there was not one
Spirit in the men of the old dispensation, and another in those who were inspired at the advent of
Christ, is most clearly taught throughout the
Churches. (Preface, 4)

•Let us now ascertain how those statements which
we have advanced are supported by the authority of
the holy Scripture. The Apostle Paul says, that the
only-begotten Son is the "image of the invisible
God," and "the first-born of every creature." And
when writing to the Hebrews, he says of Him that
He is "the brightness of His glory, and the express
image of His person." Now, we find in the treatise
called the Wisdom of Solomon the following
descriptions of the wisdom of God: "For she is the
breath of the power of God, and the purest efflux of
the glory of the Almighty." Nothing that is polluted
can therefore come upon her. For she is the splendour of the eternal light, and the stainless mirror of
God's working, and the image of His goodness.
Now we say, as before, that Wisdom has her existence nowhere else save in Him who is the beginning of all things: from whom also is derived everything that is wise, because He himself is the only
one who is by nature a Son, and is therefore termed
the Only-Begotten. . . .

Now this image contains the unity of nature and
substance belonging to Father and Son. For if the
Son do, in like manner, all those things which the
Father doth, then, in virtue of the Son doing all
things like the Father, is the image of the Father
formed in the Son, who is born of Him, like an act
of His will proceeding from the mind. And I am
therefore of opinion that the will of the Father ought
alone to be sufficient for the existence of His will.
He employs no other way than that which is made
known by the counsel of His will. And thus also the
existence of the Son is generated by Him.

> For the Son is the Word, and therefore we are not to
> understand that anything in Him is cognisable by
> the senses. He is wisdom, and in wisdom there can
> be no suspicion of anything corporeal. He is the true
> light, which enlightens every man that cometh into
> this world; but He has nothing in common with the
> light of this sun. Our Savior, therefore, is the image
> of the invisible God, inasmuch as compared with the
> Father Himself He is the truth: and as compared
> with us, to whom He reveals the Father, He is the
> image by which we come to the knowledge of the
> Father, whom no one knows save the Son, and he to
> whom the Son is pleased to reveal Him. And the
> method of revealing Him is through the understand-
> ing. For He by whom the Son Himself is under-
> stood, understands, as a consequence, the Father
> also, according to His own words: "He that hath
> seen Me, hath seen the Father also." (Book I, Chap.
> II, 5, 6)

The remainder of Origen's writings cited here are from his major
work, *Against Celsus.*

The second group of readings discusses Jesus' role in healing sickness and sin. They refer frequently to early teachings in the Old Testament. These excerpts also include Origen's explanations of the differences between Christian healing and the healing methods which seek
to rely on Greek philosophy and Greek gods. Part of his writings on
Christian healing replies to the charges of opponents of Christianity
that Jesus' signs and wonders were similar to the magic-miracles of
jugglers and "dealers in magical arts." Origen likewise explains the
very important role of Christian healing in elevating human morals
and character.

> •Let us see the manner in which this Celsus, who
> professes to know everything, brings a false accusa-
> tion against the Jews, when he alleges that "they
> worship angels, and are addicted to sorcery, in
> which Moses was their instructor." Now, in what
> part of the writings of Moses he found the lawgiver
> laying down the worship of angels, let him tell, who
> professes to know all about Christianity and

Judaism; and let him show also how sorcery can exist among those who have accepted the Mosaic law, and read the injunction, "Neither seek after wizards, to be defiled by them." Moreover, he promises to show afterwards "how it was through ignorance that the Jews were deceived and led into error."

Now, with respect to this point — His prior existence a few years ago — we have to remark as follows. Could it have come to pass without divine assistance, that Jesus, desiring during these years to spread abroad His words and teaching, should have been so successful, that everywhere throughout the world, not a few persons, Greeks as well as Barbarians, learned as well as ignorant, adopted His doctrine, so that they struggled even to death in its defence, rather than deny it, which no one is ever related to have done for any other system?

I indeed, from no wish to flatter Christianity, but from a desire thoroughly to examine the facts, would say that even those who are engaged in the healing of numbers of sick persons, do not attain their object — the cure of the body — without divine help; and if one were to succeed in delivering souls from a flood of wickedness, and excesses, and acts of injustice, and from a contempt of God, and were to show, as evidence of such a result, one hundred persons improved in their natures (let us suppose the number to be so large), no one would reasonably say that it was without divine assistance that he had implanted in those hundred individuals a doctrine capable of removing so many evils. (Book I, Chap. XXVI)

•For the law and the prophets are full of marvels similar to those recorded of Jesus at His baptism, viz., regarding the dove and the voice from heaven. And I think the wonders wrought by Jesus are proof

of the Holy Spirit's having then appeared in the
form of a dove, although Celsus, from a desire to
cast discredit upon them, alleges that He performed
only what He had learned among the Egyptians.
And I shall refer not only to His miracles, but, as is
proper, to those also of the apostles of Jesus. For
they could not without the help of miracles and
wonders have prevailed on those who heard their
new doctrines and new teachings to abandon their
national usages, and to accept their instructions at
the danger to themselves even of death.

And there are still preserved among Christians
traces of that Holy Spirit which appeared in the
form of a dove. They expel evil spirits, and perform
many cures, and foresee certain events, according to
the will of the Logos. And although Celsus, or the
Jew whom he has introduced, may treat with mock-
ery what I am going to say, I shall say it nevertheless, — that many have been converted to Christianity as if against their will, some sort of spirit having
suddenly transformed their minds from a hatred of
the doctrine to a readiness to die in its defence, and
having appeared to them either in a waking vision or
a dream of the night.

Many such instances have we known, which, if we
were to commit to writing, although they were seen
and witnessed by ourselves, we should afford great
occasion for ridicule to unbelievers, who would
imagine that we, like those whom they suppose to
have invented such things, had ourselves also done
the same. But God is witness of our conscientious
desire, not by false statements, but by testimonies of
different kinds, to establish the divinity of the doctrine of Jesus. (Book I, Chap. XLVI)

•After the above, this Jew of Celsus, as if he were a
Greek who loved learning, and were well instructed
in Greek literature, continues: "The old mythologi-
cal fables, which attributed a divine origin to

Perseus, and Amphion, and Aeacus, and Minos, were not believed by us. Nevertheless, that they might not appear unworthy of credit, they represented the deeds of these personages as great and wonderful, and truly beyond the power of man; but what hast thou done that is noble or wonderful either in deed or in word? Thou hast made no manifestation to use, although they challenged you in the temple to exhibit some unmistakable sign that you were the Son of God."

In reply to which we have to say: Let the Greeks show to us, among those who have been enumerated, any one whose deeds have been marked by a utility and splendour extending to after generations, and which have been so great as to produce a belief in the fables which represented them as of divine descent. But these Greeks can show us nothing regarding those men of whom they speak, which is even inferior by a great degree to what Jesus did; unless they take us back to their fables and histories, wishing us to believe them without any reasonable grounds, and to discredit the Gospel accounts even after the clearest evidence.

For we assert that the whole habitable world contains evidence of the works of Jesus, in the existence of those Churches of God which have been founded through Him by those who have been converted from the practice of innumerable sins. And the name of Jesus can still remove distractions from the minds of men, and expel demons, and also take away diseases; and produce a marvellous meekness of spirit and complete change of character, and a humanity, and goodness, and gentleness in those individuals who do not feign themselves to be Christians for the sake of subsistence or the supply of any mortal wants, but who have honestly accepted the doctrine concerning God and Christ, and the judgment to come. (Book I, Chap. LXVII

•But after this, Celsus, having a suspicion that the great works performed by Jesus, of which we have named a few out of a great number, would be brought forward to view, affects to grant that those statements may be true which are made regarding His cures, or His resurrection, or the feeding of a multitude with a few loaves, from which many fragments remained over, or those other stories which Celsus thinks the disciples have recorded as of a marvellous nature; and he adds: "Well, let us believe that these were actually wrought by you."

But then he immediately compares them to the tricks of jugglers, who profess to do more wonderful things, and to the feats performed by those who have been taught by Egyptians, who in the middle of the market-place, in return for a few obols, will impart the knowledge of their most venerated arts, and will expel demons from men, and dispel diseases, and invoke the souls of heroes, and exhibit expensive banquets, and tables, and dishes, and dainties having no real existence, and who will put in motion, as if alive, what are not really living animals, but which have only the appearance of life. And he asks, "Since, then, these persons can perform such feats, shall we of necessity conclude that they are 'sons of God,' or must we admit that they are the proceedings of wicked men under the influence of an evil spirit?"

You see that by these expressions he allows, as it were, the existence of magic. I do not know, however, if he is the same who wrote several books against it. But, as it helped his purpose, he compares the (miracles) related of Jesus to the results produced by magic. There would indeed be a resemblance between them, if Jesus, like the dealers in magical arts, had performed His works only for show; but now there is not a single juggler who, by means of his proceedings, invites his spectators to reform their manners, or trains those to the fear of God who are amazed at what they see, nor who tries to persuade them so to live as men who are to be justified by God. And jugglers do none of these things, because they have neither the power nor the will, nor any desire to busy themselves about the reformation of men, inasmuch as their own lives are full of the grossest and most notorious sins.

But how should not He who, by the miracles which He did, induced those who beheld the excellent results to undertake the reformation of their characters, manifest Himself not only to His genuine disciples, but also to others, as a pattern of most virtuous life, in order that His disciples might devote themselves to the work of instructing men in the will of God, and that the others, after being more fully instructed by His word and character than by His miracles, as to how they were to direct their lives, might in all their conduct have a constant reference to the good pleasure of the universal God? And if such were the life of Jesus, how could any one with reason compare Him with the sect of impostors, and not, on the contrary, believe, according to the promise, that He was God, who appeared in human form to do good to our race? (Book I, Chap. LXVI-II)

•"But." continues Celsus, "what great deeds did Jesus perform as being a God? Did he put his enemies to shame, or bring to a ridiculous conclusion what was designed against him?" Now to this question, although we are able to show the striking and miraculous character of the events which befell Him, yet from what other source can we furnish an answer than from the Gospel narratives, which state that "there was an earthquake, and that the rocks were split asunder, and the tombs opened, and the veil of the temple rent in twain from top to bottom, and that darkness prevailed in the day-time, the sun failing to give light?"

But if Celsus believe the Gospel accounts when he thinks that he can find in them matter of charge against the Christians, and refuse to believe them when they establish the divinity of Jesus, our answer to him is: "Sir, either disbelieve all the Gospel narratives, and then no longer imagine that you can found charges upon them; or, in yielding your belief to their statements, look in admiration on the Logos of God, who became incarnate, and who desired to confer benefits upon the whole human race. And this feature evinces the nobility of the work of Jesus, that, down to the present time, those whom God wills are healed by His name. (Book II, Chap. XXXIII)

•And again, when it is said of Aesculapius that a great multitude both of Greeks and Barbarians acknowledge that they have frequently seen, and still see, no mere phantom, but Aesculapius himself, healing and doing good, and foretelling the future; Celsus requires us to believe this, and finds no fault with the believers in Jesus, when we express our belief in such stories, but when we give our assent to the disciples, and eye-witnesses of the miracles of Jesus, who clearly manifest the honesty of their convictions (because we see their guilelessness, as far as it is possible to see the conscience revealed in writing), we are called by him a set of "silly" individuals, although he cannot demonstrate that an incalculable number, as he asserts, of Greeks and Barbarians acknowledge the existence of Jesus.

And some give evidence of their having received through this faith a marvellous power by the cures which they perform, invoking no other name over those who need their help than that of God of all things, and of Jesus, along with a mention of His history. For by these means we too have seen many persons freed from grievous calamities, and from distractions of mind, and madness, and countless other ills, which could be cured neither by men nor devils. (Book III, Chap. XXIV)

•For with what purpose in view did Providence accomplish the marvels related of Aristeas? And to confer what benefit upon the human race did such remarkable events as you regard them, take place? You cannot answer. But we, when we relate the events of the history of Jesus, have no ordinary defence to offer for their occurrence; — this, viz., that God desired to commend the doctrine of Jesus as a doctrine which was to save mankind, and which was based, indeed, upon the apostles as foundations of the rising edifice of Christianity, but which increased in magnitude also in the succeeding ages, in which not a few cures are wrought in the name of Jesus, and certain other manifestations of no small moment have taken place. . . .

But both Jesus Himself and His disciples desired that His followers should believe not merely in His Godhead and miracles, as if He had not also been a partaker of human nature, and had the human flesh which "lusteth against the Spirit;" but they saw also that the power which had descended into human nature, and into the midst of human miseries, and which had assumed a human soul and body, contributed through faith, along with its divine elements, to the salvation of believers, when they see that from Him there began the union of the divine with the human nature, in order that the human, by communion with the divine, might rise to be divine, not in Jesus alone, but in all those who not only believe, but enter upon life which Jesus taught, and which elevates to friendship with God and communion with Him every one who lives according to the precepts of Jesus. (Book III, Chap. XXVIII)

•After this, through the influence of some motive which is unknown to me, Celsus asserts that it is by the names of certain demons, and by the use of

incantations, that the Christians appear to be possessed of (miraculous) power; hinting, I suppose, at
the practices of those who expel evil spirits by
incantations. And here he manifestly appears to
malign the Gospel. For it is not by incantations that
Christians seem to prevail (over evil spirits), but by
the name of Jesus, accompanied by the announcement of the narratives which relate to Him; for the
repetition of these has frequently been the means of
driving demons out of men, especially when those
who repeated them did so in a sound and genuinely
believing spirit. Such power, indeed, does the name
of Jesus possess over evil spirits, that there have
been instances where it was effectual, when it was
pronounced even by bad men, which Jesus Himself
taught (would be the case), when He said: "Many
shall say to Me in that day, In Thy name we have
cast out devils, and done many wonderful works."

Whether Celsus omitted this from intentional malig-
nity, or from ignorance, I do not know. And he next
proceeds to bring a charge against the Savior Himself, alleging that it was by means of sorcery that He
was able to accomplish the wonders which He performed; and that foreseeing that others would attain
the same knowledge, and do the same things, making a boast of doing them by help of the power of
God, He excludes such from His kingdom. And his
accusation is, that if they are justly excluded, while
He Himself is guilty of the same practices, He is a
wicked man; but if He is not guilty of wickedness in
doing such things, neither are they who do the same
as He. But even if it be impossible to show by what
power Jesus wrought these miracles, it is clear that
Christians employ no spells or incantations, but the
simple name of Jesus, and certain other words in
which they repose faith, according to the holy Scriptures. (Book I, Chap. VI)

CHAPTER 14

CYPRIAN

(200 - 258)

Thascius Caecilius Cyprianus was born into an upper class pagan family in Carthage around 200. He received a good education in law and rhetoric and became a leading member of the urban society. He acquired considerable property and seemed destined toward a career as a high-ranking government official. Yet his growing personal dissatisfaction with moral and social conditions in this north African city caused him to become a Christian in 246. Cyprian's former social status and his intense devotion to Christianity aided him in obtaining rapid advances in the church hierarchy. He was ordained a priest within one year after his conversion, and in 248 he became the Bishop of Carthage. Following his admission to membership in the church, he sold his property and distributed his wealth to the poor.

In considerable degree, Cyprian was influenced by the writings of Tertullian, and he referred to the first Latin church father as "his master." Yet the new bishop was much different from his mentor, and he exerted a decidedly different influence on the church. Cyprian was more moderate and disciplined than Tertullian in both his writings and his participation in church activities. Cyprian was essentially an administrator and activist, more than a theologian and creative writer. Ernest Leigh-Bennett describes Cyprian's ecclesiastical and humanitarian role in his study *Handbook of the Early Christian Fathers* as follows:

> It is not so much as a theologian or writer that we have to regard St. Cyprian, but as a great administrator; the greatest in fact that the Church had known since St. Paul. Under him the power of the Episcopate was thoroughly consolidated, and what is known as monarchical Episcopacy, in contrast to the presidential Episcopacy attributed to earlier times, became an established and permanent fact.

> He was essentially an organizer and a statesman.
> Under him we find the Church going forth as an
> organized body of active workers to relieve suffer-
> ing. From him we get an account of the diseased
> state of the body politic and of the attitude the
> Church should take towards social questions. By
> him the essential unity of the Church was empha-
> sized, and the importance of the sacramental system
> as a bond of that union. (p. 114)

Cyprian assumed the leadership of the north African church at a
time of renewed persecution and during a period when a more stable
and efficient organization of the growing church was urgently needed.
His new form of unified episcopal structure shaped the organization of
the Christian church for more than one thousand years. It aided in
making the church an authoritarian hierarchy of bishops rather than a
charismatic order of martyrs.

During the Decian persecution (249 - 251) Cyprian fled into hiding
in the countryside to evade imprisonment and martyrdom, and he confronted numerous controversies and schisms in the church on his
return. A major issue was readmission to church membership by the
surprisingly large number of Christians who had renounced their religious faith during the persecution. Cyprian led a faction within the
church which demanded strict standards for readmission by church
members who had yielded to paganism, including rebaptism by clergy
loyal to the teachings of orthodox Christianity. A renewal of persecution under Emperor Valerian erupted in 258, and this time Cyprian
refused to flee to safety. After a brief trial, he was martyred for refusing to repudiate Christian teachings.

At the time of his death, Cyprian had become one of the most popular of the church fathers in both the western and eastern regions of the
church. His impact on western Christianity was not surpassed until the
time of Augustine. He became one of the most influential of the Ante-
Nicene Fathers for his concept of the church as an organic whole in
the form of the body of Christ and a religious order in which every
member of the clergy and laity had an important role.

Cyprian's writings depict a transitional stage of the Christian church
near the end of Roman persecution. During a short ten-year career as a
member and leader of the early church, he wrote numerous letters,
treatises, and epistles. His major works were *On the Unity of the
Church* and *On the Lapsed*. His writings are significant as they show

the trend of the church toward more worldly power and the turbulence caused by intense struggles between the Bishop of Rome (later the Pope) and the leadership in regional churches.

In considerable degree, Cyprian's writings on Christian healing reveal a declining emphasis on the church's role in spiritual healing and a growing trend toward ritual and ceremony in seeking the cure of disease.

The first reading from the writings of Cyprian is from a treatise titled *On the Dress of Virgins*. It emphasizes God's desire to impart health and well-being to man and repeats Paul's message that man's body is the "temple" of God. Cyprian tells us that in a spiritual sense we are "worshippers" and "priests" in these temples.

> •But if in Holy Scripture discipline is frequently and everywhere prescribed, and the whole foundation of religion and of faith proceeds from obedience and fear; what is more fitting for us urgently to desire, what more to wish for and to hold fast, than to stand with roots strongly fixed, and with our houses based with solid mass upon the rock unshaken by the storms and whirlwinds of the world, so that we may come by the divine precepts to the rewards of God? considering as well as knowing that our members, when purged from all the filth of the old contagion by the sanctification of the laver of life, are God's temples, and must not be violated nor polluted, since he who does violence to them is himself injured.

> We are the worshippers and priests of those temples; let us obey Him whose we have already begun to be. Paul tells us in his epistles, in which he has formed us to a course of living by divine teaching, "Ye are not your own, for ye are bought with a great price; glorify and bear God in your body." Let us glorify and bear God in a pure and chaste body, and with a more complete obedience; and since we have been redeemed by the blood of Christ, let us obey and give furtherance to the empire of our Redeemer by all the obedience of service, that nothing impure or profane may be brought into the temple of God, lest

He should be offended, and forsake the temple
which He inhabits.

The words of the Lord giving health and teaching,
as well curing as warning, are: "Behold, thou art
made whole: sin no more, lest a worse thing come
unto thee." He gives the course of life, He gives the
law of innocency after He has conferred health, nor
suffers the man afterwards to wander with free and
unchecked reins, but more severely threatens him
who is again enslaved by those same things of
which he had been healed, because it is doubtless a
smaller fault to have sinned before, while as yet you
had not known God's discipline; but here is no further pardon for sinning after you have begun to
know God.

And, indeed, let as well men as women, as well
boys as girls; let each sex and every age observe
this, and take care in this respect, according to the
religion and faith which they owe to God, that what
is received holy and pure from the condescension of
the Lord be preserved with a no less anxious fear.
(2)

The second group of passages is from Cyprian's major work, *On
the Lapsed*. It describes the declining standards and values of the
Christian church during his lifetime, and some of the reasons for its
reduced role in spiritual healing.

•Each one was desirous of increasing his estate; and
forgetful of what believers had either done before in
the times of the apostles, or always ought to do,
they, with the insatiable ardour of covetousness,
devoted themselves to the increase of their property.
Among the priests there was no devotedness of religion; among the ministers there was no sound faith:
in their works there was no mercy; in their manners
there was no discipline.

In men, their beards were defaced, in women, their complexion was dyed: the eyes were falsified from what God's hand had made them; their hair was stained with a falsehood. Crafty frauds were used to deceive the hearts of the simple, subtle meanings for circumventing the brethren. They united in the bond of marriage with unbelievers; they prostituted the members of Christ to the Gentiles. They would swear not only rashly, but even more,would swear falsely; would despise those set over them with haughty swelling, would speak evil of one another with envenomed tongue, would quarrel with one another with obstinate hatred.

Not a few bishops who ought to furnish both exhortation and example to others, despising their divine charge, became agents in secular business, forsook their throne, deserted their people, wandered about over foreign provinces, hunted the markets for gainful merchandise, while brethren were starving in the Church. They sought to possess money in hoards, they seized estates by crafty deceits, they increased their gains by multiplying usuries.

What do not such as we deserve to suffer for sins of this kind, when even already the divine rebuke has forewarned us, and said, "If they shall forsake my law, and walk not in my judgments; if they shall profane my statutes, and shall not observe my precepts, I will visit their offences with a rod, and their sins with scourges?" (6)

The final reading is from Cyprian's *Epistle LXXV,* which is subtitled *To Magnus, on Baptizing the Novatians, and Those Who Obtain Grace On a Sick-Bed.* This treatise relates the healing of sickness to the sacraments of the church, especially baptism.

•You have asked also. . .what I thought of those who obtain God's grace in sickness and weakness, whether they are to be accounted legitimate Christians, for that they are not to be washed, but sprin-

kled, with the saving water. In this point, my diffi-
dence and modesty prejudges none, so as to prevent
any from feeling what he thinks right, and from
doing what he feels to be right. . . .

In the sacraments of salvation, when necessity compels, and God bestows His mercy, the divine methods confer the whole benefit on believers; nor ought
it to trouble any one that sick people seem to be
sprinkled or affused, when they obtain the Lord's
grace, when Holy Scripture speaks by the mouth of
the prophet Ezekiel, and says, "Then will I sprinkle
clean water upon you, and ye shall be clean; from
all your filthiness and from all your idols will I
cleanse you. And I will give you a new heart, and a
new spirit will I put within you."

Whence it appears that the sprinkling also of water
prevails equally with the washing of salvation; and
that when this is done in the Church, where the faith
both of receiver and giver is sound, all things hold
and may be consummated and perfected by the
majesty of the Lord and by the truth of faith. (12)

•But, moreover, in respect of some calling those
who have obtained the peace of Christ by the saving
water and by legitimate faith, not Christians, but
Clinics, I do not find whence they take up this
name, unless perhaps, having read more, and of a
more recondite kind, they have taken these Clinics
from Hippocrates or Soranus. For I, who know of a
Clinic in the Gospel, know that to that paralytic and
infirm man, who lay on his bed during the long
course of his life, his infirmity presented no obstacle
to his attainment in the fullest degree of heavenly
strength. Nor was he only raised from his bed by the
divine indulgence, but he also took up his bed itself
with his restored and increased strength.

And therefore, as far as it is allowed me by faith to
conceive and to think, this is my opinion, that any

one should be esteemed a legitimate Christian, who by the law and right of faith shall have obtained the grace of God in the Church. Or if any one think that those have gained nothing by having only been sprinkled with the saving water, but that they are still empty and void, let them not be deceived, so as if they escape the evil of their sickness, and get well, they *should seek* to be baptized.

But if they cannot be baptized who have already been sanctified by ecclesiastical baptism, why are they offended in respect of their faith and the mercy of the Lord? Or have they obtained indeed the divine favour, but in a shorter and more limited measure of the divine gift and of the Holy Spirit, so as indeed to be esteemed Christians, but yet not to be counted equal with others? (13)

•But if any one is moved by this, that some of those who are baptized in sickness are still tempted by unclean spirits, let him know that the obstinate wickedness of the devil prevails even up to the saving water, but that in baptism it loses all the poison of his wickedness. An instance of this we see in the king Pharaoh, who, having struggled long, and delayed in his perfidy, could resist and prevail until he came to the water; but when he had come thither, he was both conquered and destroyed.

And that that sea was a sacrament of baptism, the blessed Apostle Paul declares, saying, "Brethren, I would not have you ignorant how that all our fathers were under the cloud, and all passed through the sea, and were all baptized unto Moses in the cloud and in the sea;" and he added, saying, "Now all these things were our examples." And this also is done in the present day, in that the devil is scourged, and burned, and tortured by exorcists, by the human voice, and by divine power; and although he often says that he is going out, and will leave the men of God, yet in that which he says he deceives, and puts

in practice what was before done by Pharoah with
the same obstinate and fraudulent deceit.

When, however, they come to the water of salvation
and to the sanctification of baptism, we ought to
know and to trust that there the devil is beaten
down, and the man, dedicated to God, is set free by
the divine mercy. For as scorpions and serpents,
which prevail on the dry ground, when cast into
water, cannot prevail nor retain their venom; so also
the wicked spirits, which are called scorpions and
serpents, and yet are trodden under foot by us, by
the power given by the Lord, cannot remain any
longer in the body of a man in whom, baptized and
sanctified, the Holy Spirit is beginning to dwell.
(15)

•This, finally, in very fact also we experience, that
those who are baptized by urgent necessity in sickness, and obtain grace, are free from the unclean
spirit wherewith they were previously moved, and
live in the Church in praise and honour, and day by
day make more and more advance in the increase of
heavenly grace by the growth of their faith. And, on
the other hand, some of those who are baptized in
health, if subsequently they begin to sin, are shaken
by the return of the unclean spirit, so that it is manifest that the devil is driven out in baptism by the
faith of the believer, and returns if the faith afterwards shall fail. (16)

CHAPTER 15

ARNOBIUS

(CIRCA 245 - 305)

The life of Arnobius is one of the most meagerly documented of any of the Ante-Nicene Fathers included in this survey. He has written nothing about his own life in his single surviving treatise, and scholars of this period of church history have no reliable information on the dates of his birth or death. There are brief references to his work as a teacher of rhetoric at Sicca Veneria, a town located southwest of Carthage. It is also believed that Arnobius was a teacher of Lactantius, the final church father included in this collection of writings on Christian healing.

Arnobius was probably a Greek and, like most of his predecessors, he was a convert to Christianity. In all likelihood, he embraced the teachings of the New Testament in his older years. There is little confirmed data on the reasons for his conversion; his writings, like those of Cyprian, imply a growing dissatisfaction with paganism. There is likewise no information on Arnobius' education. A general consensus among most scholars is that he was not as learned or erudite as most of the early church fathers. He never became a presbyter or ordained priest; it is assumed he did serve for a time in a modest church role as a catechumen. Wide agreement exists that Arnobius wrote the last surviving Christian apology just before the end of Roman persecution of the church. In all probability he was martyred for his religious convictions shortly after completing his major writing.

Arnobius' sole surviving work is titled *Adversus Gentes* or *Against the Heathen*. In spite of many shortcomings, this seven-volume series was a valuable contribution to the literature of the early church and to the development of Latin Christianity. It comprises a strong and sweeping counterattack against the slanders of Christianity made by pagan writers. It reveals much about paganism around the year 300, and it provides useful insights into the personal mental conflicts of dissenters from the dwindling ranks of paganism as they began to embrace Christian teachings.

The writings of Arnobius make no mention of the Old Testament and very few references to specific Christian writers. They show a thorough reading of the New Testament and the influence of other Ante-Nicene Fathers, especially Tertullian and Cyprian. At times Arnobius seems to be influenced by Epicureanism and Stoicism, yet in other places he attacks these Greek philosophies. It is very clear that he was greatly impressed with the healing miracles performed by Jesus. In the introductory note on Arnobius in the sixth volume of *The Ante-Nicene Fathers*, Dr. Coxe states:

> He gives us a most fascinating insight into the mental processes by which he, and probably Constantine soon after him, came to the conclusion that heathenism was outgrown and must disappear. He proves that the Church was salt that had not "lost its savour." It is true, that, reasoning with pagans, he does not freely cite the Scriptures, which had no force with them; yet his references to the facts of Scripture show that he had studied them conscientiously, and could present the truths of the Gospel clearly and with power. (pp. 405 - 406)

Arnobius is included among the Ante-Nicene Fathers in this coverage of Biblical healing because he is one of the most assertive and cogent writers stressing the healings performed by Jesus in his defense of Christianity against pagan opponents. Arnobius' writings provide accounts of Jesus' healings of serious diseases which are not recorded in the New Testament. He also presents additional information regarding Jesus imparting to his disciples the ability to heal. These achievements unfamiliar to modern Christians were probably spread by word of mouth among early Christian communities, or perhaps they were included in the writings of the apostles and other followers of Jesus which were lost after the period of Primitive Christianity.

Arnobius is also important in this study since his writings at the end of the fourth century show a second trend within Christian communities different from that taken by Cyprian and some other church leaders. This trend reveals a continuing emphasis on spiritual healing by individual Christians despite a declining interest in healing by the increasingly organized hierarchy of the church.

In *Against the Heathen*, Arnobius devotes eleven consecutive chapters to a vigorous affirmation of Christian teachings by citing the healings of Jesus achieved without the use of herbs, ceremony, or any "external things" except "the inherent might of His authority." He adds that these healing works have been performed by many Christians, including "unlearned Christians." None of the other Ante-Nicene Fathers has written about spiritual healing in such an explicit, concentrated, and forceful manner. Perhaps the language in no other writings about healing by these early church leaders attains a higher level of beauty and eloquence, even in translation from its original source.

The following readings comprise the eleven chapters from Book One of *Against the Heathen:*

•You worship, *says my opponent,* one who was born a *mere* human being. Even if that were true, as has been already said in former passages, yet, in consideration of the many liberal gifts which He has bestowed on us, He ought to be called and be addressed as God. *But* since He is God in reality and without any shadow of doubt, do you think that we will deny that He is worshipped by us with all the fervour we are capable of, and assumed as the guardian of our body? Is that Christ of yours a god, then? some raving, wrathful, and excited man will say.

A god, we reply, and *the* god of the inner powers; and — what may still further torture unbelievers with the most bitter pains — He was sent to us by the King Supreme for a purpose of the very highest moment. My opponent, becoming more mad and more frantic, will perhaps ask whether the matter can be proved, as we allege. There is no greater proof than the credibility of the acts done by Him, than the unwonted excellence of the virtues *He exhibited,* than the conquest and the abrogation of all those deadly ordinances which peoples and tribes saw executed in the light of day, with no objecting voice; and even they whose ancient laws or whose country's laws He shows to be full of vanity and of the most senseless superstition, (even they) dare not allege these things to be false. (42)

•My opponent will perhaps meet me with many
other slanderous and childish charges which are
commonly urged. Jesus was a Magician; He effected
all these things by secret arts. From the shrines of
Egyptians He stole the names of angels of might,
and the religious system of a remote country. Why,
O witlings, do you speak of things which you have
not examined, and which are unknown to you, prat-
ing with the garrulity of a rash tongue? Were, then,
those things which were done, the freaks of demons,
and the tricks of magical arts? Can you specify and
point out to me any one of all those magicians who
have ever existed in past ages, that did anything
similar, in the thousandth degree, to Christ? Who
has done this without any power of incantations,
without the juice of herbs and of grasses, without
any anxious watching of sacrifices, of libations, or
seasons?

For we do not press it, and inquire what they profess
to do, nor in what kind of acts all their learning and
experience are wont to be comprised. For who is not
aware that these men either study to know beforehand things impending, which, whether they will or
not, come of necessity as they have been ordained?
or to inflict a deadly and wasting disease on whom
they choose; or to sever the affections of relatives;
or to open without keys places which are locked; or
to seal the mouth in silence; or in the chariot race to
weaken, urge on, or retard horses; or to inspire
wives, and in the children of strangers, whether they
be males or females, the flames and mad desires of
illicit love? Or if they seem to attempt anything useful, to be able to do it not by their own power, but
by the might of those deities whom they invoke.
(43)

•And yet it is agreed on that Christ performed all
those miracles which He wrought without any aid
from external things, without the observance of any
ceremonial, without any definite mode of procedure,

but solely by the inherent might of His authority;
and as was the proper duty of *the* true God, as was
consistent with His nature, as was worthy of Him, in
the generosity of His bounteous power He bestowed
nothing hurtful or injurious, but *only that which is*
helpful, beneficial, and full of blessings good for
men. (44)

•What do you say again, oh you - ? Is He then a
man, is He one of us, at whose command, at whose
voice, raised in the utterance of audible and intelli-
gible words, infirmities, diseases, fevers, and other
ailments of the body fled away? Was He one of us,
whose presence, whose very sight, that race of
demons which took possession of men was unable
to bear, and terrified by the strange power, fled
away? Was He one of us, at whose order the foul
leprosy, at once checked, was obedient, and left
sameness of colour to bodies formerly spotted? Was
He one of us, at whose light touch the issues of
blood were stanched, and stopped their excessive
flow?

Was He one of us, whose hands the waters of the
lethargic dropsy fled from, and that searching fluid
avoided; and did the swelling body, assuming a
healthy dryness, find relief? Was He one of us, who
bade the lame run? Was it His work, too, that the
maimed stretched forth their hands, and the joints
relaxed the rigidity acquired even at birth; that the
paralytic rose to their feet, and persons now carried
home their beds who a little before were borne on
the shoulders of others; the blind were restored to
sight, and men born without eyes now looked on the
heaven and the day? (45)

•Was He one of us, I say, who by one act of inter-
vention at once healed a hundred or more afflicted
with various infirmities and diseases; at whose word
only the raging and maddened seas were still, the
whirlwinds and tempests were lulled; who walked

over the deepest pools with unwet foot; who trod the ridges of the deep, the very waves being astonished, and nature coming under bondage; who with five loaves satisfied five thousand of His followers; and who, lest it might appear to the unbelieving and hard of heart to be an illusion, filled twelve capacious baskets with the fragments that remained?

Was He one of us, who ordered the breath that had departed to return to the body, persons buried to come forth from the tomb, and after three days to be loosed from the swathings of the undertaker? Was He one of us, who saw clearly in the hearts of the silent what each was pondering, what each had in his secret thoughts? Was He one of us, who, when He uttered a single word, was thought by nations far removed from one another and of different speech to be using well-known sounds, and the peculiar language of each?

Was He one of us, who, when He was teaching His followers the duties of a religion that could not be gainsaid, suddenly filled the whole world, and showed how great He was and who He was, by unveiling the boundlessness of His authority? Was He one of us, who, after His body had been laid in the tomb, manifested Himself in open day to countless numbers of men; who spoke to them, and listened to them; who taught them, reproved and admonished them; who, lest they should imagine that they were deceived by unsubstantial fancies, showed Himself once, a second time, aye frequently, in familiar conversation; who appears even now to righteous men of unpolluted mind who love Him, not in airy dreams, but in a form of pure simplicity; whose name, when heard, puts to flight evil spirits, imposes silence on soothsayers, prevents men from consulting the augurs, causes the efforts of arrogant magicians to be frustrated, not by the dread of His name, as you allege, but by the free exercise of a greater power? (46)

•These facts set forth in summary we have put forward, not on the supposition that the greatness of
the agent was to be seen in these virtues alone. For
however great these things be, how excessively
petty and trifling will they be found to be, if it shall
be revealed from what realms He has come, of what
God He is the minister! But with regard to the acts
which were done by Him, they were performed,
indeed, not that He might boast Himself into empty
ostentation, but that hardened and unbelieving men
might be assured that what was professed was not
deceptive, and that they might now learn to imagine,
from the beneficence of His works, what a true god
was.

At the same time we wish this also to be known,
when, as was said, an enumeration of His acts has
been given in summary, that Christ was able to do
not only those things which He did, but that He
could even overcome the decrees of fate. For if, as
is evident, and as is agreed by all, infirmities and
bodily sufferings, if deafness, deformity, and dumb-
ness, if shrivelling of the sinews and the loss of
sight happen to us, and are brought on us by the
decrees of fate, and if Christ alone has corrected
this, has restored and cured man, it is clearer than
the sun himself that He was more powerful than the
fates are when He has loosened and overpowered
those things which were bound with everlasting
knots, and fixed by unalterable necessity. (47)

•But, says some one, you in vain claim so much for
Christ, when we now know, and have in past times
known, of other gods both giving remedies to many
who were sick, and healing the diseases and infirmities of many men. I do not inquire, I do not demand,
what god did so, or at what time; whom he relieved,
or what shattered frame he restored to sound health:
this only I long to hear, whether, without the addition of any substance — that is, of any medical
application — he ordered diseases to fly away from

men at a touch; whether he commanded and compelled the cause of ill health to be eradicated, and
the bodies of the weak to return to their natural
strength.

For it is known that Christ, either by applying His
hand to the parts affected, or by the command of His
voice only, opened the ears of the deaf, drove away
blindness from the eyes, gave speech to the dumb,
loosened the rigidity of joints, gave the power of
walking to the shrivelled, — was wont to heal by a
word and by an order, leprosies, agues, dropsies,
and all other kinds of ailments, which some felt
power had willed that the bodies of men should
endure.

What act like these have all these gods done, by
whom you allege that help has been brought to the
sick and the imperilled? for if they have at any time
ordered, as is reported, either that medicine or a special diet be given to some, or that a draught be
drunk off or that the juices of plants and of blades
be placed on that which causes uneasiness or *have
ordered* that persons should walk, remain at rest, or
abstain from something hurtful, — and that this is
no great matter, and deserves no great admiration, is
evident, if you will attentively examine it — a similar mode of treatment is followed by physicians
also, a creature earth-born and not relying on true
science, but founding on a system of conjecture, and
wavering in estimating probabilities.

Now there is no *special* merit in removing by remedies those ailments which affect men: the healing
qualities belong to the drugs — not virtues inherent
in him who applies them; and though it is praise-
worthy to know by what medicine or by what
method it may be suitable for persons to be treated,
there is room for this credit being assigned to man,
but not to the deity. For it is, *at least,* no discredit
that he should have improved the health of man by

things taken from without: it is a disgrace to a god
that he is not able to effect it of himself, but that he
gives soundness and safety only by the aid of external objects. (48)

•And since you compare Christ and the other deities
as to the blessings of health bestowed, how many
thousands of infirm persons do you wish to be
shown to you by us; how many persons affected
with wasting diseases, whom no appliances whatever restored, although they went as suppliants
through all the temples, although they prostrated
themselves before the gods, and swept the very
thresholds with their lips - though, as long as life
remained, they wearied with prayers, and impor-
tuned with most piteous vows Aesculapius himself,
the health-giver, as they call him?

Do we not know that some died of their ailments?
that others grew old by the torturing pain of their
diseases? that others began to live a more abandoned life after they had wasted their days and
nights in incessant prayers, and in expectation of
mercy? Of what avail is it, then, to point to one or
another who may have been healed, when so many
thousands have been left unaided, and the shrines
are full of all the wretched and the unfortunate?
Unless, perchance, you say that the gods help the
good, but that the miseries of the wicked are over-
looked. And yet Christ assisted the good and the bad
alike; nor was there any one rejected by Him, who
in adversity sought help against violence and the ills
of fortune.

For this is the mark of a true god and of kingly
power, to deny his bounty to none, and not to consider who merits it or who does not; since natural
infirmity and not the choice of his desire, or of his
sober judgment, makes a sinner. To say, moreover,
that aid is given by the gods to the deserving when
in distress, is to leave undecided and render doubtful

what you assert: so that both he who has been made
whole may seem to have been preserved by chance,
and he who is not may appear to have been unable
to banish infirmity, not because of his demerit, but
by reason of a heaven-sent weakness. (49)

•Moreover, by His own power He not only performed those miraculous deeds which have been
detailed by us in summary, and not as the importance of the matter demanded; but, what was more
sublime, He has permitted many others to attempt
them, and to perform them by the use of His name.
For when He foresaw that you were to be detractors
of His deeds and of His divine work, in order that
no lurking suspicion might remain of His having
lavished these gifts and bounties by magic arts, from
the immense multitude of people, which with admir-
ing wonder strove to gain His favour, He chose fish-
ermen, artisans, rustics, and unskilled persons of a
similar kind, that they being sent through various
nations, should perform all those miracles without
any deceit and without any material aids.

By a word He assuaged the racking pains of the
aching members; and by a word they checked the
writhings of maddening sufferings. By one command He drove demons from the body, and restored
their senses to the lifeless; they, too, by no different
command, restored health and to soundness of mind
those labouring under the inflictions of these
demons. By the application of His hand He removed
the mark of leprosy; they, too, restored to the body
the natural skin by a touch not dissimilar.

He ordered the dropsical and swollen flesh to recover its natural dryness; and His servants in the same
manner stayed the wandering waters, and ordered
them to glide through their own channels, avoiding
injury to the frame. Sores of immense size, refusing
to admit of healing, He restrained from further feeding on the flesh, by the interposition of one word;

and they in like manner, by restricting its ravages,
compelled the obstinate and merciless cancer to
confine itself to a scar.

To the lame He gave the power of walking, to the
dark eyes sight, the dead He recalled to life; and not
less surely did they, too, relax the tightened nerves,
fill the eyes with light already lost, and order the
dead to return from the tombs, reversing the ceremonies of the funeral rites. Nor was anything calling
forth the bewildered admiration of all done by Him,
which He did not freely allow to be performed by
those humble and rustic men, and which He did not
put in their power. (50)

•What say ye, O minds incredulous, stubborn, hardened? Did that great Jupiter Capitolinus of yours
give to any human being power of this kind? Did he
endow with this right any priest of a curia, the Pon-
tifex Maximus, nay, even the Dialis, in whose name
he is *revealed as* the god of life? I shall not say, *did
he impart power* to raise the dead, to give light to
the blind, restore the normal condition of their members to the weakened and the paralyzed, but *did he
even enable any one* to check a pustule, a hang-nail,
a pimple, either by the word of his mouth or the
touch of his hand?

Was this, then, a power natural to man, or could
such a right be granted, could such a licence be
given by the mouth of one reared on the vulgar produce of earth; and was it not a divine and sacred
gift? or if the matter admits of any hyperbole, was it
not more than divine and sacred? For if you do that
which you are able to do, and what is compatible
with your strength and your ability, there is no
ground for the expression of astonishment; for you
will have done that which you were able, and which
your power was bound to accomplish, in order that
there should be a perfect correspondence between
the deed and the doer. To be able to transfer to a

man your own power, share with the frailest being
the ability to perform that which you alone are able
to do, is a proof of power supreme over all, and
holding in subjection the causes of all things, and
the natural laws of methods and of means. (51)

•Come, then, let some Magian Zoroaster arrive from
a remote part of the globe, crossing over the fiery
zone, if we believe Hermippus as an authority. . .
Let them grant to one of the people to adapt the
mouths of the dumb for the purposes of speech, to
unseal the ears of the deaf, to give the natural powers of the eye to those born without sight, and to
restore feeling and life to the bodies long cold in
death.

Or if that is *too* difficult, and if they cannot impart
to others the power to do such acts, let themselves
perform them, and with their own rites. Whatever
noxious herbs the earth brings forth from its bosom,
whatever powers those muttered words and accom-
panying spells contain — these let them add, we
envy them not; *those* let them collect, we forbid
them not. We wish to make trial and to discover
whether they can effect, with the aid of their gods,
what has often been accomplished by unlearned
Christians with a word only. (52)

CHAPTER 16

LACTANTIUS

(260 - 325)

The life and works of Lactantius are only slightly better document-ed than those of Arnobius. His writings are included at the end of this survey on the Ante-Nicene Fathers because he lived for a short time after the end of Roman persecution of Christianity. The Christian church had been formally recognized by Constantine, and it was on its way to becoming the only official religion of the empire. Lactantius also saw the beginning of the decline of discipline and spiritual vitali-ty within the church which soon changed many practices by church members, including healing the sick.

Lactantius was born into a pagan family in north Africa, and he was converted to Christianity late in his life. His full name was Lucius Caelius Firmianus Lactantius, and as previously cited, he was proba-bly a pupil of Arnobius. Like his mentor, Lactantius acquired a reputa-tion as a teacher of rhetoric at Sicca Veneria, near the city of Carthage. While still a pagan, he was sent by Emperor Diocletian to teach in the Greek-speaking region at Nicomedia. Yet he soon abandoned his pro-fession and became a writer. For a time Lactantius lived in poverty, and it is likely that he became a Christian during this period. In 315 he moved to southern Gaul, where he tutored the oldest son of Constan-tine. He died at Treves, probably around 325, at the same time as the Council of Nicea.

Lactantius' expositions were intended to instruct the pagan leader-ship and intellectuals of the Roman empire on the basic teachings of Christianity. His major work is titled *The Divine Institutes or An Introduction to True Religion;* it was written between 305 and 313. This treatise comprising seven volumes was the most comprehensive apology of Christianity in Latin up to that time. It was an attempt at a systematic exposition of Christian doctrine in the author's language, much as Origen had previously written in Greek.

Lactantius also began to explore important political issues con-fronting the church, and he assessed its early activities as it was becoming more involved in secular as well as spiritual affairs. His writings, however, lacked depth and insight, and he remained primarily a competent rhetorician rather than a major theologian or religious writer. Lactantius' major contribution was his ability to write Latin in an elegant, lucid, and dignified style. His written works elevated the quality of Christian treatises in the Latin language to their highest level until the time of Jerome and Augustine. In the seventh volume of *The Ante-Nicene Fathers,* Dr. William Fletcher has stated:

> Lactantius has always held a very high place among the Christian Fathers, not only on account of the subject-matter of his writings, but also on account of the varied erudition, the sweetness of expression, and the grace and elegance of style, by which they are characterized. . . .His writings everywhere give evidence of his varied and extensive erudition, and contain much valuable information respecting the systems of the ancient philosophers. But his claims as a theologian are open to question; for he holds peculiar opinions on many points, and he appears more successful as an opponent of error than as a maintainer of the truth. (pp. 5, 7)

In contrast to the writings of Arnobius, the studies by Lactantius on Christian healing are meager and sporadic. They do not reveal the same enthusiasm or devotion to the healing mission of the church as the works of most previous Ante-Nicene writers. Yet they show that healing in the church around the time of the Council of Nicea had not totally disappeared. They likewise reveal the conflicting attitudes among church leaders regarding spiritual healing at the beginning of the fourth century.

The following selections written by Lactantius are from *The Divine Institutes.*

The first excerpts consist of explanations of the nature of God, Jesus, and the Word of God.

> •God, therefore, the contriver and founder of all things, as we have said in the second book, before He commenced this excellent work of the world, begat a pure and incorruptible Spirit, whom He called His Son. And although He had afterwards

created by Himself innumerable other beings, whom
we call angels, this first be-gotten, however, was the
only one whom He considered worthy of being
called by the divine name, as being powerful in His
Father's excellence and majesty. (Book IV, Chap.
VI)

•And shortly afterwards to His Son: "There is, O
Son, a secret word of wisdom, holy respecting the
only Lord of all things, and the God first perceived
by the mind, to speak of whom is beyond the power
of man." But although His name, which the supreme
Father gave Him from the beginning, is known to
none but Himself, nevertheless He has one name
among the angels, and another among men, since
He is called Jesus among men: for Christ is not a
proper name, but a title of power and dominion.
(Book IV, Chap. VII)

•With good reason, therefore, is He called the
Speech and the Word of God, because God, by a
certain incomprehensible energy and power of His
majesty, enclosed the vocal spirit proceeding from
His mouth, which he had not conceived in the
womb, but in His mind, within a form which has life
through its own perception and wisdom, and He also
fashioned other spirits of His into angels. (Book IV,
Chap. VIII)

The next group of passages comprise a general commentary on the
healings done by Jesus and his disciples.

•Having spoken of the second nativity, in which He
showed Himself in the flesh to men, let us come to
those wonderful works, on account of which, though
they were signs of heavenly power, the Jews
esteemed Him a magician. When He first began to
reach maturity He was baptized by the prophet John
in the river Jordan, that He might wash away in the
spiritual laver not His own sins, for it is evident that
He had none, but those of the flesh, which He bare;

that as He saved the Jews by undergoing circumcision, so He might save the Gentiles also by baptism — that is, by the pouring forth of the purifying dew. Then a voice is found to have been foretold by David. And the Spirit of God descended upon Him, formed after the appearance of a white dove.

From that time He began to perform the greatest miracles, not by magical tricks, which display nothing true and substantial, but by heavenly strength and power, which were foretold even long ago by the prophets who announced Him; which works are so many, that a single book is not sufficient to comprise them all.

I will therefore enumerate them briefly and generally, without any designation of persons and places, that I may be able to come to the setting forth of His passion and cross, to which my discourse has long been hastening. His powers were those which Apollo called wonderful: that whenever He journeyed, by a single word, and in a single moment, He healed the sick and infirm, and those afflicted with every kind of disease: so that those who were deprived of the use of all their limbs, having suddenly received power, were strengthened, and themselves carried their couches, on which they had a little time before been carried.

But to the lame, and to those afflicted with some defect of the feet, He not only gave the power of walking, but also of running. Then, also, if any had their eyes blinded in the deepest darkness, He restored them to their former sight. He also loosened the tongues of the dumb, so that they discoursed and spake eloquently. He also opened the ears of the deaf, and caused them to hear; He cleansed the polluted and the blemished. And He performed all these things not by His hands, or the application of any remedy, but by His word and command, as also Sibyl had foretold: "Doing all things by His word, and healing every disease."

Nor, indeed, is it wonderful that He did wonderful
things by His word, since He Himself was the Word
of God, relying upon heavenly strength and power.
Nor was it enough that He gave strength to the feeble, soundness of body to the maimed, health to the
sick and languishing, unless He also raised the dead,
as it were unbound from sleep, and recalled them to
life.

And the Jews, then, when they saw these things,
contended that they were done by demoniacal
power, although it was contained in their secret writings that all things should thus come to pass as they
did. They read indeed the words of other prophets,
and of Isaiah, saying: "Be strong, ye hands that are
relaxed; and ye weak knees be comforted. Ye who
are of a fearful heart, fear not, be not afraid: our
Lord shall execute judgment; He Himself shall
come and save us. Then shall the eyes of the blind
be opened, and the ears of the deaf shall hear: then
shall the lame man leap as a deer, and the tongue of
the dumb speak plainly: for in the wilderness water
hath broken forth, as a stream in the thirsty land."
But the Sibyl also foretold the same things in these
verses: —

"And there shall be a rising again of the
dead; and the course of the lame shall be
swift, and the deaf shall hear, and the blind
shall see, the dumb shall speak."

On account of these powers and divine works
wrought by Him when a great multitude followed
Him of the maimed, or sick, or of those who desired
to present their sick to be healed, He went up into a
desert mountain to pray there. And when He had
tarried there three days, and the people were suffering from hunger, He called His disciples, and asked
what quantity of food they had with them. But they
said that they had five loaves and two fishes in a
wallet.

Then He commanded that these should be brought
forward, and that the multitude, distributed by
fifties, should recline *on the ground.* When the disciples did this, He Himself broke the bread in
pieces, and divided the flesh of the fishes, and in
His hands both of them were increased. And when
He had ordered the disciples to set them before the
people, five thousand men were satisfied, and moreover twelve baskets were filled from the fragments
which remained. (Book IV, Chap. XV)

•But when He had made arrangements with His disciples for the preaching of the Gospel and His name,
a cloud suddenly surrounded Him, and carried Him
up into heaven, on the fortieth day after His passion,
as Daniel had shown that it would be, saying: "And,
behold, one like the Son of man came with the
clouds of heaven, and came to the Ancient of days."

But the disciples, being dispersed through the
provinces, everywhere laid the foundations of the
Church, themselves also in the name of their divine
Master doing many and almost incredible miracles;
for at His departure He had endowed them with
power and strength, by which the system of their
new announcement might be founded and confirmed. (Book IV, Chap.XXI)

The remaining readings depict the ability of early Christians to rely
on the power of God in destroying demons in spite of deception and
trickery by pagan priests. These passages also relate the failure of
pagan gods to cast out demons or heal persons possessed with this
mental illness.

•And the nature of all these deceits is obscure to
those who are without the truth. For they think that
those demons profit them when they cease to injure,
whereas they have no power except to injure. Some
one may perchance say that they are therefore to be
worshipped, that they may not injure, since they
have the power to injure. They do indeed injure, but

those only by whom they are feared, whom the powerful and lofty hand of God does not protect, who are uninitiated in the mystery of truth.

But they fear the righteous, that is, the worshippers of God, adjured by whose name they depart from the bodies *of the possessed:* for, being lashed by their words as though by scourges, they not only confess themselves to be demons, but even utter their own names — those which are adored in the temples — which they generally do in the presence of their own worshippers; not, it is plain, to the disgrace of religion, but *to the disgrace* of their own honour, because they cannot speak falsely to God, by whom they are adjured, nor to the righteous, by whose voice they are tortured.

Therefore ofttimes having uttered the greatest howlings, they cry out that they are beaten, and are on fire, and that they are just on the point of coming forth: so much power has the knowledge of God, and righteousness! Whom, therefore, can they injure, except those whom they have in their own power?

In short, Hermes affirms that those who have known God are not only safe from the attacks of demons, but that they are not even bound by fate. "The only protection," he says, "is piety, for over a pious man neither evil demon nor fate has any power: for God rescues the pious man from all evil; for the one and only good thing among men is piety." And what piety is, he testifies in another place, in these words: "For piety is the knowledge of God." (Book II, Chap. XVI)

•At present it is sufficient to show what great efficacy the power of this sign [the cross] has. How great a terror this sign is to the demons, he will know who shall see how, when adjured by Christ, they flee from the bodies which they have besieged. For as

He Himself, when He was living among men, put to flight all demons by His word, and restored to their former senses the minds of men which had been excited and maddened by their dreadful attacks; so now His followers, in the name of their Master, and by the sign of His passion, banish the same polluted spirits from men. And it is not difficult to prove this.

But since they [pagan priests] can neither approach those in whom they shall see the heavenly mark, nor injure those whom the immortal sign as an impregnable wall protects, they harass them by men, and persecute them by the hands of others: and if they acknowledge the existence of these demons, we have overcome; for this must necessarily be the true religion, which both understands the nature of demons, and understands their subtlety, and compels them, vanquished and subdued, to yield to itself. . . What, then, is the power of the gods, if the demons are not subject to their control? But, in truth, the same demons, when adjured by the name of the true God, immediately flee. (Book V, Chap. XXVII)

•They [pagan priests] do not therefore rage against us on this account, because their gods are not worshiped by us, but because the truth is on our side, which (as it has been said most truly) produces hatred. What, then, shall we think, but that they are ignorant of what they suffer? For they act with a blind and unreasonable fury, which we see, but of which they are ignorant.

For it is not the men themselves who persecute, for they have no cause of anger against the innocent; but those contaminated and abandoned spirits by whom the truth is both known and hated, insinuate themselves into their minds, and goad them in their ignorance to fury.

For these, as long as there is peace among the people of God, flee from the righteous, and fear them;

and when they seize upon the bodies of men, and harass their souls, they are adjured by them, and at the name of the true God are put to flight. For when they hear this name they tremble, cry out, and assert that they are branded and beaten; and being asked who they are, whence they are come, and how they have insinuated themselves into a man, confess it. Thus, being tortured and excruciated by the power of the divine name, they come out of the man. (Book V, Chap. XXII)

PART THREE

HISTORICAL COMMENTARY ON PRIMITIVE CHRISTIANITY

HISTORICAL COMMENTARY ON

PRIMITIVE CHRISTIANITY

The study of spiritual healing during the era of Primitive Christianity has been enriched by the writings of professional historians. Unlike the religious leaders who founded and expanded the Christian Church, these writers have collected documents and compiled chronological records for the express purpose of informing present and future generations about major ecclesiastical developments during this period.

Historians are not without their own personal dispositions and predilections. Yet their observations and judgments add an element of objectivity to this survey since their assessments are guided more by a scholarly than a theological orientation. They tend to be more concerned with the presentation and interpretation of historical facts than with the advocacy of a particular religious doctrine.

This concluding coverage of Primitive Christianity includes additional information and insights on Christian healing from a church historian writing in the third and fourth centuries, an English historian of the Roman empire writing in the eighteenth century, an English historian of Biblical and classical literature writing in the nineteenth century, and a contemporary American historian specializing on the religions of the Western classical period.

CHAPTER 17

EUSEBIUS

(CIRCA 260 - 340)

Eusebius has been called "the Father of Church History." He was born in Palestine in the early 260's and served as a researcher in Origen's library at Caesarea. His career shortly after the end of the Ante-Nicene era gave him an important vantage point and perspective on the development of the Christian church from the time of Jesus to the imperial rule of Constantine. He wrote his historical studies in a period when Christianity had already spread throughout much of the Roman empire and was gaining influence at the end of the persecution of Christians.

By modern professional standards, Eusebius was not always a scholarly writer. He wrote the first major historical work on the evolution of the church, and thus started a serious study of church history by later writers. He also collected and preserved many church documents that would probably have been lost were it not for his scholarly research.

Yet Eusebius was also a devout Christian, and in 313 he achieved the high church position of bishop of Caesarea. He likewise wrote numerous treatises and apologies defending Christian teachings and opposing Judaism and paganism. During the bitter controversy over the Nicene Creed, he supported the heretic Arius and was excommunicated for a time from the church. He later recanted and formally accepted the decision of the Council of Nicea, although he believed it had many deficiencies as a statement of Christian doctrine. He was a great admirer of Constantine and voiced strong approval of the emerging Christian empire embracing both the church and the state. He died in 339 or 340.

Despite his shortcomings as a historian, Eusebius made a contribution of immense value. His writings include a *Chronicle* of the history of the world, and *The Martyrs of Palestine,* which relates in detail the sufferings of Christians during the years of the Diocletian persecution. He also wrote a *Life of Constantine* and other shorter works. His greatest study was *The History of the Church,* which traces the growth of the church from the time of Jesus to Constantine. In some respects this major work was not well written. Yet it provided a basic framework for the studies of later church historians. It also gave some useful accounts of the healing activities of the early Christians. In his book *Saints and Sinners: Men and Ideas in the Early Church,* Kurt Aland has written: "It is simply impossible to write any kind of account of the history of the church during the first three centuries without resorting again and again to the works of Eusebius. His *Church History* gives us access to a host of sources and traditions otherwise long since lost." (p. 155)

The following writings by Eusebius are from *The History of the Church.*

The first excerpt relates some of the healing work performed by Philip in Samaria when confronting the machinations of a sorcerer named Simon Magus and also the oppression of Christians by Saul (Paul) prior to his conversion to Christianity.

•Stephen's martyrdom was followed by the first and greatest persecution by the Jews themselves of the Jerusalem church. All the disciples except the Twelve alone were dispersed about Judea and Samaria. Some, as the inspired record says, travelled as far as Phoenica, Cyprus, and Antioch; but they could not yet venture to share the message of the Faith with Gentiles, and proclaimed it to Jews alone. At that time also Paul was still raging against the Church, entering the houses of the faithful, dragging off men and women, and handing them over for imprisonment.

But Philip, one of the men already ordained with Stephen to the diaconate, was among the dispersed. He went down into Samaria, and filled with divine power was the first to preach the word there. So great was the divine grace working with him that even Simon the Magus with very many others was won over by his words. Such a name had Simon obtained at that time by the sorceries with which he got his dupes into power that he was believed to be the Great Power of God, but now even he was struck dumb by the miracles performed by divine power, and slipped in; he actually received baptism, in his hypocritical pretence of belief in Christ. . . .

While every day the saving message spread farther afield, some providence brought from Ethiopia, a country traditionally ruled by a woman, one of the queen's principal officers. The first Gentile to receive from Philip by revelation the mysteries of the divine word, and the first-fruits of the faithful throughout the world, he is believed to have been the first to go back to his native land and preach the gospel of the knowledge of the God of the universe and the life-giving sojourn of our Savior among men. (Book 2, 1)

•Thus with the powerful cooperation of Heaven the whole world was suddenly lit by the sunshine of the saving word. At once, in accordance with the Holy Scriptures, the voice of its inspired evangelists and apostles went forth into all the earth, and their words to the ends of the world. In every town and village, like a well-filled threshing floor, churches shot up bursting with eager members.

Men who through the error they had inherited from generations of ancestors were in the grip of the old spiritual sickness of idol-worship, by the power of Christ and through the teaching of His followers and the miracles they wrought were freed, as it were, from cruel masters and found release from galling fetters. They turned their backs on devilish polytheism in all its forms, and acknowledged that there was one God only, the Fashioner of all things. Him they honoured with the ordinances of true religion through that divine, reasonable worship of which our Savior sowed the seed in the life of men. (Book 2, 3)

The next passage cites an observation made by Philo, a Christian, of healing practices among Christian ascetics living in Egypt.

•It is also recorded that under Claudius, Philo came
to Rome to have conversations with Peter, then
preaching to the people there. This would not be
improbable, as the short work to which I am referring, and which he produced at a considerably later
date, clearly contains the rules of the Church still
observed in our own day. And again, when he
describes the life of our ascetics with the greatest
precision, it is plain enough that he not only knew
but welcomed with whole-hearted approval the
apostolic men of his day, who it seems were of
Hebrew stock and therefore, in the Jewish manner,
still retained most of their ancient customs.

In the work that he entitled *The Contemplative Life,
or The Suppliants,* he first assures us that he will
add nothing that goes beyond the truth, nothing of
his own invention, to the account he is about to
give. Then he says that they are called *Therapeutae*
and their womenfolk *Therapeutrides,* and goes on
to explain this title. It was conferred either because
like doctors they rid the souls of those who come to
them from moral sickness and so cure and heal
them, or in view of their pure and sincere service
and worship of God. (Book 2, 17)

In his own research Eusebius often confirmed incidents already
related in the New Testament. The following statement discusses
some of the healing work done by the apostles which had already been
reported by Luke and was being repeated by Paul.

•Luke, by birth an Antiochene and by profession a
physician, was for long periods a companion of Paul
and was closely associated with the other apostles as
well. So he has left us examples of the art of healing
souls which he learnt from them in two divinely
inspired books, the Gospel and the Acts of the
Apostles. The former, he declares, he wrote in
accordance with the information he received from
those who from the first had been eyewitnesses and
ministers of the word, information which, he adds,

he had followed in its entirety from the first. The
latter he composed not this time from hearsay but
from the evidence of his own eyes. (Book 3, 4)

The early Christians continued the practice of raising persons from
death. They also prevented death caused by poison. The following
excerpt tells of two incidents of these kinds of healings.

•We must go on, from the remarks of Papias already
quoted, to other passages in which he tells us of certain miraculous events and other matters, on the
basis, it would seem, of direct information. It has
already been mentioned that Philip the Apostle
resided at Hierapolis with his daughters: it must
now be pointed out that their contemporary Papias
tells how he heard a wonderful story from the lips of
Philip's daughters.

He describes the resurrection of a dead person in his
own lifetime, and a further miracle that happened to
Justus, surnamed Barsabas, who swallowed a dangerous poison and by the grace of the Lord was
none the worse. After the Savior's ascension, this
Justus was put forward with Matthais by the holy
apostles, who prayed over them before drawing lots
for someone to full up their number in place of the
traitor Judas. (Book 3, 39)

In some places Eusebius quotes from the writings of other Christians who sought to defend their religion and protect the church. Some
of these written works were addressed to the Roman authorities in an
effort to stop or curtail the persecution of Christians. The following
excerpt includes a brief statement in a pamphlet written by Quadratus
citing the healing works of Jesus as a defense against further persecution.

•When Trajan had ruled for six months short of
twenty years Aelius Hadrianus succeeded to the
throne. To him Quadratus addressed and sent a pamphlet which he had composed in defence of our religion, because unscrupulous persons were trying to

get our people in trouble. Many of the brethren still possess copies of this little work; indeed, I have one myself. In it can be found shining proofs of the author's intellectual grasp and apostolic correctness. He reveals his very early date by the wording of his composition.

> Our Savior's works were always there to see, for they were true — the people who had been cured and those raised from the dead, who had not merely been seen at the moment when they were cured or raised, but were *always* there to see, not only when the Savior was among us, but for a long time after His departure; in fact some of them survived right up to my own time. (Book 4, 3)

Eusebius also quotes at times from the writings of the Ante-Nicene Fathers in defending Christianity and reporting on physical healing. In the following readings, he quotes from the major work of Irenaeus.

> •In accord with the accounts which I have already given, Irenaeus demonstrates these facts in the five books entitled *Refutation and Overthrow of Knowledge Falsely So-Called,* and in Book II of the same work he makes it clear that right down to his own time manifestations of divine and miraculous power had continued in some churches.

> > But they [a group of Gnostics] fall far short of raising the dead, as the Lord raised them, and as did the apostles through prayer, and as among later Christians, because the need was so great and the whole of the local church besought God with much fasting and supplication, the spirit of the dead man has returned and his life has been granted to the prayers of God's people. . . .

But if they suggest that the Lord has done these things only in appearance, I will refer them to the prophetic writings, and prove from them that all this had been foretold about Him and really happened, and that He alone is the Son of God. So it is that in His name those who truly are His disciples, having received grace from Him, put it to effectual use for the benefit of their fellow-men, in proportion to the gift each one has received from Him.

Some drive out demons really and truly, so that often those cleansed from evil spirits believe and become members of the Church; some have foreknowledge of the future, visions, and prophetic utterances; others, by the laying-on of hands, heal the sick and restore them to health; and before now, as I said, dead men have actually been raised and have remained with us for many years.

In fact, it is impossible to enumerate the gifts which throughout the world the Church has received from God and in the name of Jesus Christ crucified under Pontius Pilate, and every day puts to effectual use for the benefit of the heathen, deceiving no one and making profit out of no one: freely she received from God, and freely she ministers.

Elsewhere Irenaeus writes:

Similarly, we hear of many members of the Church who have prophetic gifts and by the Spirit speak with all kinds of tongues, and bring men's secret thoughts to light for their own good, and expound the mysteries of God.

This will suffice to show that diversity of gifts continued among fit persons till the time I am speaking
of. (Book 5, 7)

CHAPTER 18

EDWARD GIBBON

(1737 - 1794)

Edward Gibbon was born in Surrey, England, in 1737. Poor health in his youth oriented him toward reading and a deep love of history. He studied at Magdalen College at Oxford for a brief period, where he read theology and was converted to Roman Catholicism. His disgruntled father sent him to France, where he was tutored privately by a Calvinist clergyman who brought the young Gibbon back to Protestantism. A trip to Italy in 1764 - 1765 gave him the idea of writing a historical study of the decline and fall of Rome, an enterprise he later expanded to include the entire Roman empire.

Gibbon began his monumental study titled *The Decline and Fall of the Roman Empire* in the mid - 1770's. The publication of the first volume, containing two chapters on the rise of Christianity, aroused widespread criticism for their skepticism of some aspects of the leadership of the early Christian church. Gibbon continued writing while serving in Parliament throughout England's war with the American colonies. His study was completed in 1787. It comprised a continuous history of the Roman empire from the second century A.D. to the fall of Constantinople in 1453. Gibbon's dominant thesis maintained that the material decay of Rome was the effect of a moral decay. His work is still recognized as a classic because of its breadth of vision, mastery of detail, and brilliant quality of writing. In his introduction to *The Decline and Fall,* Oliphant Smeaton has stated:

> That quality which places Gibbon in the front rank
> of historians is his marvellous power of welding
> into a homogeneous and symmetrical unity the
> widely divergent materials and topics which rise to
> confront him in his grand historic survey from Tra-
> jan to Constantine Palaeologus. Gibbon's many-
> sided culture, his tolerant catholicity, his eminently
> artistic historic method, his power of seeing to the

heart of things through super-imposed masses of
accessorial details, his marvellous general accuracy,
and his vivid power of literary portraiture, are all
qualities and excellences that are visible to every
careful reader.

Gibbon's work on the Roman empire was his final historical study.
He died in London in 1794.

Gibbon, like Eusebius, had some serious shortcomings as a historian. He belonged to the "philosophic school" of historians, which
focused largely on the growth and development of entire societies
rather than the "great man theory" also prevalent during his lifetime,
which stressed the role of individual thinkers and leaders in the evolution of human affairs. This intellectual bent induced its own personal biases and opinions. Gibbon was also influenced by a close
friendship with David Hume, an early skeptic and pragmatist, who
wrote a treatise denying the validity of the miracles recorded in the
Bible.

Gibbon's skepticism toward early Christianity was caused in some
degree by a cautious attitude toward the healing miracles of the New
Testament. He criticized the zeal and exclusiveness of the early
Christians, including several ante-Nicene leaders who were martyred.
He likewise believed the healings related in the Bible involved the
suspension of natural laws by the power of God.

Yet Gibbon's writings on Primitive Christianity are significant since
he did not deny the validity or the importance of spiritual healing in
the spread of Christianity. As a historian he stated that these healing
miracles should be carefully examined and their influence on history
should be accurately assessed. Gibbon, in brief, was fascinated yet
baffled by the healing works of the early Christian church. At the end
of his first chapter on the rise of Christianity (Chapter XV), he
expressed a deep amazement at the philosophers and pagans living
during the time of early Christianity for their "supine inattention" to
the healings performed by the Christians and their resistance to some
conviction of Christian teachings.

The following selections from *The Decline and Fall* are in Chapter
XV. These pages include Gibbon's commentary on the reaction of
Christian churches in Britain and Europe to the healing miracles of
early Christians up to his own time. He explains how differently the
general public and the clergy responded in the late eighteenth century
to the record of early Christian healing. He makes a strong case for

dispensationalism — i.e. the view that the miracles of the early church were a dispensation of God's power for only a limited period of time, and the Christian church thereafter no longer had the authority to repeat the healings and miracles done by Jesus and his followers. Yet in the end Gibbon repeats his wonder and his questions regarding the role of the healings performed by Jesus and the early Christian church.

> The supernatural gifts, which even in this life were ascribed to the Christians above the rest of mankind, must have conduced to their own comfort, and very frequently to the conviction of infidels. Besides the occasional prodigies, which might sometimes be effected by the immediate interposition of the Deity when he suspended the laws of Nature for the service of religion, the Christian church, from the time of the apostles and their first disciples, has claimed an uninterrupted succession of miraculous powers, the gift of tongues, of vision, and of prophecy, the power of expelling daemons, of healing the sick, and of raising the dead.

> The knowledge of foreign languages was frequently communicated to the contemporaries of Irenaeus, though Irenaeus himself was left to struggle with the difficulties of a barbarous dialect whilst he preached the Gospel to the natives of Gaul. The divine inspiration, whether it was conveyed in the form of a waking or a sleeping vision, is described as a favour very liberally bestowed on all ranks of the faithful, on women as on elders, on boys as well as upon bishops. When their devout minds were sufficiently prepared by a course of prayer, of fasting, and of vigils, to receive the extraordinary impulse, they were transported out of their senses, and delivered in ecstasy what was inspired, being mere organs of the Holy Spirit, just as a pipe or flute is of him who blows into it. We may add that the design of these visions was, for the most part, either to disclose the future history, or to guide the present administration, of the church.

The expulsion of the daemons from the bodies of
those unhappy persons whom they had been permitted to torment was considered as a signal though
ordinary triumph of religion, and is repeatedly
alleged by the ancient apologists as the most convincing evidence of the truth of Christianity. The
awful ceremony was usually performed in a public
manner, and in the presence of a great number of
spectators; the patient was relieved by the power or
skill of the exorcist, and the vanquished daemon
was heard to confess that he was one of the fabled
gods of antiquity, who had impiously usurped the
adoration of mankind.

But the miraculous cure of diseases of the most
inveterate or even preternatural kind can no longer
occasion any surprise, when we recollect that in the
days of Irenaeus, about the end of the second century, the resurrection of the dead was very far from
being esteemed an uncommon event; that the miracle was frequently performed on necessary occasions, by great fasting and the joint supplication of
the church of the place, and that the persons thus
restored to their prayers had lived afterwards among
them many years.

At such a period, when faith could boast of so many
wonderful victories over death, it seems difficult to
account for the scepticism of those philosophers
who still rejected and derided the doctrine of the
resurrection. A noble Grecian had rested on this
important ground the whole controversy, and
promised Theophilus, bishop of Antioch, that, if he
could be gratified with the sight of a single person
who had been actually raised from the dead, he
would immediately embrace the Christian religion.
It is somewhat remarkable that the prelate of the
first eastern church, however anxious for the conversion of his friend, thought proper to decline this
fair and reasonable challenge.

The miracles of the primitive church, after obtaining the sanction of ages, have been lately attacked in a very free and ingenious inquiry; which, though it has met with the most favourable reception from the public, appears to have excited a general scandal among the divines of our own as well as of the other Protestant churches of Europe. Our different sentiments on this subject will be much less influenced by any particular arguments than by our habits of study and reflection, and, above all, by the degree of the evidence which we have accustomed ourselves to require for the proof of a miraculous event.

The duty of an historian does not call upon him to interpose his private judgment in this nice and important controversy; but he ought not to dissemble the difficulty of adopting such a theory as may reconcile the interest of religion with that of reason, of making a proper application of that theory, and of defining with precision the limits of that happy period, exempt from error and from deceit, to which we might be disposed to extend the gift of supernatural powers. From the first of the fathers to the last of the popes, a succession of bishops, of saints, of martyrs, and of miracles, is continued without interruption; and the progress of superstition was so gradual and almost imperceptible, that we know not in what particular link we should break the chain of tradition.

Every age bears testimony to the wonderful events by which it was distinguished, and its testimony appears no less weighty and respectable than that of the preceding generation, till we are insensibly led on to accuse our own inconsistency if, in the eighth or in the twelfth century, we deny to the venerable Bede, or to the holy Bernard, the same degree of confidence which, in the second century, we had so liberally granted to Justin or to Irenaeus. If the truth of any of those miracles is appreciated by their apparent use and propriety, every age had unbeliev-

ers to convince, heretics to confute, and idolatrous
nations to convert; and sufficient motives might
always be produced to justify the interposition of
Heaven.

And yet, since every friend to revelation is persuaded of the reality, and every reasonable man is convinced of the cessation, of miraculous powers, it is
evident that there must have been *some period* in
which they were either suddenly or gradually with-
drawn from the Christian church. Whatever era is
chosen for that purpose, the death of the apostles,
the conversion of the Roman empire, or the extinc-
tion of the Arian heresy, the insensibility of the
Christians who lived at that time will equally afford
a just matter of surprise. They still supported their
pretensions after they had lost their power. Credulity
performed the office of faith; fanaticism was permitted to assume the language of inspiration, and the
effects of accident or contrivance were ascribed to
supernatural causes.

The recent experience of genuine miracles should
have instructed the Christian world in the ways of
Providence, and habituated their eye (if we may use
a very inadequate expression) to the style of the
Divine artist. Should the most skilful painter of
modern Italy presume to decorate his feeble imitations with the name of Raphael or of Correggio, the
insolent fraud would be soon discovered and indig-
nantly rejected.

Whatever opinion may be entertained of the miracles of the primitive church since the time of the
apostles, this unresisting softness of temper, so con-
spicuous among the believers of the second and
third centuries, proved of some accidental benefit to
the cause of truth and religion. In modern times, a
latent and even involuntary scepticism adheres to
the most pious dispositions. Their admission of
supernatural truths is much less an active consent

than a cold and passive acquiescence. Accustomed long since to observe and to respect the invariable order of Nature, our reason, or at least our imagination, is not sufficiently prepared to sustain the visible action of the Deity.

But in the first ages of Christianity the situation of mankind was extremely different. The most curious, or the most credulous, among the Pagans were often persuaded to enter into a society which asserted an actual claim of miraculous powers. The primitive Christians perpetually trod on mystic ground, and their minds were exercised by the habits of believing the most extraordinary events. They felt, or they fancied, that on every side they were incessantly assaulted by daemons, comforted by visions, instructed by prophecy, and surprisingly delivered from danger, sickness, and from death itself, by the supplications of the church.

The real or imaginary prodigies, of which they so frequently conceived themselves to be the objects, the instruments, or the spectators, very happily disposed them to adopt with the same ease, but with far greater justice, the authentic wonders of the evangelic history; and thus miracles that exceeded not the measure of their own experience inspired them with the most lively assurance of mysteries which were acknowledged to surpass the limits of their understanding.

It is this deep impression of supernatural truths which has been so much celebrated under the name of faith; a state of mind described as the surest pledge of the Divine favour and of future felicity, and recommended as the first and perhaps the only merit of a Christian. According to the more rigid doctors, the moral virtues, which may be equally practised by infidels, are destitute of any value or efficacy in the work of our justification. . . .

•From this impartial though imperfect survey of the
progress of Christianity, it may perhaps seem proba-
ble that the number of its proselytes has been excessively magnified by fear on the one side, and by
devotion on the other. According to the irreproach-
able testimony of Origen, the proportion of the
faithful was very inconsiderable, when compared
with the multitude of an unbelieving world; but, as
we are left without any distinct information, it is
impossible to determine, and it is difficult even to
conjecture, the real numbers of the primitive Christians.

The most favourable calculation, however, that can
be deduced from the examples of Antioch and of
Rome will not permit us to imagine that more than a
twentieth part of the subjects of the empire had
enlisted themselves under the banner of the Cross
before the important conversion of Constantine. But
their habits of faith, of zeal, and of union, seemed to
multiply their numbers; and the same causes which
contributed to their future increase served to render
their actual strength more apparent and more
formidable. . . .

•How shall we excuse the supine inattention of the
Pagan and philosophic world to those evidences
which were presented by the hand of Omnipotence,
not to their reason, but to their senses? During the
age of Christ, of his apostles, and of their first disciples, the doctrine which they preached was confirmed by innumerable prodigies. The lame walked,
the blind saw, the sick were healed, the dead were
raised, daemons were expelled, and the laws of
Nature were frequently suspended for the benefit of
the church.

But the sages of Greece and Rome turned aside
from the awful spectacle, and, pursuing the ordinary
occupations of life and study, appeared unconscious
of any alterations in the moral or physical govern-

ment of the world. Under the reign of Tiberius, the whole earth, or at least a celebrated province of the Roman empire, was involved in a preternatural darkness of three hours. Even this miraculous event, which ought to have excited the wonder, the curiosity, and the devotion of mankind, passed without notice in an age of science and history.

It happened during the lifetime of Seneca and the elder Pliny, who must have experienced the immediate effects, or received the earliest intelligence, of the prodigy. Each of these philosophers, in a laborious work, has recorded all the great phenomena of Nature, earthquakes, meteors, comets, and eclipses, which his indefatigable curiosity could collect. Both the one and the other omitted to mention the greatest phenomenon to which the mortal eye has been witness since the creation of the globe.

A distinct chapter of Pliny is designed for eclipses of an extraordinary nature and unusual duration; but he contents himself with describing the singular defect of light which followed the murder of Caesar, when, during the greatest part of a year, the orb of the sun appeared pale and without splendour. This season of obscurity, which cannot surely be compared with the preternatural darkness of the Passion, had been already celebrated by most of the poets and historians of that memorable age.

CHAPTER 19

GEORGE RAWLINSON

(1812-1902)

George Rawlinson lived in England during most of the nineteenth century. He was born in 1812 and died in 1902. During the 1850's he was a Fellow and Tutor of Exeter College at Oxford. He studied extensively the ancient literature of the Middle East, and was able to decipher the early languages of Assyria, Babylonia, Persia, and Egypt. He was assisted in this research by his brother, Sir Henry Rawlinson, a famous explorer, collector, and translator of written works of antiquity. Henry Rawlinson contributed to the translation of a scholarly book entitled *Inscription of Tiglath-Pileser I, King of Assyria, B.C. 1150* which was published by the Royal Asiatic Society in 1857.

George Rawlinson's major writing was titled *The Historical Evidences of the Truth of the Scripture Records.* It was sub-titled "Stated Anew, With Special Reference to the Doubts and Discoveries of Modern Times." This book comprised the content of eight lectures which Rawlinson delivered at Oxford in 1859. He devoted almost one-half of this book to his Notes in order to provide extensive historical evidence for the facts cited in his lectures. The preface of the book explained that the author's purpose in using this unusually long documentation was "to collect into a single volume the chief testimonies to the historical truth and accuracy of the Scripture records." An American edition of the book was published in the United States in 1860.

The major objective of Rawlinson's lectures and book was to counteract the wave of skepticism and ridicule directed toward Christianity by the rising school of Historical Criticism emanating largely from German historical writers. The success of this continental movement (also called German Neology), which subtly used Christian terminology to disparage Christian teachings, had aroused misgivings about the authenticity of Biblical records among clergymen and laity in Germany, England, and the United States, a trend Rawlinson considered "a serious and growing evil." He offered to use his specialized knowledge of ancient literature and early Christian history to oppose this spread of doubt and disbelief by asking the authorities at Oxford for permission to deliver the eight lectures, which were later published in book form.

In many ways Rawlinson's book reads like an apology of Christian doctrine written by one of the Ante-Nicene Fathers. His defense of Christianity against determined critics is lucid and balanced. Portions of the lectures include important passages about Christian healing. These excerpts assume added significance in view of the extensive and careful research he conducted in verifying the credibility of written accounts in the New Testament regarding the life and works of Jesus and the apostles, including works of spiritual healing.

The following selections from Lecture One stress the unique character of the Judeo-Christian Bible based on historical facts. In portions of this lecture the author makes one of the most moving and brilliant defenses of the authenticity of the Biblical miracles ever written in the English language. He challenges the German-led school of Historical Criticism to undertake an objective and open view of historical evidence, rather than to assert an unsubstantiated claim that the records of the Old and New Testaments are based only on myths. He condemns their rejection of the Biblical miracles by upholding these "supernatural" events as the "regular, fixed, and established rule of His [God's] government." Rawlinson maintains that God's creation of the universe is a miracle "of the most surpassing greatness" and that "Revelation is itself miraculous." He adds that many people throughout history have experienced revelations from a source beyond the human realm in performing useful works for the advancement of civilization and society.

> •Christianity — including therein the dispensation of the Old Testament, which was its first stage — is in nothing more distinguished from the other religions of the world than in its objective and historical character. The religions of Greece and Rome, of Egypt, India, Persia, and the East generally, were speculative systems, which did not even seriously postulate an historical basis. If they seemed to do so to some extent, if for instance the mythological ideas of the Greeks be represented under the form of a mythological *period,* which moreover blends gradually and almost imperceptively with the historical, still in the minds of the Greeks themselves the peri-

ods are separate and distinct, not merely in time, but in character; and the objective reality of the scene and events described as belonging to each was not conceived of as parallel, or even similar, in the two cases.

The modern distinction between the legend and the myth, properly so called, was felt, if not formally recognized, by the Greek mind; and the basis of fact, which is of the essence of the former, was regarded as absent from the latter, which thus ceased altogether to be history.

It is this peculiar feature of Christianity — a feature often noticed by its apologists — which brings it into such a close relation to historical studies and investigations. As a religion of fact, and not merely of opinion, — as one whose chief scene is this world, and whose main doctrines are events exhibited openly before the eyes of men — as one moreover which, instead of affecting a dogmatic form, adopts from first to last, with very rare exceptions, the historical shape, it comes necessarily within the sphere of the historical inquirer, and challenges him to investigate it according to what he regards as the principles of his science.

Moreover, as Christianity is in point of fact connected intimately with certain records, and as those records extend over a period of several thousands of years, and "profess to contain a kind of abridgement of the history of the world," its points of contact with profane history are (practically speaking) infinite; and it becomes impossible for the historical inquirer to avoid the question, in what light he is to view the documents which, if authentic, must exercise so important an influence over his studies and conclusions.

Christianity then cannot complain if, from time to time, as historical science advances, the question is

raised afresh concerning the real character of those
events which form its basis, and the real value of
those documents on which it relies. As an historical
religion, it invites this species of inquiry, and is glad
that it should be made and repeated. It only com-
plains in one of two cases — when either principles
unsound and wrong in themselves, having been
assumed as proper *criteria* of historic truth, are
applied to it for the purpose of disparagement; or
when, right principles are assumed, the application
of them, of which it is the object, is unfair and ille-
gitimate. (pp. 25 - 27)

•The portion of the Scripture history which was the
first subjected to the application of the new principles was the historical part of the Old Testament. It
was soon declared that a striking parallelism existed
between this history and the early records of most
heathen nations. The miracles in the narrative were
compared with the prodigies and divine appearances
related by Herodotus and Livy. The chronology was
said to bear marks, like that of Rome and Babylon,
of artificial arrangement; the recurrence of similar
numbers, and especially of round numbers, particularly indicating its unhistorical character. (p. 31)

•When the historical character of the Old Testament,
assailed on all sides by clever and eloquent pens,
and weakly defended by here and there a single hes-
itating apologist, seemed to those who had conducted the warfare irretrievably demolished and
destroyed, the New Testament became, after a
pause, the object of attack to the same school of
writers. It was felt, no doubt, to be a bold thing to
characterize as a collection of myths the writings of
an age of general enlightenment — nay, even of
incredulity and scepticism; and perhaps a lingering
regard for what so many souls held precious, stayed
the hands of those who nevertheless saw plainly,
that the New Testament was open to the same
method of attack as the Old, and that an inexorable

logic required that both should be received or neither.

A pause therefore ensued, but a pause of no long duration. First, particular portions of the New Testament narrative, as the account of our Lord's infancy, and of the Temptation, were declared to possess equal tokens of a mythic origin with those which had been previously regarded as fatal to the historical character of Old Testament stories, and were consequently singled out for rejection.

Then, little by little, the same system of explanation was adopted with respect to more and more of the narrative; till at last, in the hands of Strauss, the whole came to be resolved into pure myth and legend, and the historical Christ being annihilated, the world was told to console itself with a "God-man, eternally incarnate, not an individual, but an idea;" which, on examination, turns out to be no God at all, but mere man — man perfected by nineteenth-century enlightenment — dominant over nature by the railroad and the telegraph, and over himself by the negation of the merely natural and sensual life, and the substitution for it of the intellectual, or (in the nomenclature of the school) the spiritual. (pp. 32 - 33)

•I propose at the present time, in opposition to the views which I have sketched, to examine the Sacred Narrative *on the positive side*. Leaving untouched the question of the inspiration of Scripture, and its consequent title to outweigh all conflicting testimony whatever, I propose briefly to review the historical evidence for the orthodox belief. My object will be to meet the reasoning of the historical sceptics on their own ground.

I do not, indeed, undertake to consider and answer their minute and multitudinous cavils, which would be an endless task, and which is moreover unnecessary, as to a great extent the cavillers meet and answer one another; but I hope to show, without assuming the inspiration of the Bible, that for the great facts of revealed religion, the miraculous history of the Jews, and the birth, life, death, and resurrection of Christ, as well as for his miracles and those of his apostles, the historical evidence which we possess is of an authentic and satisfactory character.

I shall review this evidence in the light and by the laws of the modern historical criticism, so far as they seem to be established. Those laws appear to me to be sound; and their natural and real bearing is to increase instead of diminishing the weight of the Christian evidences. It is not from a legitimate and proper application of them that faith has suffered, but partly from their neglect or misapplication, partly from the intrusion among them of a single unproved and irrational opinion. (pp. 38 - 39)

•"No just perception of the true nature of history is possible," we are told, "without a perception of the inviolability of the chain of finite causes, and of the *impossibility of miracles*." And the mythical interpreters insist, that one of the essential marks of a mythical narrative, whereby it may be clearly distinguished from one which is historical, is, its "presenting an account of events which are either absolutely or relatively beyond the reach of (ordinary) experience, such as occurrences connected with the spiritual world, or its dealing in the supernatural."

Now, if miracles cannot take place, an inquiry into the historical evidences of Revealed Religion is vain; for Revelation is itself miraculous, and therefore, by the hypothesis, impossible. But what are the grounds upon which so stupendous as assertion is made, as that God cannot, if He so please, suspend the working of those laws by which He commonly acts upon matter, and act on special occasions dif-

ferently? Shall we say that He cannot, because of
His own immutability — because He is a being
"with whom is no variableness, neither shadow of
turning?" But, if we apply the notion of a Law to
God at all, it is plain that miraculous interpositions
on fitting occasions may be as much a regular, fixed,
and established rule of His government, as the
working ordinarily by what are called natural laws.

Or shall we say that all experience and analogy is
against miracles? But this is either to judge, from
our own narrow and limited experience, of the
whole course of nature, and so to generalize upon
most weak and insufficient grounds; or else, if in the
phrase "all experience" we include the experiences
of others, it is to draw a conclusion directly in the
teeth of our data; for many persons well worthy of
belief have declared that they have witnessed and
wrought miracles. Moreover, were it true that all
known experience was against miracles, this would
not even prove that they had not happened — much
less that they are impossible. If they are impossible,
it must be either from something in the nature of
things, or from something in the nature of God.

That the immutability of God does not stand in the
way of miracles has been already shown; and I
know of no other attribute of the Divine Nature
which can be even supposed to create a difficulty.
To most minds it will, if I do not greatly mistake,
rather appear, that the Divine Omnipotence includes
in it the power of working miracles. And if God created the world, He certainly once worked a miracle
of the most surpassing greatness.

Is there any thing in the nature of things to make
miracles impossible? Not unless things have an
independent existence, and work by their own
power. If they are in themselves nought, if God
called them out of nothing, and but for His sustain-
ing power they would momentarily fall back into

nothing; if it is not they that work, but He who
works in them and through them; if growth, and
change, and motion, and assimilation, and decay, are
His dealings with matter, as sanctification, and
enlightenment, and inward comfort, and the gift of
the clear vision of Him, are His dealings with ourselves; if the Great and First Cause never deserts
even for a moment the second Causes, but He who
"upholdeth all things by the word of His power,"
and is "above all and *through* all," is also (as Hook-
er says) "the Worker of all in all" — then certainly
things in themselves cannot oppose any impediment
to miracles, or do aught but obsequiously follow the
Divine fiat, be it what it may.

The whole difficulty with regard to miracles has its
roots in a materialistic Atheism, which believes
things to have a force in and of themselves; which
regards them as self-sustaining, if not even as self-
caused; which deems them to possess mysterious
powers of their own uncontrollable by the Divine
Will; which sees in the connection of physical cause
and effect, not a sequence, not a law, but a necessity; which, either positing a Divine First Cause to
bring things into existence, then (like Anaxagoras)
makes no further use of Him; or does not care to
posit any such First Cause at all, but is content to
refer all things to a "course of nature," which it con-
siders eternal and unalterable, and on which it lav-
ishes all the epithets that believers regard as appro-
priate to God, and God only.

It is the peculiarity of Atheism at the present day
that it uses a religious nomenclature — it is no
longer dry, and hard, and cold, all matter of fact and
common-sense, as was the case in the last century,
— on the contrary, it has become warm in expression, poetic, eloquent, glowing, sensuous, imagina-
tive — the "Course of Nature," which it has set up
in the place of God, is in a certain sense deified, —
no language is too exalted to be applied to it, no

admiration too great to be excited by it — it is "glorious," and "marvellous," and "superhuman," and "heavenly," and "spiritual," and "divine" — only it is "IT," not "HE," — a fact or set of facts, and not a Person; — and so it can really call forth no love, no gratitude, no reverence, no personal feeling of any kind — it can claim no willing obedience — it can inspire no wholesome awe — it is a dead idol after all, and its worship is but the old nature worship, — man returning in his dotage to the follies which beguiled his childhood — losing the Creator in the creation, the Workman in the work of his hands.

It cannot therefore be held on any grounds but such as involve a real, though covert Atheism, that miracles are impossible, or that a narrative of which supernatural occurrences form an essential part is therefore devoid of an historic character. Miracles are to be viewed as in fact a part of the Divine Economy, — a part as essential as any other, though coming into play less frequently. It has already been observed, that the creation of the world was a miracle, or rather a whole array of miracles; and any true historical account of it must "deal in the supernatural."

A first man was as great a miracle — may we not say a greater miracle? — than a raised man. Greater, inasmuch as to create and unite a body and soul is to do more than merely to unite them when they have been created. And the occurrence of miracles at the beginning of the world established a precedent for their subsequent occurrence from time to time with greater or less frequency, as God should see to be fitting.

Again, all history abounds in statements that miracles have in fact from time to time occurred; and though we should surrender to the sceptic the whole mass of Heathen and Ecclesiastical miracles, which I for one do not hold to be necessary, yet still ficti-

tious miracles imply the existence of true ones, just
as hypocrisy implies that there is virtue. To reject a
narrative, therefore, simply because it contains
miraculous circumstances, is to indulge an irrational
prejudice — a prejudice which has no foundation,
either in *a priori* truths or in the philosophy of experience, and which can only be consistently held by
one who disbelieves in God. . . .

It seems to be time to bid the nations of the earth
once more "bring forth their witnesses," and
"declare" and "show us" what it is which they
record of the "former things" — that they may at
once justify and "be justified" — in part directly
confirming the Scripture narrative, in part silent but
not adverse, content to "hear, and say, 'It is truth.'"
"Ye are my witnesses, saith the Lord" — even "the
blind people, that have eyes; and the deaf, that have
ears" — "Ye are my witnesses — *and* my servant
whom I have chosen." The testimony of the sacred
and the profane is not conflicting, but consentient —
and the comparison of the two will show, not dis-
cord, but harmony. (pp. 42 - 48)

The next set of passages is from Lecture Six. They explain the reasons for upholding the validity of the historical events recorded in the
New Testament as well as the authenticity of the healings performed
by Jesus and the apostles.

•It has been well observed, that, even if all the difficulties and discrepancies, which this writer has
thought to discover in the Gospels, were real and
not merely apparent — if we were obliged to leave
them as difficulties, and could offer no explanation
of them — still the general credibility of the Gospel
History would remain untouched, and no more
would be proved than the absence of that complete
inspiration which the Church has always believed to
attach to the Evangelical writings. The writers
would be lowered from their preeminent rank as
perfect and infallible historians, whose every word

may be depended on; but they would remain historical authorities of the first order — witnesses as fully
to be trusted for the circumstances of our Lord's
life, as Xenophon for the sayings and doings of
Socrates, or Cavendish for those of Cardinal
Wolsey.

The facts of the miracles, preaching, sufferings,
death, resurrection, and ascension, would therefore
stand firm, together with those of the choice of the
Apostles, the commission given them, and the communication to them of miraculous powers; and these
are the facts which establish Christianity, and form
its historical basis — a basis which can be over-
thrown by nothing short of proof that the New Testament is a forgery from beginning to end, or that
the first preachers of Christianity were a set of
impostors.

For the truth of the Gospel facts does not rest solely
upon the Gospels — they are stated with almost
equal distinctness in the Acts, and are implied in the
Epistles. It is not denied that a companion of St.
Paul may have written the account of the early
spread of the Gospel which is contained in the Acts
of the Apostles. But the Acts assume as indisputable
the whole series of facts which form the basis on
which Christianity sustains itself.

They set forth "Jesus of Nazareth, a man approved
of God by miracles and wonders and signs, which
God did by Him in the midst of you, *as you yourselves also know* " — a man "who went about doing
good, and healing all that were oppressed of the
devil" — who, "beginning from Galilee, after the
baptism which John preached, published the word
throughout all Judea;" whom yet "they that dwelt at
Jerusalem, and their rulers, because they knew him
not, nor yet the voices of the Prophets which are
read every Sabbath day, condemned, finding no
cause of death in him, yet desiring of Pilate that he

should be slain" — who was "taken and crucified by wicked hands" — "hanged upon a tree and slain" — then "taken down from the tree and laid in a sepulchre," but "raised up the third day, and showed openly," "by many infallible proofs during the space of forty days," "not to all the people, but unto witnesses chosen before of God, who did eat and drink with him after he rose from the dead" — and who, finally, "while his disciples beheld, was taken up into heaven, a cloud receiving him out of their sight."

The Acts further show that to the chosen "witnesses" — the Apostles to whom "the promise of the Father" had been given, and to those whom they associated with them in the direction of the infant Church miraculous gifts were communicated, so that they prophesied, cured lameness by a word or touch, spake languages of which they had no natural knowledge, restored the bedridden to health, handled serpents, cast out devils, inflicted blindness, raised the dead to life, and finally even in some cases cured men by the touch of their shadows or by handkerchiefs and aprons from their persons. (pp. 169 - 171)

The following brief excerpt from Lecture Seven cites a historical fact already mentioned several times in this study, namely, the tragic loss of many writings and documents of the early Christian leaders and their opponents which contained important discussions about early Christian healing. The next passage is an example of this type of historical record. It refers to the official report of Pilate regarding the healing works of Jesus as well as the events leading to his crucifixion.

•In estimating the value of that direct evidence of adversaries to the main facts of Christianity which remains to us, we must not overlook the probability that much evidence of this kind has perished. The books of the early opponents of Christianity, which might have been of the greatest use to us for the confirmation of the Gospel History, were with an unwise zeal destroyed by the first Christian Emperors. Other testimony of the greatest importance has perished by the ravages of time. It seems certain that Pilate remitted to Tiberius an account of the execution of our Lord, and the grounds of it; and that this document, to which Justin Martyr more than once alludes, was deposited in the archives of the empire.

The "Acts of Pilate," as they were called, seem to have contained an account, not only of the circumstances of the crucifixion, and the grounds upon which the Roman governor regarded himself as justified in passing sentence of death upon the accused, but also of the Miracles of Christ, his cures performed upon the lame, the dumb, and the blind, his cleansing of lepers, and his raising of the dead. If this valuable direct testimony had been preserved to us, it would scarcely have been necessary to enter on the consideration of those indirect proofs of the historical truth of the New Testament narrative arising from the incidental allusions to the civil history of the times which must now occupy our attention. (pp. 184 - 185)

In Lecture Eight, Rawlinson presents a general coverage of the actions and writings of the early church leaders, including the apostles and the Ante-Nicene Fathers. These passages include evidence of the important role of healing miracles in gaining new converts — "thousands upon thousands" — to the Christian church. They likewise relate the personal, social, and moral challenges which confronted the early Christians as well as the blessings which came from their membership in the new church.

•If it be still said — Why are we to believe as they? — why are we in this enlightened nineteenth century to receive as facts, what Greeks and Romans in an uncritical and credulous age accepted without inquiry, or at least without any searching investigation — the answer is two-fold.

Allowing that the bulk of men in the first and sec-

ond centuries were uncritical and credulous with
respect to remote times, and to such tales as did not
concern action or involve any alteration of conduct,
we may remark that it is untrue to represent them as
credulous where their worldly interests were at
stake, or where any practical result was to follow
upon their belief of what they heard. They are not
found to have offered themselves a ready prey to
imposters, or to have allowed themselves to be carried away by the arts of pretenders, where such
weakness would have brought them into trouble. . .
The Romans, and still more the Greeks, had plenty
of shrewdness; and there was no people less likely
than they to accept on slight grounds a religion
involving such obligations as the Christian.

It is important to bear in mind what conversion really meant in the early times. It meant the severing of
family and social ties — the renunciation of worldly
prospects — abstinence from all gayeties and
amusements — perpetual exposure to insults —
cold looks, contemptuous gestures, abusive words,
injurious suspicions, a perpetual sense of danger, a
life to lead which was to "die daily."

"The early Christians," it has been well said, "were
separate from other men. Their religion snapped
asunder the ties of common intercourse. It called
them to a new life; it gave them new sentiments,
hopes, and desires, a new character; it demanded of
them such a conscientious and steady performance
of duty as had hardly before been conceived of; it
subjected them to privations and insults, to uncer-
tainty and danger; it required them to prepare for
torments and death. Every day of their lives they
were strongly reminded of it by the duties which it
enforced and the sacrifices which it cost them."

Before accepting such a position, we may be well
assured that each convert scanned narrowly the evidence upon which he was invited to make a change

in every way so momentous. When they first heard
the doctrine of resurrection, the Athenians
"mocked." Yet after a while Dionysius and others
"clave to Paul and believed" — surely because they
found the evidence of the resurrection of Christ such
as could not be resisted.

It must be remembered that the prospect of his own
resurrection was all that the new convert had to sustain him. "If in this life only we have hope, we are
of all men most miserable," says St. Paul. And the
prospect of his own resurrection was bound up
inseparably with the fact of Christ's having risen. If
Christ were not risen, preaching was vain, and faith
was vain — then all who fell asleep in Christ perished. The Christian was taught to base his hope of a
happy future for himself solely and entirely upon
the resurrection and ascent to heaven of Jesus. Surely the evidence for these facts must have been
thousands of times closely sifted by converts who
could fairly demand to have the assurances on the
point of eye-witnesses.

Further, we must not forget that the early converts
had a second ground of belief, besides and beyond
their conviction of the honesty and trustworthiness
of those who came forward to preach the Gospel,
declaring themselves witnesses of the "mighty
works" which Christ had wrought, and preeminently
of his resurrection. These preachers persuaded, not
merely by their evident truthfulness and sincerity,
but by the miraculous powers which they wielded.

There is good evidence that the ability to work miracles was not confined to the apostolic age. The bishops and others who pressed to see Ignatius on his
way to martyrdom, "expected that he would com-
municate to them some spiritual gift." Papias related
various miracles as having happened in his own lifetime — among others that a dead man had been
restored to life. Justin Martyr declares very simply

that in his day both men and women were found
who possessed miraculous powers. Quadratus, the
Apologist, is mentioned by a writer of the second
century as exercising them. Irenaeus speaks of miracles as still common in Gaul when he wrote, which
was nearly at the close of the second century. Tertullian, Theophilus of Antioch, and Minucius Felix,
authors of about the same period, are witnesses to
the continuance to their day of at least one class of
miracles.

Thus the existence of these powers was contempora-
neous with the great spread of the Gospel; and it
accounts for that speedy conversion of thousands
upon thousands — that rapid growth of the Church
in all quarters — which would be otherwise so
astonishing. The vast number of the early converts
and the possession of miraculous powers — which
are both asserted by the primitive writers — have
the relation of effect to cause, and lend countenance
to one another. The evidence of the Catacombs, and
the testimony of Pagans, confirm the truth of the
representations made in the one case. Unless we
hold miracles to be impossible, we cannot reasonably doubt them in the other.

But the possession of miraculous powers by those
who spread the Gospel abroad in the first ages,
would alone and by itself prove the divinity of the
Christian Religion. God would not have given
supernatural aid to persons engaged in propagating a
lie, nor have assisted them to palm a deceit upon the
world in His name.

If then there be good evidence of this fact — if it be
plain from the ecclesiastical writers that miracles
were common in the Christian Church for above
two centuries — we have herein an argument of an
historic character, which is of no small weight and
importance, *additional* to that arising from the mere
confirmation by early uninspired writers of the

Sacred Narrative. We find in their statements with respect to these contemporary facts, to which they are unexceptionable witnesses, a further evidence of the truth of the Religion whereof they were the ministers — a further proof that Christianity was not of man, but of God. (pp. 221 - 224)

•The inquiry in which we have been engaged here terminates. We have found that the historical Books of the New Testament are the productions of contemporaries and eye-witnesses — that two at least of those who wrote lives of Christ were his close and intimate friends, while the account of the early Church delivered in the Acts was written by a companion of the Apostles — that the truth of the narrative contained in these writings is evidenced by their sober, simple, and unexaggerated tone, and by their agreement, often undesigned, with each other — that it is further confirmed by the incidental allusions to it which are found in the speeches of the Apostles and in their epistolary correspondence with their converts — that its main facts are noticed, so far as it was to be expected that they would be noticed, by profane writers, while a comparison of its secondary or incidental facts with the civil history of the times, as otherwise known to us, reveals an agreement which is at once so multitudinous and so minute as to constitute, in the eyes of all those who are capable of weighing historical evidence, an overwhelming argument in proof of the authenticity of the whole story — that the narrative was accepted as simple truth, soon after it was published, in most parts of the civilized world, and not by the vulgar only, but by men of education and refinement, and of good worldly position — that it was received and believed, at the time when the truth of every part of it could be readily tested, by many hundreds of thousands, notwithstanding the prejudices of education, and the sacrifices which its acceptance involved — and finally, that the sincerity of these persons' belief was in many cases tested in the most

searching of all possible ways, by persecutions of
the cruelest kind, and triumphantly stood the test —
so that the Church counted her Martyrs by thousands.

We have further seen, that there is reason to believe
that not only our Lord Himself and His Apostles,
but many (if not most) of the first propagators of
Christianity had the power of working miracles; and
that this, and this only, will account for the remarkable facts, which none can deny, of the rapid spread
of the Gospel and the vast numbers of the early converts. All this together — and it must be remembered that the evidence is *cumulative* — constitutes
a body of proof such as is seldom producible with
respect to any events belonging to remote times; and
establishes beyond all reasonable doubt the truth of
the Christian Story.

In no single respect — if we except the fact that it is
miraculous — has the story a mythic character. It is
a single story, told without variation, whereas myths
are fluctuating and multiform; it is blended inextri-
cably with the civil history of the times, which it
every where represents with extraordinary accuracy,
whereas myths distort or supercede civil history; it
is full of prosaic detail, which myths studiously
eschew; it abounds with practical instruction of the
plainest and simplest kind, whereas myths teach by
allegory.

Even in its miraculous element, it stands to some
extent in contrast with all known mythologies —
where the marvellous has ever a predominant character of grotesqueness, which is entirely absent from
the New Testament miracles. Simple earnestness,
fidelity, painstaking accuracy, pure love of truth, are
the most patent characteristics of the New Testament writers, who evidently deal with facts, not
with fancies, and are employed in relating a history,
not in developing an idea.

They write "that we may know the certainty of those things" which were "most surely believed" in their day. They bear record of what they have seen, and assure us that their "testimony is true." "That which they have heard, which they have seen with their eyes, which they have looked upon, which their hands have handled of the Word of Life, that was manifested unto them — that which they have seen and heard" declare they unto us. And such as were not eye-witnesses, deliver only "that which they also received."

I know not how stronger words could have been used to preclude the notion of that plastic growing myth which Strauss conceives Christianity to have been in Apostolic times, and to convince us of its Historic character. And the declarations of the Sacred writers are confirmed by modern research. In spite of all the efforts of an "audacious criticism" — as ignorant as bold — the truth of the Sacred Narrative stands firm, the stronger for the shocks that it has resisted; "the boundless store of truth and life which for eighteen centuries has been the aliment of humanity" is not (as Rationalism boasts) "dissipated."

God is not "divested of his grace, or man of his dignity" — nor is the "tie between heaven and earth broken." The "foundation of God" — the "Everlasting Gospel" — still "standeth sure" — and every effort that is made to overthrow, does but more firmly establish it. (pp. 226 - 228)

CHAPTER 20

RAMSAY MACMULLEN

Ramsay MacMullen received his doctorate at Harvard University in 1957. He taught at the University of Oregon as well as at Brandeis University, where he served as chairman of the Department of Classics. He has taught in the Department of History at Yale University since 1967. He was awarded the endowed chair of Dunham Professor of History and Classics in 1979.

Professor MacMullen has also been a Fellow at the Princeton Institute for Advanced Study. He is a member of the Society for Promotion of Roman Studies, and for three years he held the position of President of the Association of Ancient Historians. He is the author of eight books on the Roman empire.

Professor MacMullen's book most relevant to this survey of Biblical healing is titled *Christianizing the Roman Empire A.D. 100 - 400* . His research is directed toward the causes for the dominant religious role of the Christian church in the Roman empire by the end of the fourth century. He pursues this topic from a secular rather than a religious perspective. He states early in his study that his object is history, not theology. His major conclusion is that several causes were involved in the mass conversions to Christianity during this period, one of which was the appeal of its physical and mental healings. Of special importance, he states, was the demonstration effect caused by the confident ability of Christians to exorcise demons from numerous victims.

The following excerpts are from Chapters III and IV in *Christianizing The Roman Empire*.

> •What *did* Christianity present to its audience? For plainly the process of conversion that interests me took place in people's minds on the basis of what they knew, or thought they knew. It is useless to consider in the process all the things *we* know,

which might have been discovered by a convert
after he had picked up some further instructions and
further experience of the new faith. Accordingly,
those and only those precise impressions must be
isolated which were manifestly and for certain trans-
mitted by members of the church to persons outside,
and through which Christianity worked its spell. . . .

Writings originally directed or later offered from
within the church to an audience beyond did not
include, of course, any pages that are now canonical
or, for that matter, apocryphal; for those pages were
rather for internal consumption. At best, the occasional outsider who investigated them was an
enemy, like Celsus or Porphyry. That leaves nothing
but Apologetic literature for a wider readership. On
the basis of a statement by Tertullian and on general
probability, however, the experts today are generally
agreed that that literature likewise served chiefly for
internal consumption. And there was little enough
reading of any sort anyway. Three quarters or more
of the population was illiterate. Points of contact
and media of communication that we take for granted in our world simply did not exist in antiquity.

We are thus thrown back on face-to-face encounters
as very nearly the only kind of meeting-point
through which a knowledge of church teachings
might be gained. In due course, I will return to these
meetings, to see what might have happened when
they occurred. It was exiguous: monotheism, to
begin with. That was taught, and God was compared, in familiar fashion, to a monarch with his
companies of servants about him; and contrast was
drawn between Him and mere imitations, the daimones that passed for gods by animating idols and
so forth. Word was spread of divine wrath and pun-
ishments, the more readily imagined through being
leveled at evildoers resurrected in the flesh; while
immortal delights were also known to await the
blessed. The very stark blacks and whites of this

whole crude picture of Christianity, and the very unsteady focus on the role of Jesus, are most striking.

To this picture remains to be added a very much fuller kind of instruction, long and patient, gained by a few individuals. . . .What we already have before us, however, even if it appears stark to a point almost unrecognizable, sufficed and more than sufficed for conversion — which, after all, is the target of my inquiry. It sufficed because conversion in the sense specified above, and within the non-Christian world, did not require doctrine of the least elaboration, nor a divine biography, nor very much more than the certainty that truth was being proposed for acceptance, not some silly or wicked fiction. That much being fixed, all else followed. It followed for Marcus Aurelius, describing the foundations of his own beliefs, as it did for the stupidest stable-boy. Rather to expect that non-Christians would be converted *both* to new convictions *and* by new means, is too much — and beyond that, quite needless. It was rather their general instinct, I suppose, as it is generally everybody's instinct, to make the least possible tear in the fabric of already held beliefs, when obliged to admit some urgent novelty. At any rate, we do in fact see them acting along exactly those lines.

The fact appears first in an earlier period than my chosen one, in New Testament scenes. "The gospels represent Jesus as attracting attention primarily as a miracle worker, and winning his followers" — or, in other terminology, producing conversions — "by miracles. The gospels do so because *he* did so." Their purpose in preserving the record was also conscious: "These [manifestations] have been recorded *in order that you may believe* that Jesus is the Messiah, the Son of God" (Jn 20: 30f.). Likewise in the next generation, the Apostles' success in winning recruits arose from their deeds, above all, in healing.

"Although laymen in their language," says the very educated Eusebius, "they drew courage from divine, miraculous powers." Even Simon Magus through miracles made converts — meaning persons ready to obey him out of the conviction that he was a supernatural being (Acts 8: 11).

These passages force a choice, in our modern world a rather uncomfortable choice, between two possible interpretations. Either we must suppose the laws of nature to have been really and truly suspended, or we must try to accommodate the record within interpretations "scientific" but as little Procrustean as possible. Of the two alternatives, the first seems to need a great deal of discussing and defining and adjusting to. Why so much? The answer lies in our own encumbered imaginations. We cannot easily divest ourselves of our great knowledge and superior reasoning, so as to think more nearly like the people of the Roman Empire. They, however, took miracles quite for granted. That was the general starting point. *Not* to believe in them would have made you seem more than odd, simply irrational, as it would have seemed irrational seriously to suppose that babies are brought by storks. (pp. 19 - 22)

•Eusebius, the great first church historian, recounts how, around the turn of the first century in the province Asia, there were "many. . .who amplified the Message, planting the saving seed of the heavenly kingdom far and wide in the world. . . evangelizing. . . with God's favor and help, since wonderful miracles were wrought by them in those times also through the Holy Spirit. As a result, assembled crowds, every man of them on the first hearing, eagerly espoused piety toward the maker of all things." The scene is easily expanded from Saint Paul's writings, with their accounts of his own "signs, marvels, and miracles" matched against his competitors. Unlike the latter, the "super-preachers" as he calls them, he relies "not on plausible, clever argument but on manifestations of the Holy Spirit and of supernatural power."

There was, however, in Paul's day and in the time that Eusebius describes, a lot of coming and going also of inconsequential visionaries, evangelists, and fakes, of whom Peregrinus is a late descendant in Palestine (he is described by Lucian) and of whom we shall also hear. . .in other eastern areas. Celsus may have similar types in mind (or perhaps he was caricaturing Christians) when he speaks of "many, who are nameless, who prophesy at the slightest excuse for some trivial cause both inside and outside the temples; and there are some who wander about begging and roaming around cities and military camps, and they pretend to be moved as if giving some oracular utterance." These in turn blend into an even more miscellaneous population of visionaries, doomsayers, sorcerers, and the like, all in touch or actually filled and brimming over with divine powers.

Powers which must be seen to be believed, naturally. The population and religious expectations that encouraged the pullulation of such wandering wonder-workers could discriminate and tell the fakes from the genuine. There was a good deal of discussion about how to do that, in Christian Apologetic writings and elsewhere, too. For most purposes, however, it was enough that the wonder-worker should merely work his wonders. Then he gained credit. Otherwise, not.

At Ephesus, so told the Acts of John, the Apostle encountered unbelievers but, with miracles of healing, won them over. More effectively yet, in the very temple of Artemis himself, he prayed, "O God. . . . at whose name every idol takes flight and every demon and every unclean power: now let the demon that is here take flight at thy name. . . And while John was saying this, of a sudden the altar of

Artemis split in many pieces. . .and half the temple
fell down. Then the assembled Ephesians cried out,
'[There is but] one God, [the God] of John!. . .We
are converted, now that we have seen thy marvellous works! Have mercy on us, O God, according to
thy will, and save us from our great error!' And
some of them lay on their faces and made supplication, others bent their knees and prayed; some tore
their clothes and wept, and others tried to take
flight."

I don't think the explanatory force of this scene
should be discounted on the grounds that it cannot
have really happened, that it is fiction, that no one
was meant to believe it. I suppose instead that it was
quite widely believed in the second and third centuries with which we are concerned at the moment;
and I assume that its substance, mostly in oral form,
led on through belief to conversion. Why not? Such
wonderful stories were most reliably reported. . . .

Driving all competition from the field head-on was
crucial. The world, after all, held many dozens and
hundreds of gods. Choice was open to everybody. It
could thus be only a most exceptional force that
would actually displace alternatives and compel
allegiance; it could be only the most probative
demonstrations that would work. We should therefore assign as much weight to this, the chief instru-
ment of conversion, as the best, earliest reporters do.
True, "historians. . .of the church have declared that
such phenomena (of divine confrontations) 'are
more problems of crowd psychology than of Christian piety.' In so doing, they have declared the study
of exorcism, possibly the most highly rated activity
of the early Christian church, a historiographical
'no-go' area." But we have Justin boasting "how
many persons possessed by demons, everywhere in
the world *and in our own city,* have been exorcized
by many of our Christian men"; Irenaeus asserting
that "some people *incontestably and truly* drive out

demons, so that those very persons often become believers"; Tertullian issuing the challenge, "let a man be produced *right here before your court* who, it is clear, is possessed by a demon, and that spirit, commanded by any Christian at all, will as much confess himself a demon in truth as, by lying, he will elsewhere profess himself a 'god'"; and Cyprian once again declaring that demons in idols, "when they are adjured by us in the name of the true God, yield forthwith, and confess, and admit they are forced also to leave the bodies they have invaded; and *you may see them,* by our summons and by the workings of hidden majesty, consumed with flames."

Jesus' authority over the fiercest infestations of satanic power, making them do whatever he wished by a mere word of command, he passed on to his disciples, with the instructions to use it. They did. Exorcists by title became early established in the churches. Eusebius says theirs is "an office of special labor." Rome itself still had twenty-two of them at the turn of the fifth to the sixth century. The institution had taproots in Judaism, exorcism was of little account otherwise; but in Christianity it found an extraordinary flowering and produced that string of decisive, specific assertions just quoted. They cover experiences of roughly the mid-second to the mid-third century. . . .

The manhandling of demons — humiliating them, making them howl, beg for mercy, tell their secrets, and depart in a hurry — served a purpose quite essential to the Christian definition of monotheism: it made physically (or dramatically) visible the superiority of the Christian's patron Power over all others. One and only one was God. The rest were *daimones* demonstrably, and therefore already familiar to the audience as nasty, lower powers that no one would want to worship anyway.

It is important to bear in mind the full consequences
of these scenes. Where they persuaded, they produced a special loyalty. For stories of wonders
wrought by other deities certainly circulated as
much, making believers in just as large numbers (if
we total up the new devotees of Sabazius, Jupiter of
Doliche, Mithra, and so forth during the second and
third centuries); but these new devotees were
thenceforth not lost to paganism. They only focused
a particular conviction and gratitude on one more
god. Christian converts, by contrast, denied the
name and even the very existence of all those gods,
from the moment of believing.

On occasion, exorcisms are specified as the cause of
conversion — in Ephesus, as we have seen, in
Palestine, Italy, Africa, or Gaul. Persuasion lay in
the simplest of facts: "In religious usage, miracle is
an event in which one knows one is dealing with
God." So the yielding of North African droughts to
Christian prayer also induced a shout from "the populace, hailing, "The God of Gods!" In Palestine,
where the wonders of healing by the young Hilarion
"were on everyone's lips far and wide, the people
flocked in to him from Syria and Egypt, so that
many believed in Christ." And Eusebius, in the passages cited above, mentions unspecified kinds of
miracles in the command of the subapostolic mis-
sionaries and later, in his own day, the miracle at
Caesarea. The various bits and pieces of evidence
gathered in the preceding pages constitute, to my
knowledge, the sum of our information on how
groups (not individuals) turned to the church prior
to the opening up of toleration — that is, before A.D.
312.

Is it necessary to distinguish between moments that
gained single individuals for the church from
moments that won over large or small groups? Is
there a special sort of crowd psychology at work in
the scenes preserved for us or, for that matter, in

those producing adherents to non-Christian deities? But no differences appear in the way people reason and respond. The only purpose served by the distinction is to explain better the *rate* of change we are observing. In the whole process, very large numbers are obviously involved. For reasons that will appear shortly, it would be hard to picture the necessary scale of conversion if we limited ourselves to contexts and modes of persuasion that concerned only single individuals talking to each other. If the evidence for steady evangelizing in private settings, however, is combined with the evidence for successes en masse, the two in combination do seem to me adequate to explain what we know happened. (pp. 25 - 29)

•To return to our proper subject: we have taken our measure of the mass scenes and the quite narrowly intellectual scenes, trying to understand what is going on in them or, in more accurate terms, what are the thoughts and feelings that lead to a change of religious loyalties. What we have discovered is, as anyone might have predicted, entirely in accord with long established — that is, non-Christian — patterns. It remains to translate what we have found into a historical event, of however long-drawn-out development. But it is just here that more puzzling problems arise. How did it ever happen that the church could grow at such a rate, so as actually to predominate in occasional towns or districts by the turn of the second century and, by the turn of the fourth, to have attained a population of, let us say, five million. (p. 32)

•During most of the period I speak of, from around A.D. 100 to 312, Christians as such avoided attention. The fact is well known and easily illustrated. They can hardly be blamed for that, out of common prudence. Even where they were most numerous and presumably most taken for granted, there were many among their neighbors ready and willing to

cite them before a hanging court. So Pliny discovered. They avoided on religious grounds also those
occasions when their neighbors gathered for a good
time, in private or community celebrations. From
their own meetings, if by chance a stranger entered,
he was not to be expelled; but, as a limit on this tolerance and evidently after testing him, "if anyone
does not love the Lord, let him be outcast," with a
curse added to make sure. A prickly lot, just as Celsus said. They didn't marry non-Christians, or were
at least taught to think it a sin. It happened anyway,
of course, and the strictures were a little relaxed in
the fourth century. Still, and in sum, the church
before Constantine seems to have kept itself to itself
in its divine services and marital policies, as in its
schools. We cannot find in these institutions any
adequate explanation for its growth, whether or not
they may have produced an occasional convert. (p.
35)

•Urban households and groups that were poor, or at
least not rich, were obliged to live right on top of
each other. Their crowding necessarily exposed
them to ideas from their neighbors, even if their
wish was for some degree of privacy; and the larger
the city, the closer the crowding. A particularly
striking example is the meeting-place Christians
bought or leased in the western basement rooms of a
building in Rome, now Santa Prisca, toward the
start of the second century, adjoining which were
other rooms already in use by a non-Christian
group. For two centuries the two precincts appear to
have been separated only by a door, until the non-
Christian in A.D. 400 was destroyed and filled in.
Similarly, cemeteries were sometimes shared by
non-Christians and Christians. (pp. 39 - 40)

•In such settings, if the subject of religion arose, it
would be the aspects commonly most talked about;
and, given the concentration of ancient religion on
the relief of sickness or deformity, an exchange of

views might most likely begin with the wonderful cures wrought by this or that divine power. Of all worships, the Christian best and most particularly advertised its miracles by driving out of spirits and laying on of hands. Reports would spread without need of preaching throughout all the places so contemptuously catalogued by Celsus.

Testing to see if I can imagine in some detail a scene that conflicts with no point of the little that I know about conversion in the second and third centuries, I would choose the room of some sick person: there, a servant talking to a mistress, or one spouse to another, saying, perhaps, "Unquestionably they can help, if you believe. And I know, I have seen, I have heard, they have related to me, they have books, they have a special person, a sort of officer. It is true. Besides and anyway, if you don't believe, then you are doomed when a certain time comes, so say the prophecies; whereas, if you do, then they can help even in great sickness. I know people who have seen or who have spoken with others who have seen. And healing is even the least that they tell. Theirs is truly a God all-powerful. He has worked a hundred wonders." So a priest is sent for, or an exorcist; illness is healed; the household after that counts as Christian; it is baptized; and through instruction it comes to accept the first consequences: that all other cults are false and wicked, all seeming gods, the same.

The subject of this chapter cannot, however, be left at such a scene. For beyond such points of contact and persuasion, after the first shock of belief that led to a person's cry, "Great is the God of the Christians!" there lay initiation in many other possible degrees. Historians who think in terms of millions of people, and indeed contemporaries within the church, might well accept the bare moment of that cry as the making of a Christian. But everyone knows that a great depth of further experiences

remained to be tested in the church: of membership
in such a close group as second- or third-century
congregations were likely to afford; of daily life
governed by a more insistent moral standard than
could be found in any other, non-Christian, association; of introduction to an ordered system of beliefs
commanding history, cosmology, metaphysics,
ethics. There would be temperaments that specially
responded to the challenge of these experiences, no
doubt. There would be many a Lucius of Apuleius'
novel, many a Aelius Aristides, many who, being
once recruited to the church, went on the explore
and grow within it more fully. They could attain
what Festugière, Nock, and others would call "true"
Christianity. They could report about it with all the
more conviction to others like themselves. Their
words would strike an answering chord and incline
their listeners to belief. No doubt. But no reports of
this sort are attested. We cannot reasonably turn
these "many," then, into the thousands and thousands — to say nothing of millions - of persons that
make up the whole of our story. (pp. 39 - 41)

EPILOGUE

In the beginning God. . .
Genesis

Though ye believe not me, believe the works. . .
Jesus

EPILOGUE

At this point in our historical survey, it is probably wise to stop and make a few observations and assessments of the early roots of Biblical healing. The record of spiritual healing from Moses in the years 1300 - 1200 B.C. to Lactantius around 325 A.D. is impressive. While relatively few persons were restored to health and well-being by spiritual healing during the time of the Old Testament, many hundreds and thousands of lives were recovered from all kinds of diseases, from sorrow and pain, as well as from death in the period of Primitive Christianity. The impact of the healing works performed by Jesus during three brief years is unparalleled in human history.

We know the names of only a few of the individuals who were healed by the teachings of the Bible over this sixteen-hundred year period. We know of Miriam, Moses' sister, healed from leprosy by her brother; the widow's son revived from death by Elijah; the son of the Shunnamite woman recovered from death, and Naaman, the Syrian military commander, healed of leprosy by Elisha; the centurion's servant, Peter's mother-in-law, Jairus' daughter, a lunatic boy, blind Bartimaeus, a nobleman's son, Lazarus, and multitudes of others healed by Jesus; a man lame from birth, Aeneas, and Dorcas healed by Peter; a lame man, Eutychus, and Publius healed by Paul; and scores and hundreds of other people unknown to us by name restored to health and life as recorded by the Ante-Nicene Fathers. Not only was the health and well-being of this vast array of people regained, but the lives of their families and loved ones were returned to normalcy and stability.

As cited in the preface, these cases of healing are not part of the dominant message in most of the books of the Bible. Except for the first five books of the New Testament, the content of the Bible is much more concerned with the history of the people of Israel, their trials and victories, their law and morality, the advent of Christianity, a new law and a new morality, and a new religious doctrine for all mankind. Much of the healing message is implicit rather than explicit. Some of the most prolific writers such as Paul and several of the Ante-Nicene Fathers say much more about Christian doctrine than about Christian healing.

Biblical Healing and the Dignity of Individual Man

A major conclusion derived from the readings and the historical commentary presented in this study is that the record of Biblical healing imparted a specific and unique influence on the emerging concept of the dignity of individual man. This idea has been widely recognized as the core value of Western civilization. One of the great ironies and tragedies in the evolution of Western societies is the fact that this healing element interlinked with the fundamental principle of human dignity has been largely unrecognized and unappreciated by many thinking people of the classical period and the generations thereafter. Only a relatively small number of men and women have ever been aware of the special significance of spiritual healing based on important teachings of the Bible.

The very simple yet very profound doctrine that God is good and all-powerful, that He has made man in His own image and likeness, that He is a loving and caring God who created man for a life of health and wholeness, and that He has the power to destroy any form of sickness and disease has largely escaped the attention of most thinking people for many centuries.

Biblical Healing and the Role of Monotheism

Another crucial concept which linked the teachings of the Bible to spiritual healing during the classical period was the idea of monotheism, the cornerstone of both Hebrew and Christian thought. The first commandment of the Mosiac decalogue affirmed a spiritual relationship between man and his Creator, a bond which is the very source of man's existence and being. No other God or power or cause exists, the great lawgiver declared on Mount Horeb; and man is eternally governed and embraced by one and only one ever-present Deity. This fundamental relationship has been the ever-present source of man's health, wholeness, and well-being. Early Christian healing was based on this principle of monotheism. The destruction of physical and mental diseases served as demonstrative proof of the absolute and universal power of a single source of man's being. To repeat some colorful and judicious words in the historical writing by Professor MacMullen:

> The manhandling of demons - humiliating them,
> making them howl, beg for mercy, tell their secrets,
> and depart in a hurry — served a purpose quite

> essential to the Christian definition of monotheism:
> it made physically (or dramatically) visible the
> superiority of the Christian's patron Power over all
> others. One and only one was God. (p. 28)

A key question pervading this historical survey thereby emerges: What was the *specific* and *unique* influence of Biblical healing within the value system of early Western civilization? Why was healing achieved by the teachings of the Bible *different from* the preaching or speaking or professing about the teachings in this wonderful book?

The immediate and obvious role of healing was the restoration to health and wholeness in the lives of the people actually touched by the spiritually-minded men recorded in the Bible. Yet the influence of Biblical healing extends far beyond the sizeable but limited number of people who directly experienced spiritual healing during the early formation of the Judeo-Christian tradition.

Biblical Healing as Proof of Biblical Teachings

The unique and special influence of Biblical healing is the presentation of *proof* that the teachings about the nature of one ever-present God, the dignity of man, and the ability of man to exercise his God-given dominion over the universe are valid. The ability to heal imparts concrete corroboration of healing-oriented precepts in the Bible which preaching, professing, and talking about any kind of precepts by themselves cannot do.

What can be more convincing evidence of human dignity based on religious principles than the restoration of health and happiness to those afflicted with various forms of disease? What can establish more credibility about the true nature of man than a concept of his being that can be used to destroy physical and mental illnesses and preserve a life of health and well-being as part of a religious-based heritage of human worth and decency?

The vital element of proof began with Moses' curing his own hand of leprosy at the "great sight" of the burning bush on Mt. Horeb which initiated the recorded tradition of Biblical healing. As already cited in Part One, this healing followed the impressive "first sign" of converting a rod to a serpent and back into a rod to prove God would support and protect him in convincing the people of Israel of his leadership role in guiding them from captivity in Egypt to the promised land. The healing of leprosy was the second or "latter sign" of God's presence

and power. In many ways it was a more impressive and meaningful
sign than the first as it involved the cure of a dreadful "incurable"
physical disease well known to the people of the classical world. The
primary role of Moses' healing — both to himself and to his people
— was to serve as a proof of God's authority. It may be useful here to
repeat God's words to Moses cited in the book of Exodus: "And it
shall come to pass, if they will not believe thee, neither hearken to the
voice of the first sign, that they will believe the voice of the latter
sign." (4: 8)

Jesus was emphatic on the importance of healing in proving the
power of God and His loving relationship to man. When asked by a
group of Jews if he were the Christ, Jesus replied:

> I told you, and ye believed not: the works that I do
> in my Father's name, they bear witness of me. . . . If
> I do not the works of my Father, believe me not. But
> if I do, though ye believe not me, believe the works:
> that ye may know, and believe, that the Father is in
> me, and I in him. (John 10: 25, 37, 38)

Paul likewise stressed the importance of proof as tangible confirmation of Jesus' teachings which included the healing of sickness and
disease. In I Thessalonians he wrote: "Prove all things; hold fast that
which is good." (5: 21) In many of their writings, the Ante-Nicene
Fathers also cited the role of healing as proof of the verity of the
teachings of Jesus and his apostles. This proof exerted an important
influence in the early church. During the time of Primitive Christianity
much confusion and controversy existed over the meaning of many
parts of the Old Testament. The New Testament was still incomplete,
and the early church leaders were often uncertain which books should
be included in the Christian Scriptures. As already discussed, there
was considerable disagreement over aspects of Christian doctrine and
its conflict with Greek thought. In this period of ferment and change, a
major factor which gave the fledgling church a steady sense of assurance and conviction was the evidence of spiritual healing. A good
example of the role of proof in early Christian healing is the following
passage already cited by Justin Martyr in his treatise *On the Resurrection:*

> For every proof is more powerful and trustworthy
> than that which it proves: since what is disbelieved,

until proof is produced, gets credit when such proof
is produced, and is recognized as being what it was
stated to be. . . . He, therefore, is Himself both the
faith and the proof of Himself and of all things.
Wherefore those who follow Him, and know Him,
having faith in Him as their proof, shall rest in Him.
(Chap. I)

And in spite of some doubts about Christian healing, Edward Gibbon
cited in his prestigious study of the Roman empire the view of many
people that casting out demons was "the most convincing evidence of
the truth of Christianity."

The proofs of Biblical healing were a significant factor in intermittent conflicts between the men performing healing works and a vast
variety of determined opponents. From the time of Moses and the
prophets to Jesus, the apostles, and the Ante-Nicene Fathers, the ability to heal reinforced the defenders of the teachings of the Bible
against paganism, polytheism, the worship of Baal, Gnosticism,
Docetism, Mithraism, and numerous other competing religions, cults,
and followings. Jesus also used the proof of his healing power to
counteract the bitter attacks of the Pharisees, Sadducees, and other
articulate proponents of a rigid Jewish legalism.

The Proof of Biblical Healing vs. The Influence of Greek Thought

One of the most profound controversies involving the proof of spiritual healing during the classical era was the clash between the teachings of Christianity and the powerful influence of Greek philosophy.
Many aspects of this contest are still with our own generation near the
end of the twentieth century. The basic principles of Christianity are
still the same, but the early attraction of Greek thought has been
replaced by modern versions such as agnosticism, skepticism, astrolo-
gy, various forms of rationalism, various forms of determinism, tran-
scendentalism, pragmatism, New Thought, secular humanism, New
Age doctrines, et cetera. "Man is the measure of all things" was a key
slogan voiced by the ancient Greeks. "God is the measure of all
things" was a cardinal maxim of the Judeo-Christian tradition. In spite
of countless efforts to blend and blur and amalgamate these two major
sources of Western thought, a fundamental line was drawn between
them in the early crucible of Western civilization. And the proof

exhibited by healing works based on the Bible contributed much in
the process of preserving an important delineation.

An aspect of the conflict between Christianity and Greek thought
was voiced very clearly in Paul's well-known speech to a group of
Athenians on Mars Hill. He said:

> Ye men of Athens, I perceive that in all things ye are
> too superstitious. For as I passed by, and beheld
> your devotions, I found an altar with this inscrip-
> tion, TO THE UNKNOWN GOD. Whom therefore
> ye ignorantly worship, him declare I unto you.
>
> God that made the world and all things therein, see-
> ing that he is Lord of heaven and earth, dwelleth not
> in temples made with hands; neither is worshipped
> with men's hands as though he needed any thing,
> seeing he giveth to all life, and breath, and all
> things; . . .For in him we live, and move, and have
> our being; as certain also of your own poets have
> said, For we are also his offspring. (Acts 17: 22 - 24,
> 28)

Yet the Greek poets referred to in Paul's speech were not a major
influence in the complex and speculative philosophical systems of
thought emanating from the Greek and Roman cultures. As we have
already seen, several of the Ante-Nicene Fathers, especially those
from a Greek upbringing and parentage (e.g. Justin Martyr and Origen) made some attempts at various times to combine Greek thought
and the teachings of Christianity. This approach was strongly condemned by other early church leaders such as Tertullian, Cyprian,
Arnobius, and Lactantius. Tertullian, the articulate leader of Latin
Christianity, once uttered an emphatic query: "What has Athens to do
with Jerusalem?"

In his later years after much reflection on the nature of Greek philosophy, Origen himself stressed in his writings the ability of Christians to heal all kinds of physical and mental illnesses, while the
philosophies of Plato, the Stoics, and other Greek thinkers, he said,
were totally devoid of any healing power. And Arnobius, also a
Greek, was likewise outspoken in clarifying the vast gulf between
Christian doctrine and Greek philosophy. He used the works of Christian healing to illustrate the differences. In his writing already cited in
Part Two he stated:

> And since you [heathen opponents] compare Christ
> and the other deities as to the blessing of health
> bestowed, how many thousands of infirm persons
> do you wish to be shown to you by us; how many
> persons affected with wasting diseases, whom no
> appliances whatever restored, although they went as
> suppliants through all the temples, although they
> prostrated themselves before the gods, and swept
> the very thresholds with their lips — though, as long
> as life remained, they wearied with prayers, and
> importuned with most piteous vows Aesculapius
> himself, the health-giver, as they call him? (*Against
> the Heathen,* Book One, Chap. 49)

In more recent times in the United States a Protestant clergyman has
reiterated the important differences between Christianity and Greek
thought and their contrasting influences on Western culture. The Reverend Hugh Black has declared: "The birthplace of civilization is not
Athens, but Calvary."

The Proof of Biblical Healing in the Formation of Other Basic Values

The proof of Biblical healing has contributed to the evolution of
other important values in the early Judeo-Christian tradition. Many of
the thinkers whose words and writings have been included in this
study on our Hebrew and Christian roots have exerted a significant
influence on the formation of these fundamental and interrelated principles which have shaped Western civilization. These norms were dor-
mant and ignored for many centuries after the classical period, yet
their restoration has been extremely important in the advancement and
protection of spiritual healing during the past one hundred years.
These basic values are the rule of spiritual law, individual freedom
and human rights, individual equality, and the idea of progress.

The Rule of Spiritual Law

One of the most pervasive precepts embodied in the entire Bible is
the idea of a spiritual law or a binding relationship between God and
man. Over many centuries the presence and power of a divine law has
imparted a major influence on Western civilization. Professor Carl J.

Friedrich of Harvard University in his book *The Philosophy of Law in Historical Perspective,* has written: "Ancient Judaism has played a decisive role in shaping the origins of Western concepts of law." (p. 8). He has labeled this early law as "The Will of God" and "The Heritage of the Old Testament." This bond between God and man in the form of the covenants and the law has already been cited in the readings on the promises of healing in the Old and New Testaments. This important concept is specified here in the light of the proofs provided by Biblical healing.

During the classical period the proofs of Biblical healing, like the proofs of an experiment in a laboratory, became a significant basis for the discovery and verification of a general law. The accumulated evidence of spiritual healing gave greater precision to an understanding of the nature of God and man. It supplied justification for predicting healing results in the future. It enabled spiritually-minded men in the Old and New Testaments to be certain of their ability to heal all kinds of diseases. Just as the early covenant upheld by Abraham, Jacob, Moses, and other prophets was used to lead the collective nation of Israel out of the bondage and oppression imposed by foreign rulers, the new covenant inaugurated by Jesus has been able to lead individuals of all races and cultures out of the bondage and oppression imposed by the human mind.

As seen in this 1600-year survey of Biblical healing, the rule of spiritual law involves the application of a higher law than any man-made law. Its legal standards of health and wholeness are made and enforced by God. Its legal authority is available in man's consciousness through prayer, faith, and understanding. The superiority of spiritual law has been well stated by Paul in one of his epistles: "The law of the Spirit of life in Christ Jesus hath made me free from the law of sin and death." (Romans 8: 2)

The healings achieved by a higher spiritual law during the lives of the thinkers and writers included in this survey were not performed in occasional and unusual "supernatural" acts by a few specially gifted healers. They were accomplished by the power of an impersonal law which is universal and eternal. These "signs" and "wonders" have been available whenever inspired thought is expanded beyond a limited physical view of man and the universe. The relationship between healing miracles and spiritual law has been well explained by Archbishop Richard Chenevix Trench in his book *Notes on the Miracles of Our Lord.* He has stated:

> Miracles exceed the laws of *our* nature, but it does
> not therefore follow that they exceed the laws of *all*
> nature. . . . In the miracle, this world of ours is
> drawn into and within a higher order of things; laws
> are then working in it which are not the laws of its
> fallen condition, but laws of mightier range and
> higher perfection; they assert the preeminence and
> predominance which are rightly their own. (p. 13)

Individual Freedom and Human Rights

The idea of individual freedom and human rights is a second basic
value of the early Judeo-Christian tradition, shaped in considerable
degree by the proof of Biblical healing. This fundamental principle
has been crucial in the evolution of human dignity. As seen in the
writings included in this book, man expresses his full dignity when he
is in excellent health and well-being. Physical infirmities in any form
impose a degree of bondage.

As previously cited, the people healed by the teachings of the Bible
during the classical era enjoyed a form of individual freedom in a life
of good health and usefulness in spite of severe political, economic,
and social oppression. Conversely, thousands of people in our own
time near the end of the twentieth century living in democratic societies in many parts of the world with extensive political, economic,
and social liberties have been deprived of portions of their human dignity by the imposition of debilitating sickness and disease.

The idea of individual freedom and human rights has come largely
from the Judeo-Christian contribution to Western culture. The long
struggle for individual liberty has received less support from Greek
thought and Roman jurisprudence. The effort of Socrates in ancient
Athens, for example, to live as an individual and to voice opinions
contrary to the public opinion of his day, resulted in his condemnation
and execution. Given an opportunity to escape this unjust sentence,
the eminent philosopher himself could not conceive of doing a greater
wrong by evading the collective will of his own city-state. The erudite
writings of philosophers such as Plato, Aristotle, Cicero, and Seneca
on politics, ethics, education, et cetera, also included no support for
individual freedom and human rights separate from the "higher good"
of the corporate state. In a book entitled *Athens and Jerusalem: An
Interpretative Essay on Christianity and Classical Culture,* Professor
E.G. Weltin has explained the dominant view of human freedom in
ancient Greece and Rome as follows:

Today's assumption that individual rights have pri-
ority over communal ones would be a novelty in
ancient Greece and Rome; at the very best such
rights would be reciprocal. Since no revealed
anthropology in Classical thought guaranteed that
each individual was a personality of great value, an
end in himself, an integral link in a divine economy,
an entity destined for individual divine recognition,
Classical man was largely forced to equate his
meaning, his *raison d'être*, his worth, with the
extent to which he was privileged to enjoy participation in the affairs of the whole, generally expressed
by service to the polis as the custodian of the public
consensus. (pp. 22 - 23)

In sharp contrast was the gradual evolution of the idea and practice
of some aspects of individual freedom during the classical period
based on the teachings of the Bible and often buttressed by the proof
of spiritual healing. Almost from the beginning of the Judeo-Christian
tradition, men have attempted to carve out an area of individual privacy where they can think and act and live according to the dictates of
their own conscience without unwanted interference from the authority of the community or state. They have endeavored to establish some
kind of institutionalized limits on the exercise of governmental power.
They have sought to guarantee human rights by various forms of constitutional rule. In early Hebrew society an important source of human
rights and dignity was the Ten Commandments. In a book titled *The
Ten Commandments and Human Rights,* Professor Walter Harrelson of
the Vanderbilt Divinity School has declared:

The Ten Commandments are much more akin to
statements about the character of life in community
than they are to cases of violations of the law of the
community, and what punishment is to be dealt out
when the violations occur. Put in constitutional
terms, the Ten Commandments are much more like
the Bill of Rights and its amendments than the United States Code. (p. 12 - 13)

The movement toward individual freedom was often hampered during the time of the Old Testament by the prevailing orthodox doctrine

upholding a righteous but punitive God of the chosen people of Israel. Yet as already discussed in Chapter 4, the time-honored epic of Job depicts an early pioneer of individualism protesting this authoritarian and vindictive idea of Deity. Job claimed his innocence from sin and appealed for justice and healing. Other affirmations of individual rights and freedom are included in some parts of Psalms, Proverbs, and Isaiah.

As shown in the readings and commentary included in this book, the beginning of Primitive Christianity marked a major breakthrough in establishing individualism and human freedom. Jesus often protested against the rigid legalism of Judaism at the same time that he performed some of his most impressive healings. His words "Ye shall know the truth, and the truth shall make you free" (John 8: 32) depict very vividly his view of individual rights and freedom completely fulfilled by the enjoyment of excellent health and well-being. His own resurrection might be described as the highest achievement in human history linking spiritual healing with human rights and individual freedom. Regarding Jesus' healing role in expanding the Western concept of human freedom, Professor Harrelson has also written:

> Christianity. . . can rightly be seen as a religion in which an essential ingredient is the freedom of the human spirit with which God's raising of Jesus from death is inseparably connected. The Christian community of those who are witnesses of the Resurrection is a community marked by a new perception of the possibilities of human life and human community. Human beings need no longer live under compulsions and constraints that long have bound and sometimes enslaved them. They need no longer live only in hope of a time of freedom and joy and blessedness in God's presence. They need not do so, because what God has promised God now has brought to reality. (p. 6)

Some of the protests by the apostles against both Jewish and Roman authority likewise combined acts of healing with declarations of individual rights and freedom. Paul was stoned severely by the actions of "certain Jews" after healing a crippled man at Lystra. He recovered the following day and continued on his mission of preaching and healing. He later voiced the famous words "I was free born"

(Acts 22: 28) which reinforced the Christian emphasis on individual freedom and physical wholeness.

The teachings of Primitive Christianity, in brief, conceived of man as the image and likeness of God whose fundamental purpose is to express God-like qualities, including health, strength, and soundness. Man is thereby created for a noble and worthy purpose. His human rights are based on his divine rights. His true freedom comes from an inseparable relationship to God, not from any secular or philosophical source. Man's salubrity and security are ends, not means, for the welfare of himself as an individual and for the good of his community. His rights and freedom are not to be denigrated or abused by any human authority. All political, economic, and social institutions of society are expected to promote man's inherent rights and freedom, including the right to wholeness and well-being.

The idea of individual freedom and human rights was weak and subdued for many centuries after the era of Primitive Christianity, yet it reemerged in the form of man's "natural rights" largely in the writings of English-speaking thinkers in the seventeenth century. Important treatises of John Locke, for example, are interlaced with references to God and to key precepts contained in the Bible. In an essay on Civil Government he declared that the end of government is "life, liberty, and property." A century later Thomas Jefferson inserted in the American Declaration of Independence the principle of "self-evident" truths, that all men "are endowed by their Creator with certain inalienable Rights" which include "Life, Liberty and the pursuit of Happiness." A few years later human rights exemplified by the American Revolution became one of the major factors in the French Revolution. Just after World War II the newly-established United Nations proclaimed a Declaration of Human Rights in its efforts to promote domestic justice and world peace. During the 1960's Dr. Martin Luther King stressed human rights in his struggle against racism in the United States. In the 1980's important strides have been made by a series of treaties in advancing human rights in the Soviet Union, Eastern Europe, and many areas of Asia, Africa, and Latin America.

This liberating trend which has brought freedom to increasing numbers of people has been fostered by many factors, including the influence of ancient Stoic law, the ideas of the Age of Enlightenment, and the powerful attraction of modern democracy. Yet a vital and often forgotten force in man's long struggle for individual freedom and human rights has been the impact of teachings in the Bible validated by the proof of spiritual healing. The words and works of religious leaders such as Moses, Elijah, Elisha, Jesus, the apostles, and the Ante-Nicene Fathers, all of whom contributed to a heritage of healing, have likewise contributed to a tradition upholding important rights and liberties for individual man.

Individual Equality

The concept of individual equality has long been a basic value in the teachings of Christianity. It was stated very clearly by the apostle Peter:

> God is no respecter of persons: But in every nation he that feareth him, and worketh righteousness, is accepted with him. (Acts 10: 34, 35)

Paul also helped define human equality in one of his epistles:

> There is neither Jew nor Greek, there is neither bond nor free, there is neither male nor female: for ye are all one in Christ Jesus. (Gal. 3: 28)

The doctrine of equality was one of the most popular appeals of the early Christians in their efforts to expand the membership of their church. It emerged in a time and region of the world where societies were steeped in various forms of national, communal, and personal inequality. A major reason Christianity overcame paganism in much of the Roman empire by the fourth century A.D. was the attraction of a higher religion readily available to people of all ages, races, nations, and classes.

Individual equality is a value confined largely to Western civilization. Although it has been extremely difficult to put into practice in the West as well as in other parts of the world, it has steadily and quietly exerted a growing influence in both secular and religious affairs in some modern societies. In the United States it has often received support from another of Jefferson's maxims stated in the Declaration of Independence: "All men are created equal."

The proof of spiritual healing during the time of Primitive Christianity has strengthened the idea of individual equality. It has done this by restoring health to persons of diverse racial, social, and economic classes. Since disease afflicts people irrespective of human status or ethnic origin, the destruction of disease by spiritual means is equally available to everyone. Jesus voiced this principle when he said: "I am come that they might have life, and that they might have it more abundantly." (John 10: 10) He used the word "they" to refer to all men, women, and children. His healing mission was not restricted to any single segment of any society.

Jesus healed persons who were poor, such as the woman afflicted with a hemorrhage for twelve years, the infirm man at the pool of Bethesda, and the demented man named Legion who lived in the tombs. He healed upper class people such as the son of a nobleman. He healed many Jews; he also healed Gentiles, such as the daughter of a woman from Syrophenicia. He healed many adults, such as Peter's mother-in-law, a man with a withered hand, Bartimaeus, and Lazarus. He healed many children, such as Jairus' daughter, a lunatic boy, and a young dead man at Nain.

Similar healings were achieved for all kinds of people by the apostles and reported in the writings of the Ante-Nicene Fathers. In Solomon's porch all the apostles healed many poor and infirm persons, and Peter and John healed a beggar man lame from his birth. Paul also healed people of all races and classes as well as young people. At the city of Thyatira he cast an evil spirit out of a young woman, and he restored a young man named Eutychus from death after he had fallen from a high loft in a temple. Arnobius tells us of healings being performed and experienced by Christians who were "unlearned."

The evidence of Christian healing, in brief, provided additional authority to the concept of individual equality. Primitive Christianity professed and verified that all mankind has equal access to a loving God and His healing power.

The Idea of Progress

One of the basic values which also characterized early Western society was the idea of progress. This fundamental principle upholds the need for each individual to continually improve himself or herself, to overcome physical and mental limitations, to elevate character, and to develop personal abilities and talents to their highest possible level. To progress means to go forward, to advance, to proceed toward a worthy objective and goal, to transform one's life and mental attitudes. It induces a distinct sense of curiosity and arouses a desire for steady change.

The concept of progress later became a source of what many modern writers have called "the Protestant ethic," "the work ethic," "achievement consciousness," and "stages of development." This idea was interlinked with the evolution of spiritual healing during the classical period; it has also been intimately involved in the revival of Christian healing since the nineteenth century.

Some aspects of Greek thought have contributed to the Western tradition of progress. The idealism of Plato's philosophy upheld various teleological doctrines asserting that the processes of human and natural forces are continually moving toward a final cause or goal. The Greek sense of dynamism was a major factor in the territorial expansion of Hellenic influence and its progressive thrust in the early classical period. In a book titled *The Western World and Japan,* Sir George B. Sansom has described this unique propensity to change as follows:

> Onward from the days of the Aegean city states it [the Western ethos] continues to manifest the restless energy that impelled Hellenic culture to expand, to reach out to other lands and peoples. There are dark and silent intervals, and sometimes the Hellenic spirit seems to be in danger of extinction; but it reasserts itself and continues to exert upon the Eastern as well as the Western World an influence that cannot be permanently resisted. (p. 9)

Yet an important conclusion drawn from the writings on Biblical healing included in this book is that another powerful influence on the progress of mankind has been the Judeo-Christian tradition based on individual dignity, monotheism, the rule of spiritual law, the concept of individual freedom and human rights, and the idea of individual equality.

From the beginning of the teachings in the Old Testament, a strong message is for man to adhere to God's covenant and His law, to obey His commandments, and to turn from evil to good. It speaks of salvation, redemption, and the hope of eternal life. Individual improvement in Hebrew thought involved an encounter with serious theological topics such as atonement, sacrifice, punishment, purification, Judgment Day, salvation, resurrection, immortality, a Messiah, and diverse apocalyptic revelations of the future. This quest for perfection is well described in Proverbs: "The path of the just is as a shining light, that shineth more and more unto the perfect day." (4: 18) The Old Testament perception of progress has been explained by Abba Eban in his book *Heritage: Civilization and the Jews* in these words:

> Progress in history is a uniquely Jewish idea. It might be called the greatest contribution of the Jewish mind to other civilizations. . . .The Hebrew messianic idea. . . is alive with a sense of hope and purpose. It is worthwhile to strive for human perfection, for social progress, for compassion, for justice, for freedom, for the protection of the poor, for universal peace. (p. 58)

A sense of curiosity and a proclivity toward searching embedded in early Hebrew culture has motivated many Jews at the forefront of discovery, innovation, and progress for many centuries.

Christian teachings sustained by proofs of spiritual healing also imparted a powerful dynamic force in early Western culture. The Christian attitude toward progress was deeply affected by the role of Jesus as a Savior, a Wayshower, a Master whose entire life on earth was intended to serve as a model for his followers. His resurrection, ascension, and promises of eternal life have given Christians a strong future-oriented purpose seeking to purify and elevate their lives according to the teachings of their religion and to expect the fulfillment of its goals.

Jesus' parables are replete with instructions to change from the ways of the world to the ways of God. The sower who reaped both tares and wheat, the seed falling on the way side, the rock, the thorns, and the "good ground," the grain of mustard seed, the leaven in three measures of meal, and the prodigal son are all exhortations to change to higher levels of thought and works.

Perhaps the most vivid statement ever made about the Christian idea of progress was Jesus' words: "He that believeth on me, the works that I do shall he do also; and greater works than these shall he do; because I go unto my Father." (John 14: 12) For many centuries Christians have hoped to achieve in some modest degree the kind of spiritual healings and other works done by Jesus as he commanded. To accomplish "greater works" has been an awesome challenge that has obviously not yet been fulfilled. Yet it upholds another high goal for the aspirations and progress of successive generations of Christians.

Jesus' followers also placed great stress on regeneration and progress. In Colossians, Paul appealed to fellow Christians to "put off the old man with his deeds" and to "put on the new man, which is renewed in knowledge after the image of him that created him." (3: 9,10) He relied heavily on the Bible as a source of inspiration and individual spiritual development. In II Timothy he added: "All Scripture is given by inspiration of God, and is profitable for doctrine, for reproof, for correction, for instruction in righteousness: That the man of God may be perfect, throughly furnished unto all good works." (3: 16, 17) And as already cited in Chapter 8, the book of Revelation contains John's foretelling of "a new heaven," "a new earth," and "a holy city" in which there will be no more death, sorrow, crying, or pain, because the "first heaven" and the "first earth" and "the former things are passed away." (21: 1 - 4)

Early Christians, in brief, were expected to practice their religion by growth in character, morality, enlightenment, usefulness, and spiritual understanding. They were counseled to repent from sin and evil, to receive baptism and purification, and to work out their own salvation by living and working closer to God. They were recruited into an evangelizing movement seeking to bring the kingdom of heaven to the whole world, an aspiration toward the perfectibility of mankind that planted some of the initial seeds of Puritanism, which emerged after the fifteenth century in western Europe and has exerted an enormous influence on modern Christian doctrine.

As seen in this survey, the idea of Christian progress has also interacted closely with Christian healing. The early Christians were active in spiritual healing, which is preeminently a form of individual purification, growth, and regeneration. The destruction of sickness by prayer and faith inevitably elevates the individual to a higher understanding of the nature of man. It supplies confidence and conviction to the Christian trust in a loving and caring God.

Progress and healing are closely related to spiritual law that upholds its own high standards and provides its own enforcement and power. This law guides mankind in the restoration of health and wholeness. Paul has declared that "the law was our schoolmaster to bring us unto Christ, that we might be justified by faith. But after that faith is come, we are no longer under a schoolmaster. For ye are all the children of God by faith in Christ Jesus." (Gal. 3: 24 - 26)

Biblical Healing in the Context of Historical Times

A final comment can be made about the conditions and circumstances existing at different times during the classical period which
affected the rise and decline of Biblical healing. A conclusion derived
from this study is that the healing of disease by prayer and an understanding of God often evolved at times of extreme human turmoil and
oppression. The struggle against these adverse conditions has been
interlinked with mankind's struggle for higher forms of freedom. The
presence of severe hardships at some periods in the Old Testament era
caused a few spiritually minded leaders to turn wholeheartedly to God
for guidance, sustenance, and protection. This probing was sufficiently deep to enable them to heal physical disease.

This broad quest for freedom was seen with Moses at the burning
bush seeking assurances from God before leading the people of Israel
out of bondage in Egypt at the same time his hand was healed of leprosy. The ability to heal was also used by Elijah and Elisha at a time
of tumult during the oppressive reign of King Ahab. A good case can
be made that the healing of disease during the time of the Old Testament was most prevalent in the early phases of Hebrew religious
development, a time of a receptive and expectant mental outlook that
might be called "primitive Hebrew thought."

A similar trend occurred with the advent of Primitive Christianity.
Jesus' healing mission took place in one of the most tumultuous and
brutal epochs in human history. Octavian-Augustus Caesar had just
changed the Roman republic to the Roman empire and inaugurated a
system of emperor worship intermixed with paganism. Judaism was
divided into several feuding sects, one of which (the Zealots) was
seeking to expel Roman rule from Judea by violent means. Roman
rulers launched harsh persecutions toward monotheistic religions, first
against the Jews and later against the Christians. For over three hundred years the outlook for the survival of Christianity appeared
extremely unfavorable.

Yet as portrayed in this study, this period witnessed the highest
level of spiritual thought in human history. The Christian church in
spite of staggering opposition became firmly established, its membership expanded, and its healing mission continued.

By time of the Council of Nicea in 325 the Christian church was
gaining secular power. Within a few short decades it changed dramatically from a persecuted religious movement to a dominant religious
order. Christianity then began to show some signs of losing its healing

vigor. Its teachings were diluted by its establishment as the official religion of the Roman empire. Pagan beliefs and worship became intermixed with Christian doctrine as barbarian invaders overran territories formerly ruled by Rome. A formal legalism aided in centralizing power in the pope and a hierarchy of professional clergy, a trend which increasingly detached the church's leadership from the laity. By the time of the Post-Nicene period the church was becoming a law unto itself. Very important in weakening the practice of spiritual healing was the inclusion in church doctrine of the belief from Old Testament theology that man is essentially a sinner and that God sends sickness as a means of punishment and repentance.

In spite of these adverse trends, Christian healing continued unchanged in the Eastern Christian church centered at Constantinople. Christian healing was also continued by individual Christians in several Western societies. A new period of controversy and change again caused a relatively small but influential group of spiritually minded thinkers to delve deeply into the teachings of the Bible and heal physical disease by faith and prayer. The mission of healing may have been lost by the Latin church, but it still appealed to some receptive hearts and minds eager to preserve this important element of their religion for future generations.

APPENDIX A

THE RECORD OF BIBLICAL HEALINGS

HEALINGS RECORDED IN THE OLD TESTAMENT

1. Abimilech's wife healed of barrenness   Genesis 20: 17, 18

2. Sarah, Abraham's wife, healed of   Genesis 21: 1 - 5
   barrenness

3. Moses healed of leprosy   Exodus 4: 1- 7
   at the burning bush

4. Miriam, Moses' sister, healed of   Numbers 12: 1 - 15
   leprosy

5. Moses stops an epidemic   Numbers 16: 41 - 50

6. Moses' instructions heal snake bites   Numbers 21: 4 - 9
   in the wilderness

7. Manoah's wife healed of barrenness   Judges 13: 2 - 24
   and gives birth to Samson

8. King Jeroboam's paralyzed hand   I Kings 13: 1 - 6
   is healed by a man of God

9. Elijah restores life to a widow's son   I Kings 17: 17 - 24

10 Elisha restores life to the son of the   II Kings 4: 8 - 37
   Shunnamite woman

11. Elisha heals Naaman of leprosy   II Kings 5: 1 - 14

12. King Hezekiah is healed of a boil   II Kings 20: 1 - 9
    and his life is prolonged by Isaiah   Isaiah 38: 1 - 8, 16 - 19

13. Job is healed of a severe skin disease   Job 42:1 - 5, 10 - 16
    and other personal losses

HEALINGS OF JESUS
RECORDED IN THE NEW TESTAMENT

1. Leper healed

Matthew 8: 1 - 4
Mark 1: 40 - 42
Luke 5: 12 - 15

2. Centurion's servant
   healed of palsy

Matthew 8: 5 - 13
Luke 7: 2 - 10

3. Peter's mother-in-law
   healed of a fever

Matthew 8: 14, 15
Mark 1: 30, 31
Luke 4: 38, 39

4. Multitudes healed

Matthew 8: 16, 17
Mark 1: 32 - 34
Luke 4: 40, 41

5. Bedridden man
   healed of palsy

Matthew 9: 2 - 8
Mark 2: 3 - 12
Luke 5: 17 - 25

6. Jairus' daughter restored to life

Matthew 9:18,19,23 - 25
Mark 5: 22 - 24, 35 - 43
Luke 8: 41, 42, 49 - 56

7. Woman healed of twelve-year
   hemorrhage

Matthew 9: 20 - 22
Mark 5: 25 - 34
Luke 8: 43 - 48

8. Two blind men healed

Matthew 9: 27 - 30

9. Dumb man healed

Matthew 9: 32, 33

10. Blind and dumb man healed

Matthew 12: 22
Luke 11: 14

11. Man with a withered hand
    healed

Matthew 12: 10 - 13
Mark 3: 1 - 5
Luke 6: 6 - 10

12. Daughter of Syrophenician woman healed	Matthew 15: 22 - 28 Mark 7: 24 - 30
13. Lunatic boy healed	Matthew 17: 14 - 18 Mark 9: 14 - 27 Luke 9: 38 - 43
14. Two blind men healed	Matthew 20: 30 - 34
15. Insane man in the tombs restored to normalcy	Matthew 8: 28 - 34 Mark 5: 1 - 15 Luke 8: 26 - 33
16. Deaf and dumb man healed	Mark 7: 31 - 35
17. Blind man at Bethsaida healed	Mark 8: 22 - 25
18. Blind Bartimaeus healed	Mark 10: 46 - 52 Luke 18: 35 - 43
19. Young man at Nain restored to life	Luke 7: 11 - 16
20. Infirm woman healed	Luke 13: 11 - 13
21. Ten lepers healed	Luke 17: 11 - 19
22. Nobleman's son healed	John 4: 46 - 53
23. Infirm man at Bethesda healed	John 5: 1 - 9
24. Man blind from birth healed	John 9: 1 - 7
25. Lazarus restored to life	John 11: 1 - 44
26. Man with unclean spirit healed	Mark 1: 23 - 26 Luke 4: 33 - 35
27. Multitudes healed	Matthew 8: 16, 17
28. Many demons at Galilee healed	Mark 1: 32

29. Multitudes healed

Matthew 12: 15, 16
Mark 3: 10, 11

30. A few unbelieving persons
near Nazareth healed

Matthew 13: 58
Mark 6: 5, 6

31. Multitudes healed in the land of
Gennesaret

Matthew 14: 34 - 36
Mark 6: 55, 56

32. Multitudes healed at Galilee

Matthew 4: 23
Luke 6: 17 - 19

33. Multitudes healed

Matthew 9: 35

34. Multitudes healed to convince
two disciples of John the Baptist

Luke 7: 19 - 23

35. Multitudes healed in a desert

Matthew 14: 13, 14
Luke 9: 11
John 6: 2

36. Multitudes healed in a
mountain near Galilee

Matthew 15: 29 - 31

37. Multitudes healed in the coasts
of Judea beyond Jordan

Matthew 19: 1, 2

38. Blind and lame people
healed in a temple

Matthew 21: 12 - 14

39. Severed ear of Malchus, servant
of a high priest, healed at
Gethsemane

Luke 22: 50, 51

40. Jesus' resurrection from death

Matthew 28: 1 - 20
Mark 16: 1 - 20
Luke 24: 1 - 53
John 20: 1 - 23

HEALINGS OF THE APOSTLES
RECORDED IN THE NEW TESTAMENT

1. Jesus sends his twelve disciples to heal all   Matthew 10: 1 - 8
   manner of sickness and disease   Mark 3: 13 - 19
                                                         Luke 9: 1- 6

2. The apostles confirm the word with signs   Mark 16: 19, 20
   and healing after Jesus' ascension

3. The apostles perform many signs and   Acts 2: 41 - 47
   wonders on the day of Pentecost

4. Peter and John heal a man lame from birth   Acts 3: 1 - 8

5. The apostles perform many signs and   Acts 5: 12 - 16
   wonders in Solomon's porch

6. Stephen performs great wonders and   Acts 6: 5 - 15
   healing miracles in Jerusalem

7. Philip exorcises demons and heals lame   Acts 8: 4 - 8
   and paralyzed persons in Samaria

8. Ananias heals Saul (Paul) of blindness   Acts 9: 10 - 18
   after his vision on the road to Damascus

9. Peter heals Aeneas of palsy at Lydda   Acts 9: 32 - 35

10. Peter restores Dorcas to life at Joppa   Acts 9: 35 - 42

11. Paul heals a lame man at Lystra   Acts 14: 8 - 18

12. Paul is restored to life after stoning   Acts 14: 19, 20

13. Paul casts out evil spirit from a young   Acts 16: 14 - 18
    woman at Thyatira

14. Paul exposes and destroys the false   Acts 19: 13 - 20
    practice of exorcism

15. Paul restores life to Eutychus after a severe   Acts 20: 7 - 12
    fall

16. Paul heals himself of a bite from a venomous   Acts 28: 1 - 6
    viper at Malta

17. Paul heals the father of Publius of a fever at   Acts 28: 8, 9
    Malta

APPENDIX B

ANNOTATED BIBLIOGRAPHY

ANNOTATED BIBLIOGRAPHY

The following bibliography includes publications which have been useful to laymen, scholars, and clergy of many denominations. These books relate numerous healings of physical and mental diseases which have been achieved by reliance on the teachings of the Bible during the past 3000 years. They may be obtained from the publishers whose addresses are listed at the end of the bibliography.

Blue, Ken. *Authority to Heal*. Downers Grove, Illinois: InterVarsity Press, 1987. 168 pp.

The author is the pastor of the Vineyard Christian Fellowship in Vancouver, Canada, and the director of the Kingdom Ministries which sponsors training conferences for evangelical churches. Since 1979 he has been active in promoting healing ministries in North America. In his book, Dr. Blue explains the "hindrances" within the Christian church to spiritual healing. His authority for healing is the teachings of Jesus in the New Testament. The book contains specific guidance for starting healing services in the Christian community.

Bosworth, F. F. *Christ The Healer*. New Jersey: Fleming H. Revell Company, 1973. 241 pp.

This work is a collection of sermons delivered in cities throughout the United States and Canada during healing revivals conducted by the author early in the twentieth century. The present edition is a republication issue by the author's son, R.V. Bosworth, who is continuing the missionary work started by his father. The primary message in this study is to rely on a deep and abiding faith in God's word and to follow the healing example of Jesus.

Drahos, Mary. *To Touch the Hem of His Garment*. New York: Paulist Press, 1983. 215 pp.

The author is a successful playwright and writer for radio and the popular press. Her healing work has been influenced by both Catholic and Protestant authors. Her book explains healing methods based on a "search for wholeness." It includes a discussion of the role of meditation and healing services in the church.

Drury, Michael. *The Adventure of Spiritual Healing*. New York: Walker and Company, 1978. 203 pp.

The author of this very readable book is a woman with extensive experience as a professional writer. Her work is the probing and affirmation of a devout layperson detached from the teachings of any specific Christian denomination. She emphasizes a simple thesis that everyone has the right to a life of good health. If disease comes, she states, it can be overcome by the teachings of Jesus and the New Testament.

Eddy, Mary Baker. *Science and Health With Key to the Scriptures*. Boston: The Christian Science Publishing Society, 1906. 700 pp.

This is the textbook of the Christian Science church first authored in 1875 by the woman who founded this religion. It contains an explanation of the healing methods of Christian Science and the reasons for claiming that this religion is a science. This book and the Bible are the "Pastor" of the church designed, according to its founder, to "reinstate primitive Christianity and its lost element of healing."

_____. *Prose Works Other Than Science and Health*. Boston: The Christian Science Publishing Society, 1925. 1267 pp.

This book comprises a collection of all of the writings by the founder of Christian Science except the textbook cited above. It includes a brief autobiography of Mary Baker Eddy's life narrating the events leading to her establishment of this new religion. It also contains a sermon titled "Christian Healing" delivered in Boston affirming that her method of healing relies entirely on "the omnipotence of the Supreme Being. . . Truth, Life, and Love" rather than the use of drugs or other medical means.

Feldman, David M. *Health and Medicine in the Jewish Tradition.* New York: The Crossroad Publishing Company, 1986. 121 pp.

The author is a spokesman of the conservative tradition midway between the orthodox and reform versions of Judaism. His book is an early issue of the series on health and medicine sponsored by the Lutheran General Health Care System and the Lutheran Institute of Human Ecology at the Park Ridge Center in Illinois. Professor Feldman's book is sub-titled "L'HAYYIM - TO LIFE," and it explains the long-standing Jewish emphasis on individual and social well-being. The author likewise discusses the close relationship between ethical behavior according to the laws and customs of Judaism and general mental and physical health. He cites the many contributions Jews have made in the field of medicine over a period of many centuries.

Garland, George F. *The Power of God to Heal.* New Jersey: Robert H. Sommer, 1973. 239 pp.

This work is a collection of all the healings cited in both the Old and New Testaments. Its definition of healing includes the accomplishment of many kinds of miracles reported in the Bible besides the cure of physical and mental illnesses. On this basis Mr. Garland cites a total of 383 healings of a vast variety within the pages of the Bible.

Harrell, David Edwin, Jr. *All Things Are Possible.* Bloomington, Indiana: Indiana University Press, 1975. 304 pp.

This scholarly study of the healing and charismatic revival ministries in the United States covers the period from the early post-World War II period until the 1970's. The author has done extensive research and conducted personal interviews with leading figures in this healing movement including William M. Branham, Oral Roberts, Gordon Lindsay, Jack Coe, T.L. Osborn, W.V. Grant, and A.A. Allen. In spite of the diversity of opinion surrounding this colorful phase in American religious history, Professor Harrell's book maintains a high degree of balance and objectivity.

Holifield, E.Brooks. *Health and Medicine in the Methodist Tradition*. New York: The Crossroad Publishing Company, 1986. 198 pp.

The author is a distinguished professor of American church history at Emory University. His book is one of the series of studies funded by the Lutheran General Health Care System and the Lutheran Institute of Human Ecology. Professor Holifield's work is sub-titled "Journey Toward Wholeness," and it contains extensive information on the healing works of John Wesley during his establishment of the Methodist Church in the eighteenth century. The book places considerable emphasis on the role of Methodist hospitals in providing health care and healing services.

Kee, Howard Clark. *Medicine, Miracle, and Magic in New Testament Times*. New York: Cambridge University Press, 1986. 163 pp.

The author is a distinguished professor of Biblical Studies in the School of Theology at Boston University. His work analyzes in considerable depth the competition between various methods of healing cited in the Old Testament and practiced in the Greek and Roman traditions prior to the Christian era. Only a modest portion of Professor Kee's study is devoted to the healing works of the New Testament. Yet in his concluding observations, he emphasizes the "sharp contrast" between healing in the works of Jesus and his followers and the practices of medicine and magic in the surrounding Hellenistic culture.

Kelsey, Morton T. *Psychology, Medicine, and Christian Healing*. New York: Harper and Row, 1989. 363 pp.

This book is a revised and expanded version of the author's seminal study entitled *Healing and Christianity* published in 1973 which has made him one of the leading scholars in the field of Christian healing. The new study provides a wealth of historical information on the healing mission of Jesus and his followers as well as the healing works of medieval and modern Christians. Reverend Kelsey again makes a strong case for a revitalized healing mission in Christian churches today. He explains his views relating Christian healing to the latest advances in psychology and medicine with special emphasis on the healing methods of C.G. Jung.

_____. *Prophetic Ministry: The Psychology and Spirituality of Pastoral Care.* New York: The Crossroad Publishing Company, 1986. 210 pp.

This book consists largely of a personal account of Reverend Kelsey's quest for a spiritual alternative to the "rationalist point of view and the essentially materialistic philosophy" of Western culture which has rejected much of the movement toward Christian healing. The author bases his own healing ministry on a combination of Christian doctrine and the principles of psychology of C.G. Jung. He explains the role of faith in the healing ministry and pastoral counseling of the Christian church.

Lawrence, Roy. *Christian Healing Rediscovered.* Downers Grove, Illinois: InterVarsity Press, 1980. 128 pp.

This very readable book is an explanation of Christian healing in the Anglican Church in Great Britain. The author is a vicar of St. Stephen's Church and one of the leaders in its healing ministry. He explains the growth in healing services in his own congregation, and provides numerous examples of persons healed by relying on Christian teachings. In his healing ministry, Reverend Lawrence places great emphasis on the example of Jesus' works and the power of devout prayer.

MacMullen, Ramsay. *Christianizing the Roman Empire: A.D. 100 - 400.* New Haven: Yale University Press, 1984. 183 pp.

This work already cited in this survey of Biblical healing is authored by a professor of history and classics at Yale University. It is written for nonspecialists in ancient history, and it contains numerous useful insights into the interaction between paganism and Christianity during the tumultuous demise of the Roman empire. The author's assessment of the influence of spiritual healing on the expansion of the Christian church is unique among most professional historians.

MacNutt, Francis. *Healing*. Notre Dame, Indiana: Ave Maria Press, 1974. 333 pp.

This book comprises an explanation of the healing approach and methods by a former pioneer in the charismatic movement of the Roman Catholic Church. The author explains how his healing mission was influenced by the writings of Agnes Sanford and other Protestant leaders in the field of Christian healing. Father MacNutt's study rejects many common "prejudices against healing," and it appeals to all Christian churches to accept the responsibility to heal the sick. Some portions of this book are oriented toward the teachings and practices of Roman Catholics, yet its overall message is directed to all Christians concerned about spiritual healing. Since writing this book, the author has further expanded his healing mission after his conversion to the Episcopal Church and the establishment of the Christian Healing Ministries in Jacksonville, Florida.

_____. *The Power to Heal*. Notre Dame, Indiana: Ave Maria Press, 1977. 254 pp.

This work is a sequel to Father MacNutt's first book on healing cited above. In the words of the author, it contains "new insights into healing," including the need for patience, persistence, and the use of "soaking prayer." The latter form of prayer, he explains, involves the application of prayer over an extended period of time to penetrate the thought of the patient with God's healing love and power.

McCormick, Richard A. *Health and Medicine in the Catholic Tradition*. New York: The Crossroad Publishing Company, 1985. 171 pp.

The author of this book is a professor of Christian ethics at Georgetown University in Washington, D.C. His work is the initial study in the "Project Ten" series sponsored by the Lutheran Institute of Human Ecology. Father McCormick's work explains the ethical guidelines for Catholic health care institutions as well as Catholic views on "well-being," morality, and sexuality. Like other authors in this scholarly series, he presents a denominational definition of key "passages" in human life, including pre-natal existence, infancy, aging, and death.

Marty, Martin E. *Health and Medicine in the Lutheran Tradition.*
New York: The Crossroad Publishing Company, 1986. 178 pp.

The author is a professor of theology at the University of Chicago
and the President of the Executive Staff of the Park Ridge Center, a
special research institute established by the Lutheran General Health
Care System. His book explains the Lutheran attitude toward health
and illness as well as the role of the church, the medical profession,
and the community in caring and healing. Professor Marty discusses
aspects of the healing works by Martin Luther near the end of his
career. He likewise provides Lutheran insights into the meaning of
family, sexuality, and death.

Neal, Emily Gardner. *The Healing Ministry: A Personal Journal.*
New York: The Crossroad Publishing Company, 1985. 171 pp.

This book is by a prolific writer and leader in the healing ministry
of the Episcopal Church. She is an ordained minister and was the only
lay person on the first Commission on Healing established by her
denomination. Her personal journal reads much like a diary of a gradual movement toward a major role in the practice of Christian healing.
It explains specific methods of healing by faith and prayer. Mrs. Neal
emphasizes the influence of love and expectancy in achieving physical
and mental healing.

Numbers, Ronald L. and Amundsen, Darrel W. (eds.). *Caring and
Curing: Health and Medicine in the Western Religious Traditions.*
New York: Macmillan Publishing Company, 1986. 601 pp.

This book consists of twenty chapters explaining the teachings of
specific Western religious "traditions" regarding problems of health,
medicine, and healing. These chapters are written by a specialist in the
history and healing mission of Judaism or a single Christian denomination. They contain brief historical information as well as discussions
of denominational attitudes toward current issues regarding healing
and health. The role of medicine and modern hospitals in the healing
work of many Christian churches is frequently discussed.

Osborn, T. L. *Healing the Sick.* Tulsa: Harrison House, Inc. 1986. 540 pp.

The author is a widely traveled evangelist preacher who has taken his healing crusades to many parts of the world. His book is sub-titled "A Living Classic," and it was first published in 1951. It contains an appeal to rely on faith and the word of God to achieve healing. Much emphasis is placed on Jesus as Healer and Savior. The author cites numerous cases of healing from many kinds of diseases.

Peel, Robert. *Health and Medicine in the Christian Science Tradition.* New York: The Crossroad Publishing Company, 1988. 154 pp.

This work by the author of a three-volume series on the life of Mary Baker Eddy adds the Christian Science viewpoint to the series of denominational studies sponsored by the Park Ridge Center of the Lutheran General Health Care System. It explains why the founder of this religion placed a strong emphasis on a search for truth as well as a system of healing. Mr. Peel likewise provides reasons for claiming that Christian Science comprises a "science" of healing based on a fundamental spiritual law which practices healing without the use of surgery or drugs.

_____. *Spiritual Healing in a Scientific Age.* New York: Harper and Row, 1987. 203 pp.

This book examines briefly the issue between the scientific community with its adherence to physical laws and the slowly expanding religious perspective upholding the validity of spiritual healing. Mr. Peel's response to these divergent approaches consists of a presentation of numerous testimonies of physical healing by Christian Scientists. Most of the cases cited in his book are detailed accounts of healings which have been verified through diagnosis and examination by the medical profession.

Roberts, Oral. *A Daily Guide to Miracles.* Tulsa: Oral Roberts Evangelistic Association, 1975. 576 pp.

This widely distributed book consists of a thirteen-week daily study guide to pray for miracles which are most likely to come in the form of guidance, prosperity, and healing. The author's commentary for each day of the seventh week is oriented directly to the use of a deep faith in God and the miracles performed by Jesus in achieving healing from all kinds of diseases.

Sanford, Agnes. *The Healing Power of the Bible*. New York: Harper and Row, 1969. 221 pp.

The author was the wife of an Episcopalian minister and one of the leading authors and advocates of Christian healing in the United States after World War II. In this book she relates the inspiration and healing power available in the Bible. Mrs. Sanford likens the Scriptures to a searchlight which leads to inspiration and healing. Most of her analysis covers key figures in the Old Testament from Adam to Ezekiel. The final chapters discuss the healing power reported in the New Testament which was exemplified in the life and works of Jesus.

_____. *The Healing Light*. New York: Ballantine Books, 1972. 174 pp.

This book is a revised version of the author's original study published in 1947 which in her own words "records my very first steps into the new world wherein Jesus Christ lives and moves in the soul of man, and through his indwelling Spirit heals mind and body." Mrs. Sanford's study contains a detailed explanation of her methods of healing, including the role of love, faith, and forgiveness. It relates the experiences of many people healed of physical and mental illnesses by relying on Christian teachings. It places great emphasis on the power of prayer.

_____. *The Healing Touch of God*. New York: Ballantine Books, 1958. 213 pp.

This work endeavors to take its readers beyond the initial message in the author's first book *The Healing Light* into a deeper study of the healing mission of Christianity. It explains in greater depth the nature of God and man as well as the efficacy of devout prayer. Mrs. Sanford focuses on common obstacles to healing prayer and the importance of forgiveness and the redemptive role of suffering. She sees healing closely related to the emergence of a "new creature in Christ Jesus."

Sanford, John A. *Healing and Wholeness*. New York: Paulist Press, 1977. 162 pp.

The author is the son of Agnes Sanford and has also written extensively on Christian healing. He is an Episcopalian minister active in lecturing and pastoral counseling. His book relates health to an understanding of the "whole" man, or the person whose view of his diverse "parts and functions" is in harmony and at peace. Reverend Sanford combines healing insights from ancient traditional societies, the teachings of Jesus, and the psychology of C.G. Jung.

Seybold, Klaus and Mueller, Ulrich B. *Sickness and Health*. Nashville: Abingdon Press, 1981. 205 pp.

This book is a translation of a study published in 1978 in West Germany. The authors are Bible scholars at the University of Kiel conducting research on Old and New Testament writings relevant to attitudes and methods of religious healing. Their conclusion upholds a diversity of interpretations toward healing disease rather than a common view in the Old Testament, and a theological rather than a physical approach to healing in the New Testament. This study is based on a carefully developed method of classification of all healings recorded in the Bible.

Shlemon, Barbara Leahy. *Healing Prayer*. Notre Dame, Indiana: Ave Maria Press, 1976. 85 pp.

This relatively short book is written by a Roman Catholic lay woman who has been active in the healing ministry since 1964. She has worked with clergymen in both Catholic and Protestant healing missions, and she has lectured on Christian healing in the United States and abroad. Mrs. Shlemon is a registered nurse and the mother of five children. Her writings stress the role of prayer and love in the healing process. She likewise emphasizes the need for forgiveness and humility in achieving spiritual healing.

Shlemon, Barbara Leahy, Linn, Dennis, and Linn, Matthew. *To Heal as Jesus Healed.* Notre Dame, Indiana: Ave Maria Press, 1978. 107 pp.

This book contains personal statements by Mrs. Shlemon and two Roman Catholic priests active in healing work within the Catholic church and various ecumenical ministries. The authors provide practical advice on different healing methods, including the laying on of hands, anointing with oil, and various kinds of prayer. They also cite many examples of successful spiritual healing.

Sipley, Richard M. *Understanding Divine Healing.* Wheaton, Illinois: Victor Books, 1986. 162 pp.

The author is a pastor of the Hillsdale Alliance Church in Regina, Saskatchewan, and an active preacher in the healing revival movement in the United States and Canada. His approach to healing relies on the close relationship between the human mind and body as well as a "divine life" bestowed on each person by God. Reverend Sipley explains the processes which cause and heal both sin and disease.

Trench, Richard Chenevix. *Notes on the Miracles of our Lord.* Grand Rapids, Michigan: Baker Book House, 1949. 298 pp.

This widely used book contains an explanation of thirty-three miracles performed by Jesus. It defines miracles in a broad sense to include Jesus' mastery over many natural laws, including walking on the water, stilling the stormy sea, and feeding five thousand people from a few loaves and fishes. Archbishop Trench's scholarly study relates twenty-four cases of physical healing in this survey of the miracles recorded in the New Testament. He maintains these healings are not violations of the laws of nature. Instead they are "laws of mightier range and higher perfection; they assert the preeminence and predominance which are rightly their own."

Vaux, Kenneth. *Health and Medicine in the Reformed Tradition.* New York: The Crossroad Publishing Company, 1984. 149 pp.

The author is a professor of ethics and medicine at the University of Illinois Medical Center and a director of the studies in Project Ten sponsored by the Park Ridge Center and the Lutheran General Health Care System. His book explores the doctrine of the Protestant Reformed teachings regarding healing in Calvinist and Presbyterian churches. Professor Vaux cites an appeal made by Paul Tillich in 1963 urging a stronger healing ministry within the Presbyterian Church. This book discusses the role of prayer and confession in the healing process.

Wimber, John. *Power Healing*. San Francisco: Harper and Row, 1987. 293 pp.

This popular book contains an account of the author's experience in establishing healing ministries in evangelical churches beginning in 1964 after an impressive healing of his small son. For many years he has led the healing services of the Vineyard Christian Fellowship in Anaheim, California. This study explains his methods of healing as well as specific steps in forming a healing service in Christian churches. It likewise includes useful information on the healing works of early Christian leaders.

Worrall, Ambrose A. and Olga N. *The Gift of Healing*. Columbus, Ohio: Ariel Press, 1985. 240 pp.

This book is a personal account of the healing work done by a husband and wife in Baltimore, Maryland over a period of forty years. Their healing methods included a combination of personal "gifts" of intuition, clairvoyance, and the application of "scientific laws" of healing. The Worralls conducted their healing activity as an avocation, and refused compensation for their healing work. Mrs. Worrall established the New Life Clinic in Baltimore which has continued a healing mission since her death in 1985.

ADDRESSES OF PUBLISHERS

Abingdon Press
201 Eighth Avenue, S
Nashville, TN 37202

Ariel Press
3391 Edenbrook Court
Columbus, OH 43220

Ave Maria Press
Notre Dame, IN 46556

Avon Books
1790 Broadway
New York, NY 10019

Ballantine Books
400 Hahn Road
Westminster, MD 21157

Baker Book House
P.O. Box 6287
Grand Rapids, MI 49506

The Christian Science
Publishing Society
Reading Room Center
P.O. Box 1875
Boston, MA 02117

Cambridge University Press
32 E. 57th Street
New York, NY 10022

Crossroad Publishing Company
370 Lexington Avenue
New York, NY 10017

Fleming H. Revell Company
Old Tappan, NJ 07675

Harper & Row
Keystone Industrial Park
Scranton, PA 18512

Harrison House
P.O. Box 35035
Tulsa, OK 74153

Indiana University Pre
Bloomington, IN 47402

InterVarsity Press
P.O. Box 1
Downers Grove, IL 60515

Macmillan
. Publishing Company
866 Third Avenue
New York, NY 10022

Oral Roberts Evangelistic
Association, Inc.
Tulsa, OK 74171

Paulist Press
9825 W. Roosevelt Road
Mahwah, NJ 07430

Robert H. Sommer
The Mail Box
27 Blauvelt Drive
Harrington Park, NJ 07640

Victor Books
1825 College Avenue
Wheaton, IL 60187

Walker & Company
720 Fifth Avenue
New York, NY 10019

Yale University Press
92A Yale Station
New Haven, CT 06520

INDEX

INDEX